FAMILY VIOLENCE

FAMILY VIOLENCE

Research and Public Policy Issues

Edited by Douglas J. Besharov

THE AEI PRESS

Publisher for the American Enterprise Institute
Washington, D.C.

Distributed by arrangement with

University Press of America, Inc.
4720 Boston Way   3 Henrietta Street
Lanham, Md. 20706   London WC2E 8LU England

Library of Congress Cataloging-in-Publication Data

Family violence : research and public policy issues / Douglas J.
  Besharov, editor.
    p.   cm.
  ISBN 0-8447-3707-0.
  1. Family violence—United States.   I. Besharov, Douglas J.
HQ809.3.U5F347   1990
362.82'92'0973—dc20   89-18431
                                                 CIP

1 3 5 7 9 10 8 6 4 2

AEI Studies 500

The AEI PRESS
Publisher for the American Enterprise Institute
1150 Seventeenth Street, N.W., Washington, D.C. 20036

Printed in the United States of America

Contents

Acknowledgments

This book would not have been possible without the generous support of the Harry Frank Guggenheim Foundation. The foundation is committed to the fullest possible inquiry into violence and its impact on human social life.

Special thanks go to Karen Colvard, the Guggenheim Foundation's program officer for this project. She helped identify many of the exceptional researchers who contributed to this volume, helped select and structure the conference, and shared her experience and wisdom with the group. Clark McCauley served valiantly as conference moderator; he kept us to our task with grace and good humor.

Two people at AEI energetically and cheerfully helped bring this book together. Gail Owens administered the first half of the project and helped organize a smoothly running and convivial conference. Kelty Barber administered the second half of the project and ably guided the various papers forward to the point of publication.

Finally, I want to express my appreciation to the authors themselves. Without their fine work, there would be no book.

DOUGLAS J. BESHAROV

Foreword

Family violence, that is, assaultive behavior against spouses, children, and other family members, is a serious—and apparently growing—national problem. Each year hundreds of thousands of wives are abused by their husbands, and over a million children suffer various forms of physical, sexual, and emotional maltreatment.

Despite the seriousness of family violence, little is known about this tragedy. Only now are we gaining an appreciation of its magnitude and its causes. Moreover, our ability to prevent or treat such behavior is rudimentary, at best. Thus research on the incidence and etiology of family violence and on effective means of intervention is indispensable to efforts to protect its victims better.

Unfortunately, as described in this volume, the quality of current research on family violence leaves much to be desired. Too often appropriate public policy making has been stymied by the absence of crucial data.

It is impossible to summarize the diverse contents of a book like this, but a few points should be emphasized:

1. *Research on the extent and sequelae of family violence must be evaluated within the context of the study's definitions and methodology.* Widely varying estimates of the incidence of child abuse or spouse abuse are a direct result of differences in definition and methodology. Similarly, one cannot expect to determine the sequelae (or effects) of a behavior if one cannot define it reliably and consistently. Standardization of terms should be a first priority.

2. *Research will not find the cause of family violence.* Dozens of well-funded research projects have tried and failed to discover the specific cause or causes of family violence. As for all forms of human behavior, there is no one cause. Research should seek to identify and understand better the different mixes of social and individual factors that lead some individuals, but not others, to violence. No research is likely to be any more definitive.

3. *Research will not discover a "cure" for family violence.* Just as there is no single cause of family violence, no single therapeutic technique or

service can cure it. Instead, many effective treatment approaches can break patterns of abuse; success depends on the family, its situation, the quality of the therapist, and a host of other variables. Research should pursue this kind of multifaceted approach to assessing treatment efforts.

4. *Research on the operational functioning of programs is not glamorous, but it is essential.* Many spouses and children suffer serious injury *after* public agencies have learned of their situations. In cases of child abuse, for example, agency malfunctions usually come to light only when a child's death is widely reported by the media. Research on program evaluation can reveal points of delay, staff inadequacies, decision-making problems, and administrative weaknesses so that they can be corrected before a child's unnecessary death. In this area a small amount of research money can produce a great deal of program improvement.

5. *Special demonstration programs may do more harm than good.* What better way to combat family violence than to create a new program to provide treatment services? Unfortunately, such demonstration programs are a costly and often counterproductive duplication of pre-existing services. Almost invariably, they last only as long as special funding is available. They spend an inordinate amount of time in getting started, finding clients, and winding down. And because they are so short-lived, they have difficulty in recruiting well-qualified therapists.

Often these new programs do more harm than good. They seem to promise a quick cure for parents—when long-term, intensive services are needed. And they siphon off funds that would ordinarily go to such services. Too many of these projects "coordinate" the services of established agencies thus create interagency antagonisms and discourage other coumunity-based agencies from becoming involved with abusive families. Instead, funding should enhance the capacity of existing mental health, social, and family service agencies to serve families in trouble.

Before closing, a few words are in order about the relevance of research to policy. We are a people particularly enamored of numbers; no other constitution requires a census that counts not just people but also things. Research can be crucial to policy making because it gives us numbers. Research on the incidence of family violence, showing that child abuse and spouse abuse are widespread, has galvanized public and political support for tougher laws and expanded programs.

Sometimes research merely sanctions or justifies an existing policy preference. Larry Sherman's research, for example, on the effect of arrests in domestic violence cases facilitated a policy change that was already occurring. At the time his findings were published, advocates around the country were arguing for more arrests, and, suddenly, there appeared this research that conveniently sanctioned their position. Advocates, politicians, and police departments needed a reason to change their policy, and Sherman's study provided it. Thus research can provide powerful leverage for change.

Research findings can also block change. In effect they can be used to sanction inaction or the refusal to change direction. For every constituency that wants to make a reform, a corresponding group usually prefers the status quo. Research can provide a reason—or an excuse—for saying no to a change in policy. The policy maker can say, "I would like to help you, but there is research that shows that it would not be wise to do so." Research does not have to be definitive; it can even be flawed, just not embarrassing. The point is that research can provide political cover.

Research is often irrelevant to policy, of course. When it comes to research on child abuse, for example, no program evaluation shows any treatment program making more than a small difference in the behavior of the parents involved. People believe that treatment makes a difference, but no systematic, properly controlled study has shown an impact. If one had, the program would have been replicated across the nation. This absence, however, has not prevented the expansion of treatment programs because we believe in helping parents care better for their children.

Does research matter? Yes. But not as much as many researchers would like—partly because of political and other factors and partly because of shortcomings in the research itself. If we want policy makers to pay more attention to research, we will have to improve our product. That is what this volume has been all about, that improvement.

Douglas J. Besharov

Contributors

Douglas J. Besharov
Resident Scholar
American Enterprise Institute for Public Policy Research

Ellen G. Cohn
University of Maryland
Crime Control Institute

Karen Colvard
Program Officer
Harry Frank Guggenheim Foundation

R. Emerson Dobash
Department of Sociology and Social Policy
University of Stirling

Russell P. Dobash
Department of Sociology and Social Policy
University of Stirling

Jeffrey L. Edleson
Associate Professor
School of Social Work
Director of Evaluation and Research
Domestic Abuse Project
University of Minnesota

Zvi Eisikovits
Senior Lecturer
School of Social Work
Director
Youth Policy Research Center
University of Haifa

Jeffrey Fagan
Senior Research Fellow
New York City Criminal Justice Agency

Diane Follingstad
Associate Professor
University of South Carolina

Joel Garner
Program Manager
National Institute of Justice
U.S. Department of Justice

Charles P. Gershenson
Senior Evaluator
Center for the Study of Social Policy

Sally A. Lloyd
Associate Professor
Department of Family and Consumer Studies
University of Utah

David W. Moore
Professor of Political Science
Director
University of New Hampshire poll
University of New Hampshire

Einat Peled
University of Haifa

Carol Petrie
Program Specialist
National Institute of Justice,
U.S. Department of Justice

Lawrence W. Sherman
Professor
University of Maryland
President
Crime Control Institute

Betty Stewart
Assistant Commissioner for Children, Youth and Families
U.S. Department of Health and Human Services

James K. Stewart
Director
National Institute of Justice
U.S. Department of Justice

Murray A. Straus
Professor of Sociology
Director
Family Research Laboratory
University of New Hampshire

Cathy Spatz Widom
Professor
Departments of Criminal Justice and Psychology
Indiana University

1
Qualitative Research on Spouse Abuse

Zvi Eisikovits and Einat Peled

*Grown-ups love figures. When you tell them that you have made a
new friend, they never ask you any questions about essential matters. They never say to you "what does his voice sound like? What
games does he love best? Does he collect butterflies?" Instead they
demand: "How old is she? How many brothers has he? How much
does he weigh? How much money does his father make?" Only from
these figures they think they have learned anything about him. . . .
They are like that. One must not hold it against them. Children
should always show great forbearance toward grown-up people. But
certainly, for us who understand life, figures are a matter of indifference.*

—Antoine de Saint-Exupery, *The Little Prince*

Our choice of quotation as the motto for this chapter certainly does not
spring merely from reverence toward the Little Prince's candidness
and intellectual honesty. It reflects our obvious preference for the
naturalistic paradigm. We make no claim of "objective scholarship";
rather we hope to make our bias explicit and to be able to defend it.

The qualitative-quantitative debate has often been presented as a
methodological one. Attempts have been made to show the advantages and disadvantages of both modes of inquiry, their appropri-
ateness in a variety of research situations, and their usefulness in
building and testing theory as well as in guiding various stages of the
research enterprise. In this continuing tour de force we tend to lose
sight of the obvious: that the debate is paradigmatic rather than
simply methodological. The qualitative-quantitative debate grew out
of two divergent sets of beliefs and ideas about the naure of reality,
the ways of knowing and understanding it, and the values as criteria
underlying both the ontological and the epistemological choices. One
is what has traditionally been known as the positivistic paradigm; the

other is interchangeably termed the qualitative, the naturalistic, or the phenomenological paradigm.

The two paradigms maintain opposite positions on most of their essential components. Positivists argue for one "true" reality, naturalists for multiple ones; positivists believe that researcher and research should be separate and independent from each other, naturalists that they should be interactive entities; positivists hold causes to be temporally precedent to or simultaneous with effects, naturalists that cause and effect cannot be separated; finally, positivists assert that inquiry should attempt to make knowledge value free, naturalists that all inquiry is value laden.[1]

This brief juxtaposition shows clearly that the nature of truth—whether empirical, logical, ethical, or metaphysical—will be largely a function of the underlying paradigm. Much of the reasoning behind family violence research is rooted in the positivistic paradigm. It both maps and creates a considerable part of the context and boundaries of this domain of study, shaping it in specific ways. At the same time a small but rich body of naturalistic research on spousal abuse is beginning to be assembled. In spite of the valuable insights that have been drawn from these works, their effect on the field is incommensurate with their substantive contribution.[2]

The purpose of this chapter is to examine some of the shortcomings of the positivistic paradigm in the study of spouse abuse and to show the potential of the naturalistic one. We do this by examining some empirical and theoretical evidence stemming from both methodological traditions.

Single Reality or Multiple Realities

The positivistic paradigm postulates a single, tangible reality that can be broken down into its components. Two elements are inherent in this assumption. First, as in Aristotle's "law of the excluded middle" and "law of contradiction," there is only one truth, and what is not true is false. The nature of truth is not negotiable. Second, the exploration of truth is achieved by analyzing its constituents. The subsequent synthesis is based on the assumption that reassembling the pieces will yield a veridical picture of reality.

The literature on risk factors in the etiological tradition of research on spouse abuse is illustrative. Ninety-seven potential risk markers found in fifty-two case comparison studies were reviewed by G. T. Hotaling and D. B. Sugarman in an attempt to assess the empirical evidence concerning causes and prediction of spouse abuse.[3] Most of the studies used a clear-cut definition of the risk factors chosen for the investigation, based on theoretical, empirical, or clinical orientations, and devised adequate measures to weigh the extent of the phenomena. Although definitions and measures were shaped as an extension of the researchers' reality, an assumption was made that the nature, meaning, and boundaries of the phenomena are captured by them. A. Rosenbaum and K. D. O'Leary's study, for example, chose to compare couples who were violent, nonviolent and well adjusted, and nonviolent but in conflict on measures of adjustment, alcoholism, attitudes to sex roles, personal history, and demographic variables.[4] Those measures were expected to distinguish between the entire realities of abusive and nonabusive couples. While the relationship of some variables to violence is implied by previously found correlates (for example, alcohol and violence), the choice of this specific constellation neither is grounded in a theoretical rationale nor reflects the reality of the subjects' experience in spouse abuse. Further, assigning the subjects to a place on, for example, a five-point scale for the phenomenon being measured fragments their reality into five possibilities, no more, no less. Using quantifiable measures in this way is based on the assumption that if two or more persons fall on the same place along the scale, their experience in the measured phenomenon is similar or identical. If two men score similarly on marital adjustment measures, for example, their experience of marital adjustment is expected to be similar. The reality is more complex, however. Here are two statements from men who scored identically on G. B. Spanier's Diadic Adjustment Scale but had very different views to convey on the meaning of adjustment.[5]

> Look, she and I differ on practically everything. If I say it's night, she'll say it's day. . . . we never make common decisions.

> She and I always agree . . . because she does what I tell her. Things have been that way ever since we married.

Thus defining risk factors and homogenizing them through standardized measures creates the illusion of a single objective reality. In fact, at least three realities are at work, not necessarily overlapping for each subject: the subjects' reality as the researcher is aware of it, their reality in their own awareness, and the reality composed of issues beyond the actors' or the researcher's awareness as framed in a given time or situation.[6]

> Informant: You gave me that form? What is it supposed to find out? . . . If I answered or something?
> Researcher: Things that happened to you so we can know how much stress you live in.

3

Informant: Most of these don't happen to anybody. For me
they don't matter.
Researcher: O.K. So mark NO.
Informant: But other things that are worse happened and
they are not in here.

Accepting the existence of multiple realities constructed in the minds
of the actors implies to the researchers the need for a paradigmatic
shift. The nature of the issues to be addressed within the new paradigm will shift accordingly.

The complexity of multiple realities in family violence can be
illustrated by several issues. For many couples, living in violence
comes to be ordinary and hence taken for granted. Violence is expected; it occurs and becomes part of the actors' everyday experience.
Suffering evolves into a regular state of affairs, and with time
awareness of the relationships between violence and suffering becomes blurred. In the relatively unstructured interaction between the
naturalist researcher and his or her informant, some aspects of violence that have been taken for granted are rediscovered by the actors
and become part of their awareness. Hence a new reality emerges.
One of our informants commented on the interview situation as
follows:

You know those conversations we have? I was thinking about
them. For me it's like a playback movie. Except if I want to be
honest I don't really know if it's replay or a new movie.
Before you asked me I never stopped to think about that
stuff.

Another aspect of the actors' multifaceted reality is expressed in
linguistic structures. Those structures can be understood on the immediate level of analyzing what is being said in a specific context or by
extracting underlying themes and metaphors that transcend the specific context. On the immediate level, when listening to spouses talk
about their violent interaction, the researcher often finds that even
when violence has no behavioral expression, it is still there in the
actors' experience. One can be terrorized by the specter of violence.
Thus in time violence is transformed in the actors' minds into fear,
guilt, and expectation, which ultimately create an ecology of terror. A
man talked about his wife's experience of beating as follows:

As I told you . . . five years ago, that's the story . . . she left
home. . . . That's the one and only time it happened. But it
stays with her because every woman that will go through
such trauma . . . the marks stay forever. . . . What I am
trying to do is to influence her to change everything. I keep

telling her: "Forget it, it happened, it passed." I'll tell you, there is no cure for it, just time. It's not like a disease: you giving a shot and it's over.

On a more general level, two kinds of underlying linguistic structures are metaphors and accounts. Metaphors are linguistically, cognitively, and behaviorally pervasive building blocks of our reality. Essentially they enable us to understand and experience one kind of phenomenon in terms of another. For instance, the concept of "argument" is widely experienced in our culture as "war":

Your claims are *indefensible.*
He *attacks every weak point* in my argument.
His criticisms were *right on target.*
I *demolished* his argument.
I never *won* an argument with him.
You disagree? O.K.! *Shoot!*
If you *use that strategy,* he'll *wipe you out.*
He *shut down* all my arguments.[7]

Metaphors like these are not merely linguistic devices but both mirror and create reality. Argument as war metaphors, when used in the context of conjugal violence, reveal an essential component of the spouses' experience.

Accounts are another linguistic structure that can highlight the connection between the actors' reality and some tangible but external one.[8] Accounts have been defined as linguistic devices used by actors to explain untoward behavior and bridge the gap between actions and expectations. In the intersubjective reality of the family, based on shared expectations and norms, most interactions are taken for granted. When the spouses come into contact with outside factors, however (for example, when public suspicion of spouse abuse arises), much of the base that has been taken for granted disappears, and explanations or justifications are called for to prevent conflicts, to maintain a respectable social identity, or at least to save face. In spite of the heuristic potential of this concept in exploring the actor's presentation of self, its explicit use in the family violence literature is rare. K. J. Ferraro should be singled out as one of the few whose work has applied it.[9] She focused on neutralization techniques used by battered women to justify their continued involvement with the violent spouses who failed to provide them with the warmth and security that are expected from a spouse. Among the techniques identified were denial of the assaulter's responsibility, denial of the extent of injury, self-blame for the situation, denial of the possibility of leaving because of economic dependency, and appeal to moral commitment toward the partner and their children. More recently, T. Mills used the

5

concept in the context of examining battered women's strategies for coping with violence.[10]

The "rediscovery of reality" as demonstrated by such linguistic devices can be studied only by means of naturalistic inquiry, which enables the knower and the known to explore their mutual realities and the ways in which they were created. Such mutuality, however, is not universal practice in social research. The position of the knower toward what is to be known is a major point of divergence between the two paradigms.

The Knower and the Known

The old Galilean dichotomy between "doing science" (that is, the scientist is involved in applying ideas to the reality investigated) and "observing science" (that is, the investigator is an outside observer, reflecting but not interfering with the phenomenon studied) was handled in the positivist tradition by accepting in principle the compatibility of the two while rejecting it in research practice. The model of science used by positivists is one in which the scientist is objective and independent and manipulates data from "neutral territory." The idea of separating the knower from what is to be known to achieve scientific objectivity is based on the subject-object dualism, the investigator being the subject and the topic of investigation the object. How do positivistic research methods attempt to achieve this, and what are their underlying rationales? The knower defines a priori what is to be known and frames an operational definition of it. Zvi Eisikovits and J. S. Edleson, for example, in their study of spouse abuse on an Israeli sample defined the phenomenon as "the use of physical force by a man against his cohabiting spouse (i.e., hitting, pushing, shoving, throwing objects etc.), with the intent of inflicting pain, at least once during the last year; that some social control agent is cognizant of."[11]

Such operational definitions are assumed to represent the phenomenon, and appropriate sampling procedures are followed to make the study population representative of the universe of actors involved in it. As the subject of inquiry is defined, procedures are devised to eliminate potential contaminating effects arising from interaction with the researcher, the research situation, and the instruments used. For instance, the researcher's presence and procedures are known to generate in subjects various errors, such as the guinea pig effect (awareness of being tested), role selection (providing data from a set of selves irrelevant to the phenomenon), and response set (a tendency to endorse rather than oppose).[12] A variety of strategies are suggested to handle these threats to internal validity, culminating in the Solomon four-group design, the use of unobtrusive measures, or straight-out deceiving and misinforming of subjects. Procedures such as these are expected to achieve objectivity and crystallize knowledge in its purity, sediments aside. Thus separating the body of knowledge from those who generate it meets the criterion of dualism. Such dualism has proved false in other domains, such as form-substance, medium-message, mind-body, good-bad, and psyche-soma.[13] It is common knowledge now that the medium is the message, as it is that many illnesses are both psychic and somatic. Similarly, those who investigate spousal violence will quickly give up such dichotomies as violent-nonviolent, psychological-physical violence, or even agressor-victim. Hence the efforts invested in separating the knower and the known hold little promise either methodologically or substantially.

In the naturalistic paradigm the acceptance of multiple realities and intersubjectivity leads to an opposite approach: the knower and the known are seen as inseparable, interactive, and thus coconstituting each other. Holism and emergent designs, as well as purposive rather than representative sampling, are appropriate. A researcher may study a population of battered women in shelters, for example, and, instead of making statements about battered women in general, make the context explicit by showing how it interacts with those who participate in it. Further, a researcher may focus on the universality and uniqueness of being a battered woman living in a shelter. As an integral part of the data, the researcher would explain his or her role in the context under investigation, make a continuing effort to become conscious of his or her own values, and clarify those to the audience. Such investigation would imply a holistic examination of the entire system with its interacting components.

Some phenomena do not lend themselves to separating the knower from the known. Emotionality is a case in point. Violence among intimates is essentially an emotional phenomenon.[14] As enacted emotion, the experience of violence is situational, reflective, and relational.[15] Emotions cannot be given unvarying definitions; actors must communicate their own definitions of the situation and encompass those who come into their interactional field (such as the researcher). The feelings that a person expresses about himself or herself shape, influence, and reveal the feelings others have toward him or her. Thus the emotional aspects of spouse abuse are defined intersubjectively. An illustrative quotation from our research:

> If she is lying to me about something then I'm getting pissed because I hate lies. . . . Then we start arguing. . . . Suddenly

> she stops talking and then I get even more angry. . . . So
> sometimes I slap her. . . . Then, after she is crying the quar-
> rel is over. If she cries there is nothing I can do. . . . She
> starts crying because she got hurt from the fact I gave her a
> slap. . . . When one cries, usually he is sorry for what he did
> . . . so it's over.

Since emotions vary from person to person, as well as from experience to experience within the same person, the essence of understanding emotions lies in understanding the personal meaning and
interpretations brought to them. Descriptions in the actors' own language are obtained through interviewing, and then interpretations
are singled out by "bracketing," abstracting, and using theory
heuristically. Finally, the actors' experience is reconstructed and put
into context. By these means the emotional phenomenon can be
understood with minimal distortion, acknowledging the contributions of all actors to it.

Linear or Circular and Multiple Causality

Any field of inquiry, particularly one that includes intervention, in-
vests a great deal of energy in debating causality. This issue has
become synonymous with predictability, control, and therefore security. Any investigation of family violence presupposes the need to
understand its causes, to predict its occurrence successfully, and to
devise strategies to avoid or eradicate it. Within the positivistic tradition, several key issues have been identified as problematic concerning causality, particularly in the study of human beings.[16]

Temporal precedence and asymmetry. Effects should not be their own
causes, nor should they precede causes, but simultaneous and backward causation cannot be excluded in the study of human beings. We
cannot ascertain whether violence is caused by certain psychiatric
states or vice versa.

The anticipatory nature of human beings. Given this characteristic,
the temporal sequence of cause-effect is often disturbed since an effect
may be produced in anticipation of its cause and so precede it. Consider the following quotation:

> She sits there and I'll tell you I feel she's asking for it. She's
> crying and weeping. As far as I am concerned I can't get this.
> I didn't touch her yet she's crying. So I figure, I'll give you a
> reason to cry. And there goes the neighborhood.

Recurrent regularity and cause. There is predictable regularity in the
occurrence of certain phenomena that can be statistically calculated.

The phenomena are assumed not to vary among occurrences. Ruling out coincidence, however, is problematic. One of the major features of family violence is unpredictability. The assumption that regularity can be ascribed to cause does not always work with human beings. Patterns of behavior arising from habits and routine have nothing to do with the cause-effect sequence. Since at least part of spouses' lives is taken for granted and habitual, it will be difficult to distinguish between ascribed causes, actual causes, and accounts stemming from habit. Consider the following quotation:

> You see, that's the power of habit, understand? Because I'm used to find food and to find her and if I don't find her and don't find food that's again the power of habit. You are used to what you got used to, and then you don't get it. So sometimes you are getting nervous and sometimes you don't. It depends on your mood that day.

Conditional stipulation. Given the practically endless variation in time and context, the possibility of generalizing a cause related to human conditions is limited. This pulls the rug out from under intervention programs that are etiologically based.

Beyond these details, the assumption of temporal and contextual independence underlying causal models makes them most vulnerable. In the wake of such devastating attacks on causality, one would expect the naturalistic paradigm to abandon it altogether. Instead, much effort is invested in reshaping it, because of the need of the naturalistic paradigm to explain occurrences as a way of avoiding uncertainty. What changes in the naturalistic paradigm is not the interest in causality but rather methods of studying it.

While the naturalistic researcher chooses to gain depth and contextualization at the expense of generalizability, he or she uses a variety of conceptual and methodological tools to enhance the credibility of his or her data. Among these are triangulation and attempts to achieve ecological validity in multilevel and multivariate designs.[17]

A study of spouse abuse in process at the University of Haifa in Israel makes an attempt to meet both criteria in part.[18] It uses ten quantitative measures on various ecological levels, such as the Rational Behavior Inventory on the personal level, the Diadic Adjustment Scale on the interpersonal level, the Interview Schedule for Social Interaction to examine social support on the immediate environmental level, and the Beliefs about Spouse Abuse Inventory on the broader sociocultural level. In addition, a qualitative interview using a guide is administered to both spouses to capture the context and subjective experience of violence. The qualitative and quantitative data obtained by these procedures are triangulated during data analysis. For purposes of ecological validity the multivariate analysis will attempt to understand the relative contributions of the measures on various ecological levels to distinguishing violent from nonviolent spouses. Comparing materials collected from the spouses will illuminate the subjective perspectives of the actors.

Value-free or Value-laden Research

Values as used in this brief discussion are defined as criteria or perspectives brought into play when making choices or expressing preferences.[19] The neutralization of values is a central concern in the positivistic paradigms, as is their explicit use in the naturalistic one.

Positivists advocate the use of methodological procedures that enable us to sort out values from facts. Aside from returning to the old dualistic fallacy, assuming the existence of a "real" and an "apparent" reality, the positivist paradigm attempts to distinguish between facts and theory. Facts, however, are theory laden, and theory is value laden; therefore, facts are value laden.

The concern about values began to surface in the feminist spouse abuse literature illustrating that family violence research is value laden.[20] A recurring theme in this literature is the question, Why do battered women stay? D. R. Loseke and S. E. Cahill pointed out that the question is heavily value laden and reflects professionals' expectations concerning the behavior of battered women.[21] By both asking and answering the question, the experts have constructed a new deviant category, that of battered women who stay, the value expectation being to leave. Experts could ask instead, Why do men stay? but they do not.

Analyzing the theoretical, methodological, and outcome components of intervention in spousal violence dramatizes the same issue.[22] The unit, method, and theoretical orientation of intervention have shifted along the years, mirroring parallel changes in the value orientation of professionals and researchers. The focus of treatment shifted from individual women in the late 1960s and early 1970s to men's groups and community intervention programs in the 1980s. While the focus of the intervention was the woman, the underlying theoretical trend was psychodynamic. As the focus shifted to the men, the theoretical orientation shifted to cognitive-behavioral. The values underlying these changes are obvious; they stem from a belief about the location of the problem or rather its ascription as lying within the woman or the man, on the intrapsychic or the behavioral level.

I. S. Lincoln and E. G. Guba identified several sources of values, such as the researcher's values, values underlying the paradigm guiding the inquiry or the methodological choices made, and values stemming from the sociocultural context.[23] They may or may not be relevant to any specific research. In a society based on patriarchal values, for instance, if a family violence study uses a feminist substantive theory and methods that cannot account for the subjective perspective of women, the conflict among various sources of values will probably make the inquiry impossible, particularly if the research is commissioned to a man, as most of it is.

Is Qualitative Research on Spousal Violence Usable in Public Policy?

As is consistent with our ontological commitment to multiple realities, the answer to our question is yes and no. When we add to this answer the need to consider the reality of the researcher, the policy maker, and the subject, we are faced with a six-box matrix. Given our initial explicit bias in favor of qualitative research, we will briefly touch on the arguments against using this paradigm in policy and focus on the possibilities it offers.

The Cons. First, an inherent contradiction seems to exist between naturalistic research and policy: emergent design, ever-changing questions, and unpredictable findings are incompatible with the policy maker's job of planning, predicting, preventing, and controlling events.

Second, systems under investigation by naturalistic observation are exposed in a manner that is hard to control. This is not always in the policy person's interest. The question is not only whether to expose but also how much to expose. It may or may not be in the interest of policy makers to introduce sociocultural levels in addressing a social problem. Some problems are better kept as problems of individual behavior and family relations and not allowed to break loose and be defined as social problems. In Israel, for example, battering is still mainly handled as behavioral, while issues related to its sociocultural significance, such as women's position in society, are carefully evaded.

Third, naturalistic research may raise major ethical and professional dilemmas for policy makers. Such research requires hands-on intimate knowledge and rapport with settings and people engaged in deviant behavior often defined as crime. Moreover, how much violation of family privacy should be allowed must be weighed against the benefits for the families investigated. Any of these factors may constitute a hindrance to the policy maker's becoming involved with qualitative research.

The Pros. The researcher may consider the potential benefits that can be derived from this paradigm along the subject–researcher–policy maker chain. Subjects of spousal violence are difficult to identify, approach, and interview. A principal reason is that spousal violence is still hidden in the family closet behind the confusing intimacy-violence contradiction. The establishment of rapport and involvement with informants inherent in this paradigm may allow us to search the closet.

From the researcher's perspective, we have attempted to argue throughout this essay that the nature of the phenomenon as subjective, interpretive, processual, and emotional makes it particularly amenable to naturalistic study. Capturing interpretations, accounts, justifications, and existential situations that are taken for granted and mapping feelings are difficult with forced-choice questionnaires. We should add to this the need to generate grounded hypotheses and substantive grounded theory given the relative youth of the field.

Finally, policy makers as consumers of knowledge may benefit from qualitative information on several levels. Good descriptions of settings, situations, and people are like field trips for policy makers, putting them in touch with the people and problems they make policy for. Holistic, contextual information will provide the policy analyst with a universe of options for action. Finally, the ideographic nature of the qualitative paradigm makes it more accessible to clinical practitioners. This attribute may hold some promise of bridging the gap between research and practice.

A final note: the greatest damage to qualitative research comes from within; some insiders and some refugees from the other paradigm just do not do careful enough research. For some reason concern for methodological rigor is attributed to those whom the Little Prince considered "concerned with numbers." Let us attempt the same rigor in the study of words and do it in such a way that qualitative research will become indispensable because of its quality.

2
Methodological Issues and New Directions for Research on Violence in Relationships

Diane Follingstad

With the advent of research on violence in relationships, excitement was evident because a previously untouched social issue was going to be addressed by scholars. Now, years later, we stand among a myriad of books, articles, and findings and wonder just what we have to show for this flurry of effort. Does what we now know make all the effort worthwhile. Do the findings lend themselves to a cohesive theory or approach to studying this area? Unfortunately, the knowledge base appears to lack the promise of information useful for stimulating treatment and prevention programs. When in 1980 R. J. Gelles reviewed the research, he was concerned about a wide range of methodological problems, and a review of much recent research suggests that the same problems continue to plague this research area.[1]

Studying violence in relationships is inherently difficult, and any study of social issues within families and relationships finds it hard to produce lucid and cogent results. Even given the difficulties, however, the research findings have not been such as to suggest a coherent picture or a coherent policy. Numerous small, independent, isolated studies have been generated that do not appear to be based on relevant theories or past findings. Thus generalizing from the findings is difficult. In addition, studies are too often exploratory and descriptive and thus do not contribute to the need to find causal connections. Conclusions are therefore severely limited and inhibit the ability to determine future directions of research. Policy makers who want to reduce violence in relationships face confusion and an inability to turn the sometimes contradictory findings into useful directives.

This chapter covers three major areas important for addressing the problems in research on family violence. First, the chapter discusses the *general* problems characteristic of research on violence in relationships, attempting to understand the major pitfalls, the unique difficulties, and the best possibilities for conducting such research. Second, since much of the research is done through interviewing and questionnaires, a section is devoted to ideas for enhancing these devices when they are used. A final section discusses why this research does not easily lend itself to public policy and includes alternatives and suggested models for remedying the problem. The goal of the chapter is to clarify what is needed in research on violence in relationships so that funding agencies and policy makers can determine which difficulties cannot be overcome and can make informed choices of proposed studies that will advance the field.

General Problems of Research on Violence in Relationships

Difficulties Inherent in This Research Area. Any investigator attempting to tackle research on domestic violence is immediately aware of problems unique to this area of study, difficulties that discourage even the most stout-hearted researchers. Unfortunately some researchers therefore look for the easiest solutions to the problems rather than the most scientifically appropriate solutions. Today's emphasis on publishing may be partially responsible for the emphasis on finding some sample on which to conduct some measure likely to produce some results that some journal might consider for publication. The following observations are made with an eye to understanding the best possible solutions for the inherent difficulties of this field of study.

An appropriate sample is the first problem. Most researchers study women as victims after concluding that male aggressors are nearly impossible to reach as research subjects. Aggressors rarely volunteer for treatment, much less as helpful research subjects. Marital research has promoted the necessity of assessing both partners in a marriage, but in the area of domestic violence this goal can rarely be attained. Therefore, inherent problems of using only one source of information to draw conclusions about both partners are faced. Most conclusions about the personalities of abusers and the quality of marital relationships are a result of interviews only with the victims.

If a researcher decides that abused women need to be the source of data because locating abusing men may be almost impossible, further difficulties arise in choosing an appropriate sample. Battered women are not a captive population and typically must volunteer as subjects of study. Volunteers may be a unique sample, since any researcher must wonder why some abused women are willing to identify themselves for research purposes while others are not. Abuse has thus initially been defined by the women willing to admit to researchers that they have been abused and willing to be assessed. As more and more data are collected, how battered women are located and what sources may be used to identify a sample of subjects become serious concerns that must be addressed if the most representative group of subjects is to be located.

Abused women must be identified and their involvement in research solicited. Researchers have often sought out battered women staying in shelters that provide emergency lodging and other services because they constitute a ready-made group for study. In doing so, however, researchers have not always shown an awareness that this subsample may have characteristics dissimilar to those of the larger population of battered women and may be a unique group. Locating volunteers through broader recruitment (such as through the media or agencies) will often produce a preponderance of volunteers who have been in battering relationships but are no longer in them.[2] Once again, such a sample presents unique aspects that reduce the extent to which the findings can be generalized. Ethical concerns, practical difficulties of identifying and approaching battered women, and possible risks to their well-being during assessment add to the problems of locating representative samples.

Some studies have attempted to handle sampling problems by comparing subsamples of their subject populations. They may compare shelter subjects with subjects recruited from the newspaper. Although this is a step in the right direction, these studies may still not be representative of battered women, and the comparisons may not be important ones. Rather than comparing women by the way in which they are located, it might be more appropriate to use the degree of physical force directed toward the women as a basis for comparison. Unfortunately, whether more important dimensions exist has not been well documented; relating as much information about the subject population as possible should be the rule.

A recent study by L. L. Lockhart seemed to entail much more effort for the researcher but signaled the usefulness of probability sampling to locate subjects.[3] Earlier efforts by M. A. Straus and S. K. Steinmetz showed that nonclinical cases that had not been officially reported could be sampled to collect information on family violence.[4] Lockhart's effort seems parallel to the dating violence studies that sample large groups of dating persons (usually college students) to locate those who have engaged in or been subjected to violence in their relationships. To find a representative sample of battered women, Lockhart surveyed many groups of women in the community to locate a representative group of women and then asked questions about battering.

The advantages of this method appear to be the availability of a wide range of comparison groups and the locating of women rather than specifically battered women to be involved in a study. A disadvantage is that large numbers of women may need to be assessed to locate enough battered women for statistically useful information, although 35 percent of Lockhart's subjects reported at least one incident of physical force. Moreover, some of the most severely battered women have become very isolated and would not be involved in such a study; these, however, might not be located by any sampling means. A third disadvantage is that an in-depth study of battering relationships may not be possible with this method. The advantages far outweigh the disadvantages, however, and this method may be a purer one than most studies attempt. It may also be an option for finding battering men by sampling large groups in the hope that the anonymity of the procedure will induce more men who have used physical force to report it.

Although most research leans toward reporting some demographic information on subjects and the source of subjects, studies differ considerably in what information they report and where they find their subjects. The variations among studies make comparisons virtually impossible. For example, a group of rural, low-income, mainly white battered women who are studied for their problem-solving skills cannot easily be compared with a group of urban battered women from a shelter composed mostly of minority women. Some minimal standards are needed for what demographic data should be reported to have a solid understanding of the sample on which the results were based.

Because of the nature of the subject population and the difficulty of obtaining samples for research, another problem lies in the lack of experimentation that can be conducted with the subjects. A researcher may feel that merely interviewing battered women or having them fill out questionnaires is enough of an imposition. Battered women may be willing to volunteer for an interview or a questionnaire, since they see the relevance of their participation, but unwilling to be involved in an experimental manipulation whose purpose they do not understand. The interviews and questionnaires more directly related to the battering relationship may be helpful to a woman; they may allow the woman to experience catharsis or to feel understood by an interviewer. Certainly laboratory experiments on abusing men have not been conducted except for my beginning experimentation on laboratory aggression by college men with a history of dating or marital physical force. Thus, because the modes of research have seemed restricted, the paucity of experimentation is still apparent, leaving causes very much in question. The focus of researchers does not have to be as restricted as once thought, however. Even very simple experimentation that could be conducted through questionnaires has been neglected, such as describing abuse situations or marital conflict to battered women and offering them fixed alternatives to determine whether their problem-solving methods differ from those of women experiencing no abuse. More movement into experimentation appears possible and certainly seems paramount for progress in this area of research.

The reliance on questionnaires and interviews produces self-reported data with all its inherent biases and distortions. Selective memory must be considered along with an awareness that subjects may differ in their willingness to engage in self-disclosure. Although the deficiency of self-reported data may never be completely rectified, improving the quality of such data may be possible. Some quantification of information, such as having subjects complete Straus's Conflict Tactics Scale (CTS) to produce accurate frequency and severity data, would allow for comparison among subjects.[5] Attempting to find some source of validation of the subject's report, such as a relative or police reports, would add power to the information given. Another possibility, discussed in detail below, would be to allow for subjective responses but to require the subjects to fit their experience into creative precoded categories as well.

Pitfalls of Research on Violence in Relationships. Numerous pitfalls that repeatedly appear in the literature on domestic violence could and should be avoided. Reseachers must become familiar with the criticisms and suggestions that have been made so as not to repeat the mistakes. In a new and developing area, researchers must thoroughly review the literature to build on previous studies, or they will not be aware of the suggestions made in critical reviews that point out the pitfalls.

One factor that makes comparison of studies next to impossible is that samples are not typically described along the most useful dimensions. Although the source of the subjects, their ages, their education, and other demographic information may be given, often they are described as a group of battered women for whom the variation in severity and frequency of abuse is unknown. Thus inconsistencies among studies cannot be reconciled by comparing the women's history of abuse. Because the definitions of "abuse" and "battered woman" have been so varied and uncertain, we must move away from

17

lumping battered women together as a unitary group toward characterizing them by relevant dimensions of abuse. To make findings across studies more comprehensible, researchers must begin to think beyond demographic variables to such variables as severity and frequency of physical abuse, information about the women's families of origin, or the experiences of the women within the abusive relationships. Such variables as levels of intimacy, the length of the relationship, or the amount of communication may be more useful for comparisons than gross demographics data.

At this stage it is no longer forgivable to find studies that do not include a reasonable comparison or control group. So many possibilities exist for at least minimal comparison that a lack of it is not justified. At the very least, a researcher's group of subjects should be compared on a standardized measure with the norms of the original standardization group. A comparison between identifiable subgroups within a sample might clarify why certain findings appear. Researchers, for example, often use the fact that a certain percentage of their sample possesses a trait to declare that the presence of that trait is a significant factor to consider for battered women. They typically gloss over the fact that a significant portion of the sample does not possess the trait. More realistically, the researchers should compare the group possessing the trait with the other subjects on additional variables to determine what is different about the two groups that might explain the presence of the trait in some subjects but not in others. More creative comparisons have been developed and should serve as models for future research: groups of nonbattered women have served as contrasting groups; A. Rosenbaum and K. D. O'Leary included a nonviolent but maritally discordant group for comparison; and my colleagues and I have suggested comparing battered women systematically with other groups of victims.[6]

The hypotheses put forth in the research show a dismaying paucity of links between this research and broader theories in psychology. Like research on victimization, rape, and restitution, research on family violence has often been narrowly focused and issue oriented. The unfortunate result is that articles on the subject are often isolated pieces reflecting a point of view not linked to broader theory. Hypotheses set forth by program-oriented reseachers often stay narrowly confined to ideas about battered or battering persons generated from clinical experience rather than from major theoretical models. While no one would suggest that clinical experience is an erroneous source of hypotheses, we must wonder why, for example, major theories about aggression or marital interactions do not become a fertile ground for generating hypotheses on violence in relationships. Better connections between family violence research and major theories are urgently needed.

Another major pitfall of research in domestic violence lies in the aspect of measurement. Questionnaires designed specifically for one particular study and interviews are the predominant ways of assessing people with violence in their histories. Operational definitions and measurements of dependent variables vary tremendously, and little standardization occurs from one study to the next. Violence is typically treated as the dependent variable or end product, and the possibility of its being a process variable is not considered.

The measurement aspect of the research need not be as problematic as it is. Studies should make more use of measures such as Straus's CTS, even when unique measures need to be adopted for the purposes of the studies.[7] Standardized measures should be tapped more frequently even when they lengthen questionnaires. In addition, E. J. Webb, D. T. Campbell, R. D. Schwartz, L. Sechrest, and J. B. Grove have suggested that multiple operations including a variety of measurement approaches lend the greatest validity to information.[8] Only a few researchers, for example, have observed interactions of couples where battering occurs for comparison with nonbattering couples. Behavioral observations would be excellent as one kind of measurement to be contrasted with others.

Studies that just describe a group of subjects or give percentages of subjects with a certain characteristic yield little useful information. When researchers began to study violence in relationships, descriptive studies had some use in providing information on incidence, generating hypotheses, and offering ideas for testing causality. Although descriptive studies may be appearing less often in the literature, it is surprising to see them in current journals. Correlational studies are a step up in statistical sophistication, but causal connections are still missing after such studies have been conducted. D. A. Bagarozzi and C. W. Giddings have criticized correlational studies as offering "no insight for interpersonal processes, redundant patterns and escalating coercive cycles."[9]

Probably the biggest disservice of correlational studies or even studies that list multiple significant relationships of variables with domestic violence is that they do not address the relative importance of those variables. Multivariate analyses need to be used to determine the amount of variance accounted for by each variable. Such analyses can be expected to show that some variables, though significant, account for virtually no variance because of redundancy with other variables. Multivariate analyses should become much more prevalent to sort out the relative importance of the many variables suggested as being related to domestic violence. For those brave researchers who conduct ethical and sensitive experimentation in this area, inferential statistics based on large enough samples and well-delineated hypotheses should provide some of the most useful information.

Enhancement of Interviews and Questionnaires

Because interviews and questionnaires are used so frequently in research on domestic violence, special attention needs to be given to ways of enhancing their utility for research. Questionnaires and interviews have become the most common data collection devices in this area because of practical difficulties in locating subjects, especially battering men, and sensitivity toward victims of family violence. The questionnaires referred to in this section are items to be answered by the subject for the purposes of the researcher and not standardized measures already in existence. Because researchers frequently must devise measures to test unique hypotheses, their results are often based on newly developed questionnaires. Interviews and questionnaires for assessing family violence share the elements of devising questions to test hypotheses and handling responses to the items so that they become usable data. Uniquely developed items for studies immediately raise questions of reliability and validity, which individual researchers should address or at least recognize that they may not be able to resolve.

Three main aspects of interviews and questionnaires need to achieve more sophistication and complexity. These are the designation of original hypotheses, the framing of precise questions, and the development of meaningful response options.

Hypotheses about domestic violence are often not linked to broader theories of human behavior. Thus the research is at a critical point where hypotheses must move beyond narrow theories specific to domestic violence to broader theories such as aggression and marital interaction. More sophisticated hypothesis generation may require pilot testing of ideas to define the concepts being tested more adequately. Pilot testing may also be important because newly devised measures could be subjected to scale analyses in this early stage and then given to the larger sample.

Hypotheses need to be more than simple determinations of whether a factor exists to a great extent in a group of subjects. They must ask both why a particular factor is present in some subjects, and why it is not present in others and what difference this makes. A study finding that 40 percent of its battered women had parents who engaged in physical force cannot just conclude that this is an impor-

20

tant factor that may predispose women to later battering relationships. The researcher must determine whether the 40 percent differ from a random or equivalent sample of women and explain what it means that 60 percent did not experience this background. Comparisons of the two groups on additional history or other measures might suggest explanations that could lead to experiments on causes.

As the first step, hypotheses can keep the researcher focusing on causal connections and on answering why and how as the important questions for producing explanatory models. Practitioners reading the literature do not need to know just that a certain treatment program "worked" but why it worked and for which participants its effects were most beneficial. Thus hypotheses for studies should begin as more sophisticated ideas leading to more useful research designs.

As an example of increased sophistication of hypotheses, consider a researcher interested in whether a woman's early responses to violence influenced the frequency and severity of later violence by her partner. The researcher might identify women with only a few incidents (with a cessation of violence for a specified period of time) and compare their responses to early incidents with those of women who have experienced long-term battering. If the investigator hypothesized that strong sanctions (such as threatening some consequence to the abusive partner) would lower rates of aggression, she might ask subjects whether during early incidents they threatened consequences if the man ever used force again. This factual hypothesis would be incomplete, however, without determining many subjective aspects, such as whether the woman intended to carry out the threat, whether she had the skill or ability to follow through on it, whether she believed the threat sufficiently negative for the man, whether she thought the man believed her, and whether she actually carried out the threat. If the woman had threatened the man and violence had then decreased, the additional subjective information about her behavior would be more useful for understanding why her action may have worked than the simple piece of data that she did make a threat.

Plenty of anecdotal and clinical information exists about people involved in violent relationships. To move toward understanding commonalities, causes, and connections, the items devised for interviews and questionnaires need to be more standardized. Attention must be paid at this stage to devising questions that most adequately and accurately allow hypotheses to be tested. Books on questionnaire development have information that is useful in developing items for collecting data from interviews as well. Sources on item development are well aware both of the usefulness of interviews and questionnaires for tapping perceptions, beliefs, feelings, and motives and of the reluctance or inability of some people to express these. Thus researchers devising questionnaires and interviews need to be familiar with sources on questionnaire development and should have graduate education and training in this aspect of research. The goal to keep in mind is to formulate questions in such a way as to enhance the clarity, relevance, and validity of the information being collected.

While much has been written about devising questions for use in hypothesis testing, much less attention has been paid to devising the responses to the questions. Discussions about responses usually deal with quantitative rather than qualitative aspects, such as numerical scales versus rankings or odd versus even numbers of options. Much thought is given to whether to use closed questions with fixed alternatives or open questions with no alternatives given. Fixed alternatives have been said to work best when possible alternative replies are known, are limited in number, and are clear-cut, that is, when factual information and clear opinions are to be elicited. This manner of thinking, however, may severly limit the usefulness of fixed alternatives. Precoded categories for responses can certainly be more sophisticated than yes or no or indications of degrees of approval or disapproval of a statement. In pilot testing a sense of the range of alternatives may be determined through open-ended questions. The alternatives will often suggest a dimension that can be used as a model for the response options. When asking battered women how they reacted to the first incident of abuse, for example, a dimension of passivity or activity may emerge, although the actual responses may have been numerous and unique.

Dimensions are even important to consider for seemingly simple factors. Assessing how often abuse has occurred can be measured in many ways, such as the duration of abuse during the relationship, changes in the frequency of abuse over time, the total number of incidents, or the frequency of the abuse in six-month intervals. Specific interval and ratio data would be much more useful for such variables than data assessing the presence or absence of abuse.

Another way to improve response options would be to generate all possible response categories for the kinds of questions subjects find difficult to answer comprehensively. A question such as "Why did you stay in an abusive relationship?" requires a person to try to remember all possible reasons, including the most important reasons, for engaging in a certain action. A wide range of possible responses might be generated through the pilot testing and organized into categories to be presented to all subjects. Allowing them to consider many possibilities would help them decide which applied to them. They might also choose the response option they believed most important in influencing their behavior. Options for the question concerning a woman's continued presence in an abusive relationship might be "presence of children in the home," "financial dependence on the partner," or "nowhere to go." By answering each option and choosing the most important one, the subject does not have to rely solely on memory or respond with whichever option occurs to her at the moment the question is asked. Rather she can consider a range of comprehensive options and even add some of her own. *Choice*

In an interview format subjects might initially answer open-ended questions and then be led to decide on the precoded category that most accurately reflected their answer. In this manner the respondents could judge which category was appropriate for their own behavior or attitude, rather than have the interviewer or a coder interpret it. While the final precoded option might lose some subtleties of the answer to the open-ended question, what is necessary for research is meaningful and reasonable quantification of data. The researcher might prefer to avoid subtleties and subjectivity in some items (such as trying to determine the severity of the abuse in a battering relationship) and might therefore ask for very specific factual information that would later be recoded according to preset criteria (such as asking the exact kind of force used and the resulting injuries, which would later be recoded as mild, moderate, or severe). Whichever direction is taken, precoding and recoding guarantee comparability of responses among subjects because of the use of the same terms and dimensions.

Translating a Problematic Research Area into Information Usable for Public Policy

As a researcher trying to understand how policy makers might use the data generated on violence in relationships, I believe that policy makers would experience difficulty in locating a foothold in this research. The basic reason for this lies in the piecemeal approach to studying domestic violence and the focus on identifying minute factors that may be related to that violence. With little idea about which factors may be the most important, policy makers would not know where to begin. Therefore, it is not difficult to make a case for the support of studies that begin to take the mass of significant findings and turn them into variables ranked by importance and by the amount of variance they can account for. In this manner some "significant" findings may prove relatively useless for predicting aspects of domestic violence, and the more important variables will be identified. After this winnowing out, further studies would be supported to investigate what the best predictor variables actually mean for the cause, maintenance, or cessation of violence in relationships.

When considering why this research area does not lend itself easily to public policy, we must decide what kind of research best serves this purpose. Usually, research conducted to direct policy is focused on demonstrating the feasibility of an application. The paucity of studies of outcomes or of prevention of domestic violence is noticeable. Unfortunately, many studies are done not with a pragmatic goal but just to "understand" more about the participants in violent relationships. Thus many researchers reinvent the wheel. Given that treatment or prevention studies are vastly difficult to conduct, this field of study has reached a stage where money needs to be directed into larger, more complex undertakings that are theoretically based and specifically geared to produce information on outcomes. Much of the preliminary research offers suggestions for treatment or prevention programs, and these kinds of studies which should be very relevant to public policy makers.

Larger questions also need to be addressed through studies investigating such questions as how to change society's attitudes toward violence. Efforts to reduce acceptance of violence as "just part of a marriage" or to raise support for victims by society at large rather than just by social service agencies might have wide-ranging implications. Public education programs might be assessed for their effects on societal attitudes and norms and on community services and emphases. Experimental studies that might identify causal factors need funding encouragmenet even when they remain purer research, for example, on how aggressors respond to laboratory aggression variables. Field studies, such as those investigating the effects of arrest on recidivism by battering men, strongly deserve support for their information on tertiary efforts to handle domestic violence.[10] These studies have had important practical applications in changing police policies for responding to domestic violence calls.

While waiting for more pragmatic and useful research to be conducted, public policy makers may want to handle their confusion about the myriad of research results by thinking of abuse perpetrators and victims in terms of a taxonomy. Rather than looking for a universal solution, policy could begin to address the needs of various groups within the troubled population. Women who need to use shelters, for example, often have shared characteristics and distinct needs. Although D. K. Snyder and L. A. Fruchtman distinguished several types even within a shelter population, shelters can probably identify a variety of important needs of their clients that could be addressed as a unit when policy is made.[11] Different modes of intervention might be supported for serving other groups of battered women, such as television or newspaper appeals for battered women who have never been identified by any source and live alone with the knowledge of their status as victims. Relationships with very intermittent abuse might be targeted for couples' counseling different from the kinds of intervention that might be considered for relationships with long-term, high-frequency, and high-severity abuse.

Summary and Conclusions

Although domestic violence research has inherent difficulties and researchers can do many things to improve the research and avoid typical pitfalls, some of the pragmatic research that should direct public policy is probably still some years down the road. The most useful research is likely to come with a large price tag; it is no coincidence that research has largely avoided outcome, prevention, laboratory, and experimental field studies. Considering special groups of the population may be the best strategy for policy makers to adopt until larger questions are answered through research efforts. As top priorities studies of outcomes of treament and prevention programs and experimental research aimed at illuminating causal factors should be encouraged. National unified research efforts and directions can be established by funding organizations that stress these priorities.

3

Implications of Biases in Sampling Techniques for Child Abuse Research and Policy

Cathy Spatz Widom

Medical models of causes, correlates, and consequences dominated early research and writing on child abuse. In the 1970s, a major shift in emphasis took place, along with the demonstration that abusive behavior occurred in nonclinical or community samples. In the 1980s, the literature on child abuse and neglect has expanded in a number of directions. Since it is not possible to study all physically or sexually abused or neglected children, however, sampling continues to be necessary for inferences about the larger population of such children. With sampling, come decisions based on the values and assumptions of researchers.

To provide a keener sensitivity to potential sampling biases and to enhance understanding of present and future research in the field, this paper addresses ways that sampling decisions and subsequent biases influence research on child abuse. The extent to which the literature on child abuse reflects two particular problems—*criterion-dependent* and *method-dependent* biases—will be examined and recommendations for minimizing biases in future research will be made. Although this chapter is organized around criterion- and method-dependent biases, they are not mutually exclusive: clearly criteria and methods overlap.

A criterion or a method, of course, may be quite valid for one purpose and not for another. Comparisons, however, are important because they address the validity of the data gathered by these techniques. Although methods of measurement may have biases or inaccuracies, if the results of each method can be compared, then a researcher should be able to evaluate the effects of the biases and ultimately make adjustments for some of the deficiencies.

Criterion-Dependent Bias

The first problem with comparing data on child abuse is the definition of child abuse or the comparability of the populations covered by studies. Who are the populations studied? To what extent do the techniques of the studies themselves produce systematic biases in results? A key issue here is the representativeness of samples: that is, the ability to generalize accurately from a sample to the broader population.

Criterion-dependent bias refers to the extent to which definitions or criteria for inclusion of subjects influence findings in research on child abuse. Although nominal definitions are often similar, operational definitions differ. Convergence in findings would not necessarily be expected unless results are based on the same or similar populations. The list below presents a number of dimensions upon which to evaluate criteria for inclusion of subjects:

- broad or narrow definitions?
- physical abuse, neglect, and sexual abuse included?
- restricted to abuse by parents or caretakers?
- restricted to children living with natural parents?
- at least one episode of abuse necessary?
- any evidence of neurological impairment?
- abuse validated by external sources?

Broad or Narrow Definitions? In some research, abuse has been more narrowly defined and limited to a clinical condition, such as bone fractures, contusions, abrasions, welts, or burns[1] or physical injury to a child that leaves welts or bruises that remain at a minimum forty-eight hours after the incident was reported.[2] A broader definition of abuse places it on a continuum of behavior that ranges from the slight pain of mild physical punishment (such as in slaps or spankings)[3] to "severe discipline by physical means"[4] to extreme abuse at the other end of the continuum. Definitions of abuse have also included an even wider range of activities, such as failure to provide adequate food, clothing, or proper care for the child,[5] behavior more commonly called neglect.

These definitions influence some aspects of child abuse research more directly than others. Estimates of the number of child abuse and neglect cases in the United States, for example, vary significantly from approximately 500,000 per year[6] to as high as 2.3 million.[7] Not all the differences between these estimates result from bias based on criteria. The low estimates, however, are based on more rigorous and narrow criteria,[8] in contrast to the higher estimates, which are based on broader and more encompassing definitions, such as those in the national surveys of family violence.[9]

The complexity of definition is reflected by the general cultural approval of physical punishment.[10] One frequently cited finding is that 93 percent of parents surveyed reported using physical punishment, although some use it only rarely and only on young children.[11] On the one hand, clearly no one is likely to condemn a parent for spanking a child. On the other hand, if the child were spanked by a stranger, communities might respond differently.

To what extent is a particular definition of child abuse sufficiently discriminating to be useful? Is it useful to include all parents who use physical force in the form of physical punishment in a definition of abuse? Basic differences in operational definitions of abuse or neglect affect not only estimates of its frequency but also the replicability of assessment and research.

Physical Abuse, Neglect, and Sexual Abuse Included? Decisions about when (and whether) to include physical and sexual abuse and neglect influence the kinds of samples studied and, in turn, influence results. Some studies distinguish between abused and neglected children, treating them as separate groups, whereas others combine them and treat them as one. In some studies sexual abuse is treated as a separate topic, and sexual abuse cases are explicitly excluded from study. In other studies, sexual abuse cases are included with cases of physical abuse. Gil, for example, excludes incidents of sexual abuse, "unless they also involved elements of nonsexual physical abuse."[12]

Some evidence suggests that maintaining distinct categories for physical abuse, neglect, and sexual abuse is both conceptually and empirically appropriate.[13] If the sexes are victimized by different forms of early abuse, then studies need to consider the effects of gender while they are investigating the correlates, causes, and consequences of abuse. What are the effects of combining types of abuse in study samples? To what extent does the aggregation of cases obscure important behavioral or psychological differences? To what extent is it worthwhile or necessary to isolate and examine specific forms of abuse?

Restricted to Abuse by Parents or Caretakers? Criteria for many studies restrict their samples to victims of abuse or neglect by parents or caretakers, usually in the home. In Gil's national survey, the definition of abuse stipulated that the perpetrator be the parent or caretaker, usually an adult. The perpetrator could also be another relative, babysitter, teacher, or someone not related but was *always* someone at least temporarily taking care of the child. While this requirement is appropriate for some research questions, the exclusion of abuse in other contexts limits the general application of the findings. This limitation is particularly troubling for estimating the incidence and prevalence of abuse.

Abuse outside the home is rarely addressed. While parents or caretakers may represent the most frequent perpetrators, excluding abuse by others leads to an incomplete understanding of the problem. How many cases are excluded because the perpetrator was not a parent or caretaker? Are the causes of abuse by parents different from abuse by others?

A number of newspaper accounts of sensational cases of abuse in day care centers have appeared recently. In the Fells Acre case in Massachusetts, for example, a mother and daughter were recently found guilty of raping and indecently assaulting four children in their care. Previously, the son had been convicted of eight rapes and seven indecent assaults.[14] How different (if at all) are the effects on children abused by day care workers from those on children abused by parents?

The relationship of the perpetrator to the victim may differ depending on the age of the child. Infants and toddlers are more likely to be victimized by parents, whereas for older children the percentage of parent perpetrators decreases and the role of people outside the immediate family increases.[15] If we restrict abuse to caretakers only, then we lessen our ability to assess causal factors.

With some exceptions, little systematic research has examined the causes or consequences of abuse by a variety of perpetrators. Does it matter who commits the abuse—parent, stepparent, family friend, stranger, and so on? In her study of the proximate effects of sexual abuse, Adams-Tucker found that the children molested by their father appeared to suffer more than other abused children.[16] Do the long-term consequences also differ?

Restricted to Children Living with Natural Parents? A number of studies have restricted their samples to abused children who are currently living with their natural parents. Perry, Doran, and Wells studied abused children who had remained in residence with their families.[17] In contrast, one of the criteria for inclusion in a study by Wolfe and Mosk was that children must have been living with the natural or foster parent for the past six months or longer.[18] In their study, Friedrich, Einbender, and Luecke, all children were living with natural parents, each of whom was on Aid to Families with Dependent Children.[19] How representative are samples of abused chidren who remain in the homes of their natural parents? To what extent can these findings be generalized to those children not living with their biological parents, such as those living with foster or adoptive parents?

In their study of fifty abused children, Martin and Beezley reported that 34 percent of the children had had from three to eight home changes from the time of identified abuse to the followup (mean time 4 and a half years later).[20] In a three-year followup of abused and neglected children, six of the fifty were judged to be within normal limits of intellectual and emotional development at followup.[21] Interestingly, all had been living in the parental home continuously since the original identification of maltreatment.

To what extent are children who suffer extreme abuse or neglect more likely to be adopted, either by foster parents or others? To what extent are studies that omit this group representative? Because information on adopted children is difficult to obtain, we need to explore this factor's influence in studies that do not systematically address this question.

A related issue is the extent to which definitions of samples are restricted to child abuse among intact families. According to a number of sources, between 30 and 42 percent of abused children come from single-parent households.[22] These estimates of the frequency of single-parent households in abusive families are higher than that generally found in the United States, although the proportion of intact families overall has declined dramatically over the past twenty years.[23] This means that population surveys restricted to intact families, such as the Straus, Gelles, and Steinmetz survey or laboratory studies using only intact families, cannot perhaps be generalized to a substantial portion of abusive experiences.

Whether (and in what respects) the practice of restricting samples to children with natural parents or to those from intact families makes a difference is unclear at this time. Few studies have systematically examined the issue, and those that have have not been conclusive.

At Least One Episode of Abuse Necessary? Some studies require that there be at least one episode of documented abuse for inclusion in their studies.[24] In Gil's survey, at least half the sample cohort had been victims of physical abuse prior to the incident reported, suggesting a pattern of family interaction rather than an isolated incident. If one episode is required, is it reasonable to assume this is the only one? Depending on the source of the information, is it reasonable to believe there were more episodes of abuse? If the abuse happened earlier, why was it reported only now? In studying the consequences of abuse or neglect, one might hypothesize that the more episodes, the more serious the abuse and the more traumatic the consequences.

In an evaluation of research findings, it is important to know whether studies are investigating chronic behavioral patterns or infrequent explosive episodes. Can findings from studies in which the criterion is a minimum of one episode of maltreatment be applied to those studies of children who have been chronically and repeatedly abused? Criteria for abuse in relatively few studies deal with this question of whether abuse is chronic.

Any Evidence of Neurological Impairment? In developmental psychology, studies typically recognize the importance of excluding children with evidence of neurological impairment, particularly in research assessing aspects of cognitive or intellectual functioning.[25] For cognitive assessments, excluding such children is obviously necessary. At the same time, eliminating such neurologically impaired children from studies of abuse makes any differences in cognitive or intellectual functioning even more dramatic. In a study by Barahal, Waterman, and Martin, even with IQ controlled, abused children displayed lower intellectual skills and fewer social cognitive competencies than a closely matched control group of nonabused children.[26]

For other research or for public policy purposes, it is important to have base rate (how often this occurs normally or naturally in the population) information on such impairments. Do we reliably know the extent to which abused children are neurologically impaired? How many chidren are eliminated from studies because of such impairment? It would be helpful to include this information routinely in descriptions of subjects in research reports.

So far, we have discussed definitions and criteria for inclusion of subjects in studies of child abuse. One additional criterion is sometimes included in definitions of abuse and neglect that also illustrates the overlap between criterion- and method-dependent biases: the extent to which the abuse or neglect has been validated by external sources.

Abuse Validated by External Sources? In an analysis of approximately 2,400 cases gathered by the National Clearinghouse on Child Neglect and Abuse, Groeneveld and Giovannoni found that 48 percent of the cases overall were substantiated.[27] Abuse only cases were most likely to be substantiated, and the likelihood of a report being substantiated was related to both the source of the report and the nature of the complaint. Cases from professional sources (law enforcement agencies, social agencies, schools, and medical sources) were more likely to be substantiated than those reported by individuals. Groeneveld and Giovannoni suggested that the unreported cases are very likely to be less serious.

In addition to widely varying definitions of child abuse and neglect, studies have often included unsubstantiated or unvalidated cases. This is particularly troubling in surveys where nonclinical or community samples are asked about prior abusive experiences. More recently, an important improvement in the field is the tendency of investigators to require substantiation and validation of the abuse or neglect for inclusion in their studies. Without validation from external sources, estimates of the incidence of abuse or neglect are seriously open to question. Unless the abuse or neglect incident itself is verified, the question of whether the abuse or neglect actually occurred is left open. Furthermore, unsubstantiated cases are more likely to be biased toward the least serious end of the continuum.

Method-Dependent Bias

The second major problem in comparing studies of child abuse is how incidents enter records and studies. Unlike other kinds of social science research where the phenomena can be studied directly and, in some cases, even manipulated in a laboratory setting, child abuse most often occurs in private. Methods that can penetrate "behind closed doors" are necessary.[28]

How do cases come to be included in studies of child abuse and neglect? In some studies estimates of child abuse and neglect are based on sample surveys in which an interviewer asks a series of questions. In other studies, information comes from sources further removed from the incident, as in reports of incidents known to the police or from emergency room records or other official sources.

Method-dependent bias refers to the extent to which methods chosen for data collection influence outcomes in research on child abuse. To what extent do particular methods produce bias? To what extent do particular data collection methods limit the larger applicability of findings?

Four basic methods and sources of information commonly used in research on child abuse will be reviewed here: (1) the use of records of official agencies for child abuse and neglect; (2) analysis of case files of (nonabused) samples for evidence of abuse or neglect; (3) samples drawn from treatment or parent training groups; and (4) self-reported responses (through interviews, questionnaires, or surveys). Table 3–1 lists these methods and highlights the advantages and disadvantages of each.

Contact with an Official Agency for Child Abuse or Neglect. Much of the child abuse literature is based on data derived from cases where the victim becomes publicly known and labeled by official agencies involved in child abuse and neglect. This information is available from a range of agencies such as local child protective services, departments of public welfare, departments of child welfare, and departments of social services or from child abuse registries, statistical reports of child abuse from national agencies (such as the American

TABLE 3–1
METHOD-DEPENDENT BIAS

Source	Disadvantage	Advantage
Official agency for child abuse or neglect	Bias toward lower classes, more extreme cases, more serious cases. Yields underestimates.	Typically substantiated and validated, lower cost, wide geographic coverage possible
Analysis of case files for selected samples: emergency room patients, psychiatric hospital patients, institutionalized youths	Incomplete information in files, questionable validity of information. Yields underestimates.	Availability
Treatment or parent training groups	Social desirability, demand characteristics, volunteer vs. non-volunteer, intervention effects unknown.	Captive audience, in-depth study possible, long-term study possible
Self-report responses: interviews, surveys, and questionnaires	Social desirability, retrospective bias (memory decay), single-perspective reporting, nonrespondent problem, questionable validity.	Accessibility, not subject to agency bias, wide geographic coverage possible

Humane Association), or hospital or physician referrals for abuse or neglect.

A number of these sources provide information on the demographic characteristics of abused children and, in turn, illustrate method-dependent bias. The American Humane Association collects child abuse data from all over the United States on a standard reporting form completed by child protective workers at the time the initial abuse report is filed.[29] This information differs from hospital-based data not only in that a larger sample size is available but also in that a broader spectrum of abuse is reported in the national studies.

Studies based on emergency room admissions generally show that at least two-thirds of the abused children in their samples are under six years old.[30] Records of the American Humane Association indicated that approximately 40 percent of the abused and neglected children in its sample were under six. Some hospital studies have reported that as many as 60 percent of the abused children are under two years old. In contrast, Gil found that more than three-fourths of the children in his nationwide sample were over two years old and nearly half were over six.[31] Interestingly, Gil also reports that 65 percent of the children under three, as opposed to 35 percent of children over three, were either severely or fatally injured.

Together these studies illustrate how sources of information may influence research findings. Hospital settings tend to receive the more severe and medically involved abuses. Emergency room studies, in particular, are biased to reflect the more severe injuries. Thus if younger children are more susceptible to severe injuries, then it is not surprising that younger children are overrepresented in studies based on emergency room and hospital records.[32]

Clearly much child abuse and neglect do not come to the attention of official agencies, a fact of particular concern for cases of child abuse and neglect from the 1950s and 1960s. At that time, since most communities did not have child protection services, and, since there were no mandatory child abuse reporting laws as we currently have, in cases where abuse was found, it may have gone unreported. Furthermore, parents may not take their child for medical attention, repeat abusers may change hospitals, and injuries may not be clearly attributable to abuse. Thus, basing estimates of the incidence of child abuse on official agency records yields underestimates, only hinting at the true incidence.

Researchers have argued that official reports of child abuse overrepresent low-income families.[33] They argue that since community agencies are less likely to intervene in middle- or upper-class homes, estimates of child abuse based on official records are biased against the lower classes. National surveys of family violence have found, however, that those with the lowest incomes are more likely to abuse their children.[34] Others have phrased the relationship somewhat differently, suggesting that low socioeconomic status characterizes the largest portion of abusive families.[35]

On the one hand, unless we are careful, studying abuse on the basis of cases known to the police, hospital, and the like prevents us from separating factors that lead families to be identified as abusive from those factors usually related to abuse. Other factors, such as parental unemployment, alcoholism, drug problems, or other indicators of inadequate social and family functioning, may be present. As Gelles noted: "Factors causally associated with abuse become confounded with factors related to susceptibility or vulnerability to having an injury diagnosed as abuse."[36]

On the other hand, where substantiation and validation of cases are important, then dependence on official agency records is warranted. Recorded cases appear to represent the more serious and extreme ones and the more clear-cut physical abuse.[37] In addition, records of official agencies do not suffer from problems of social desirability, retrospective recall bias, and single perspective reporting that plague other sources of information. Use of official agency records also permits wide geographic coverage with minimal cost.

Analysis of Case Files for Evidence of Abuse or Neglect. Researchers have analyzed existing case files for evidence of abuse or neglect, drawing upon the medical records of hospitals[38] and psychiatric clinic admissions[39] and institutional files of youth service bureaus[40] or of delinquents or incarcerated youths.

The clear advantage to using existing case files is their accessibility and availability. The disadvantage, however, is similar to the problem with official agency records: analysis of these files yields underestimates of abuse. Kratcoski abstracted information about abuse experiences by reading case summaries of incarcerated youths written by psychologists or social workers.[41] Findings based on these analyses are open to distortion, since in many of the files those interviewing the youths never brought up issues about parent relationships or possible early abusive experiences, missing the chance to uncover possible abuse or neglect. In addition, the parents had rarely been officially charged with abuse, leaving open the question of the validation and substantiation of the abuse reported. In some instances, researchers had to determine whether abuse had occurred.

Findings based on analysis of case files created for some other purpose are also mixed in with the reason for which the case was

35

originally included. Hospital medical records yield cases that are more likely to have sustained severe physical injuries than cases gathered in some other manner. In the same way, analyzing records of incarcerated delinquents for evidence of previous abuse or neglect produces findings that are intermingled with correlates of delinquency.

Sampling from Individuals in Treatment or Parent Training Programs. Researchers have used samples of abusive parents or abused children drawn from a variety of treatment or training programs. A number of studies, for example, have examined children placed in day care centers by protective services[42] and adults in treatment,[43] in court-referred treatment programs,[44] in parent training programs,[45] or members of Parents Anonymous.[46] Others have conducted in-depth studies of abused children and their families.[47]

While the advantages of this sampling method lie in the possibilities for long-term and in-depth study with a relatively captive population, the disadvantages are significant, including the tendency to report behavior in a favorable light, the characteristics of the setting of the study, and the volunteer status of participants. In addition, the effects of the intervention or treatment are unknown.

Social desirability refers to the tendency to report behavior in more acceptable terms. A person might refer to a "punch with a closed fist" as a "slap" to the interviewer, for example. In view of society's disapproval of various forms of family violence, adults asked to provide retrospective accounts of earlier experiences might reconstruct their own childhood histories to be consistent with or to explain their present behavior. This is of particular concern here since much research on child abuse is based on self-reports by parents (often mothers) who participate in groups for abusive parents: "Stripped of all elaboration, mothers' interview responses represent self-descriptions by extremely ego-involved reporters," according to one researcher.[48]

Depending on people to volunteer for these studies also produces a bias, most likely toward the less severe cases. The more deviant mothers would probably choose not to participate. In a study by Gaines and others all eligible abuse subjects and a random selection of neglect cases and controls received letters inviting them to participate in a study of child-rearing attitudes.[49] Approximately 20 percent of all groups responded positively to the request to participate. Some nonrespondents were in institutions or jail or had left the state to avoid prosecution. Recognizing the volunteer problem, the authors believed the control group was representative of the subculture from which it was drawn. They cautioned, however, that the matched maltreatment samples may not have been sufficiently extreme on critical variables and suggested that "although it is a poor alternative to compare known abusers with 'best moms,' dramatic results will not be forthcoming if a walk-in group is contrasted with matched groups other than the most severe abusers and neglecters."[50]

Given that therapy or training programs typically address problems associated with the abusive behavior, there are *demand characteristics* of the situation that influence the way a people behave and present themselves, introduced by the situation with strong expectations to succeed in therapy.[51] Findings are further mingled with the possible effects of the interventions themselves, a particularly problematic situation in studies investigating the consequences of abuse and neglect where measurement takes place over a time period. These threats to the validity of child abuse studies need to be systematically examined.

Self-Reported Responses. The majority of research on child abuse and neglect relies on self-reports in response to questionnaires and interviews. National probability sample surveys, for example, have assessed the incidence and prevalence of family violence in general and abuse in particular.[52] Other studies administer questionnaires to students or to youths in institutions[53] or use interviews and psychiatric assessments,[54] psychiatric and neurological examinations,[55] or maternal self-reports.[56]

Survey research methods and questionnaires enabled researchers to study abuse independent of official records and agents of social control, thereby eliminating the biases inherent in dependence on official reporting agencies. Another advantage of this method is that wide geographic coverage is possible.

Some handicaps, however, are associated with sole reliance on self-reported data from surveys or interviews. One difficulty is simply that of ensuring that the same question means the same thing to respondents in different contexts. It is possible that people of diverse backgrounds and experiences interpret similar events differently. The same event may be perceived by different individuals as irrelevant, benign, or positive or as threatening and harmful. Empirical findings suggest that a person's cognitive appraisal of life events strongly influences his or her response to a situation.[57] Thus, asking people about experiences they suffered as a child runs into the problem of how they evaluated the experience initially and the additional problem of simple memory decay.

Not surprisingly, the reliability of information based on retrospective recall has been questioned by researchers because people distort or forget the past. In a preliminary report of a prospective study, for example, De Lissovoy found that abused parents interviewed by social workers reported histories of abuse in their own childhood.[58] When questioned several months later by investigators, however, the same parents described few acts that could be considered abuse or that required medical attention.

Interviews have certain demand characteristics, which may encourage forgetting, remembering, invention, or exaggeration, in addition to the problem of social desirability. If asked to recall the past, people perceive and describe events and conditions in the context of later circumstances and present situations.

A related problem is single-perspective reporting, because information in surveys is typically gathered from interviews with one member of the family. This account provides one person's perspective on the issues, and its accuracy thus depends on the perception of the person interviewed. Research comparing perceptions by family members revealed significant disagreement, clearly reflecting differences in the perception of family dynamics by different family members.[59]

A final source of bias is that of the nonrespondent, or those people who choose not to volunteer to participate. Because surveys often suffer from low response rates, one needs to be concerned about those people not surveyed or not interviewed. Individuals who move frequently, are in institutions or jails, and so on are most likely to be underrepresented in surveys like these. Without information about these nonrespondents, estimates of abuse or neglect are incomplete and biased; the wider application of the results is thus limited.

Because bias exists in any measure we choose, we should recognize the effects of our choices and minimize bias whenever possible. Recommendations for minimizing bias in the course of research on child abuse are outlined briefly below. While compliance with these recommendations would minimize bias or distortion, recognition of the deviations should also help us understand the contradictory results of different studies.

Use of Explicit Criteria. While not all researchers will define abuse and neglect identically, the rationale for decisions about the breadth of the definitions—whether physical and sexual abuse and neglect are included, the restriction to abuse by parents or caretakers or to children living with natural parents, the number of episodes necessary, and the role of neurological impairment—must be made explicit. A clear description of criteria for inclusion of cases is necessary to ensure whether the sample selected can be generalized to other collections of abuse cases. Furthermore, we also need to be more aware of the implications of decisions about criteria for inclusion. Awareness of potential biases in criteria and methods may be the first step toward elimination of such biases.

Comparison of Physical and Sexual Abuse and Neglect. Many studies restrict their samples to victims of excessive physical force by parents, usually in the home. Abuse outside the home is rarely addressed. Sexual abuse is typically treated as a separate topic, although in some studies sexual abuse cases are included along with physical abuse or neglect. Many studies fail to distinguish between abused and neglected children, treating them as one group, obscuring potentially important behavioral or psychological distinctions. While some researchers have carefully restricted their work to one form of abuse or neglect, systematic comparisons are necessary to understand the representativeness and wider applicability of these samples. Further research is needed to determine whether it is useful or necessary to distinguish between physical and sexual abuse and neglect theoretically or empirically.

Need to Validate Abuse and Neglect. Increased efforts should be made to validate information used in research, using reverse and forward record checks whenever possible. The results of self-report studies and research based on official records of crime have been fairly consistent with the correlates of crime. Hindelang, Hirschi, and Weis found that self-reports were basically reliable and valid for relatively minor offenses but that the more serious offenses are more efficiently revealed (and with fairly little bias) by some official data.[60]

Assessments of family histories should not rely solely on personal reports, which may well be unreliable, but should attempt to include information from other informed sources, such as grandparents, siblings, friends, neighbors, and teachers. Recognizing the pitfalls of social desirability, retrospective recall, single-perspective reporting, and demand characteristics of the situation, *direct observations* should be used whenever possible, particularly in research that does not involve private behavior. Thus, studies of the behavior or cognitive, emotional, or social development of abused children should use direct observation rather than rely solely on the mother's report.

Need for Appropriate Control Groups. A number of investigators have begun to provide careful and complete descriptive information about the characteristics of their samples, leading to a potential reduction in bias. Some biases, however, cannot be minimized simply by more careful subject descriptions. In these cases, control groups are necessary to assess the independent effects of abuse and neglect. Without control groups, it is difficult to assess the strength of findings or the magnitude of relationships, and factors correlated with abuse are confused or inappropriately interpreted as causes.

Low-income families, for example, may have many problems, child abuse only one of them. Inasmuch as other factors—undernutrition, parental unemployment, alcoholism, drug problems, or other inadequate social and family functioning—are often present in such multiproblem homes, control groups matched on socioeconomic status and other relevant variables become vital components of this research. The failure to include control groups (or inclusion of inappropriate ones[61] may produce misleading estimates of causes, correlates, or consequences of abuse.

This is particularly problematic because of a heavy reliance on correlational studies in the field of child abuse. While correlational designs may be internally valid and appropriate, they rarely address causes. If the purpose of a study is to differentiate between abused and nonabused children (or abusers and nonabusers) on particular dimensions, then background variables that might confuse interpretation must be controlled. Better yet, longitudinal studies designed to test alternative plausible hypotheses are needed.

Need for Longitudinal Studies. To address issues of causality, designs need to incorporate some temporal element and go beyond simple cross-sectional analyses. One possible model for such research is that referred to as specialized cohorts.[62] In prospective or cohort studies, two groups of children who are free of the outcome variable are assembled. The risk factor—presumably early abuse or neglect—is present in one group and absent in the other at the time they are selected for the study. The two groups are then observed over time to determine whether the hypothesized outcome occurs.

Use of High-Risk Groups. Since child abuse and neglect remain low-base-rate phenomena, a related strategy for future research involves studies of high-risk children. By forming risk groups in which development can be studied directly, we should be able to move beyond retrospective reconstructions of causal factors. While difficult ethical problems might occur in identifying high-risk groups, prediction for research purposes may face less formidable ethical problems than risk-studies for intervention.[63]

Use of Multiple Measures. Finally, the importance of using multiple measures of social phenomena is widely recognized in the social sciences. In the literature on child abuse, increased diversity in measurement instruments and data collection techniques needs to be encouraged and supported. One strategy or another should not be proposed as the only one for research purposes: rather, a variety of techniques should be incorporated to overcome sampling and methodological biases in single-approach designs.

Recommendations for Minimizing Bias

In contrast to the physical or natural sciences where precise measurements are possible, in studies of child abuse and neglect it is virtually impossible to establish absolute rates or unqualified statements about relationships. With one set of criteria and one set of methods, estimates may be low, and relationships weak. With different criteria and different methods, estimates and relationships may be higher and stronger.

In this chapter I have tried to show how definitions and criteria for inclusion in studies of child abuse and methods of data collection influence research results. In particular, differences in criteria and methods affect not only estimates of the incidence and prevalence of abuse and neglect but also our understanding of demographic characteristics, correlates, and consequences of these experiences.

4
Improved Research on Child Abuse and Neglect through Better Definitions

Douglas J. Besharov

In recent years, considerable funding has supported research on child abuse and neglect. Between 1974 and 1988, for example, the National Center on Child Abuse and Neglect spent more than $100 million on research, demonstration, and evaluation activities. Although many research studies have made important contributions to understanding this serious national problem, research in this area is often criticized as poorly performed and largely irrelevant to the important policy questions facing the field. In the best-known survey of research efforts, Holmes concluded that "the majority of studies are so poorly designed that no generalizations should be made from the 'findings.' "[1]

The weakness of research in child abuse and neglect is a serious concern. The ambiguity that surrounds incidence studies has prevented agreement about the nature and severity of the problem and about the consequent need for remedial action. Similarly, the inconclusiveness of efforts to document the effectiveness of promising preventive and treatment approaches has denied to planners and program advocates a concrete agenda to implement them. Better research on the subject is essential if policy makers and the general public are to understand the nature of the problems facing the existing child protective system and how to remedy them. As Giovannoni and Becerra point out: "Social policy regarding social problems can begin to take on a rational stance only when informed by valid data."[2]

Many problems plaguing research in child abuse and neglect are endemic to social science research generally; it is not the purpose of this chapter to tread over issues already well known and well described elsewhere.[3] Instead, this chapter describes how inadequate definitions of "child abuse" and "child neglect" are an additional—

and largely unnoticed—obstacle to more successful research that aggravate the impact of the more general problems.

How Definitions Fail Research

Definitions of "child abuse" and "child neglect" are the basic building blocks of many research studies. As Giovannoni asks: "If one cannot specify what is meant in operational terms by abuse and neglect, how does one specify what it is that is being studied? How are populations to be selected and how are crucial variables to be measured?"[4] Unfortunately, existing definitions often fail to meet research needs because they lack comparability, reliability, and taxonomic delineation.

Lack of Comparability. Thousands of conflicting definitions of "child abuse" and "child neglect" are in use today. Definitions have legal, social-service, medical, psychological, or sociological orientations. Some describe child maltreatment in terms of proscribed parental conduct; some focus on the harm to the child; and many are couched in terms of both. While many definitions share common approaches, elements, and even phraseology, the different combinations and permutations seem endless.

Because no one definition is widely accepted, researchers have been impelled to develop their own idiosyncratic definitions. Often, they adopt the definition of the program under study.[5] As a result, there are almost as many definitions as research projects. Unfortunately, even the slightest difference can include or exclude large and significant groups of child-rearing situations and make findings all but impossible to compare. Comparability of research findings is thus a major victim of definitional diversity:

> Valid results may thus be rejected on the ground that they are not corroborated by similar work, when in fact the studies were not comparable in the first place because the populations being studied were different. Thus research intended to inform policymakers as to the nature of the problem may simply be exasperating to them because of the unexplained, conflictual findings.[6]

Incidence studies most dramatically demonstrate the lack of comparability of research findings. A study's findings are a direct consequence of the definition used. Thus estimates of the number of children abused and neglected each year range from 60,000 to 4.5 million[7] (table 4-1). Comparing these findings is indeed like comparing apples with oranges. Giovannoni and Becerra comment:

TABLE 4–1
ANNUAL ESTIMATES OF ABUSED
AND NEGLECTED CHILDREN,
BY SELECTED INCIDENCE STUDIES

Category	Investigator	Definition	Number of Cases
Abuse	Gil[a]	Abuse that resulted in some degree of injury	2,500,000–4,070,000
	Helfer and Kempe[b]	Officially reported abuse	60,000
	Light[c]	Reanalysis of Gil's data	200,000–500,000
	Nagi[d]	Officially reported abuse	167,000
	Nagi[d]	Unreported abuse	91,000
	Gelles[e]	Parent-to-child violence	1,400,000–1,900,000
	Westet[f]	Physical, sexual, and emotional abuse	580,400
	American Humane Association[g]	Abuse officially reported to social service agencies	111,072
Neglect	Light[c]	Neglect and other forms of maltreatment excluding abuse	465,000
	Nagi[d]	Officially reported neglect	432,000
	Nagi[d]	Unreported neglect	234,000
	Westet[f]	Physical, emotional, and educational neglect	498,000
	American Humane Association[g]	Neglect officially reported	202,227

NOTE: Refer to each study for precise definitions used.
SOURCES:
a. D. Gill, *Violence against Children: Physical Child Abuse in the U.S.* (Cambridge, Mass.: Harvard University Press, 1970).
b. R. Helfer and C. H. Kempe, *The Battered Child* (Chicago: University of Chicago Press, 1972).
c. R. Light, "Abused and Neglected Children in America: A Study of Alternative Policies, *Harvard Education Review*, vol. 43, no. 4 (November 1973), pp. 556–98.
d. S. Nagi, *Child Maltreatment in the United States: A Challenge to Social Institutions* (New York: Columbia University Press, 1977).
e. R. Gelles, "Violence toward Children in the United States." Paper presented to the American Association for the Advancement of Science, Denver (1973).
f. U.S. Department of Health and Human Service, *Study Findings: Study of Natural Incidence and Prevalence of Child Abuse and Neglect: 1988* (Washington, D.C.: U.S. National Center on Child Abuse and Neglect, 1988).
g. American Humane Association, *National Analysis of Official Child Neglect and Abuse Reporting* (Washington, D.C.: U.S. National Center on Child Abuse and Neglect, 1978).

Estimates of the incidence of child abuse have been based on work using no further definition of "abuse" than that it was the label assigned to the act. There is no way of knowing whether the cases being counted represent similar or diverse phenomena, and hence no way of knowing what the numbers actually mean, save for an indication of the volume of cases being processed under particular labels through various reporting and protective systems.[8]

Yet the impact of a study's definition on its count of child maltreatment is rarely emphasized. Only those who have closely examined these studies understand that a major cause of their incomparability is the differences in the nature and quality of the definitions used and therefore in the child-rearing situations being counted.[9]

Without an accepted definition of "child maltreatment," the findings of incidence studies can be subtly manipulated by altering the study's operational definition. The feasibility study for the National Study of the Incidence and Severity of Child Abuse and Neglect defined child maltreatment in terms of harmful parental conduct without specifying a minimum level of harm, indeed without requiring the proof of any actual harm; it estimated that 30 percent of America's children were neglected.[10] Later, the study's definition was limited to parental conduct whose harm to the child could be documented according to specific criteria.[11] To qualify as neglect, a physical injury, for example, had to leave a mark on a child for at least forty-eight hours. Consequently, the study's estimate plunged to 1 percent. Which of these estimates is correct depends on the degree of harmfulness considered sufficient to amount to child abuse. The national study could as easily have selected twenty-four hours or seventy-two hours or some other criterion as the cutoff point.

Lack of Measurement Reliability. The one characteristic that all definitions in this field share is imprecision.[12] Definitions often contain such phrases as "a child who lacks proper parental care"[13] or "a child whose environment is injurious to his welfare."[14] Even relatively more precise definitions provide little guidance about their application. The noted authority C. Henry Kempe reflects the feelings of most child protective professionals when he asserts, "Child abuse is what the Courts say it is."[15]

Broad and imprecise legal definitions are sometimes defended on the ground that individuals and courts protecting children need freedom to exercise their sound judgment in determining, on a case-by-case basis, whether particular child-rearing situations should be considered child maltreatment.[16] Many court decisions take the position that since "neglect" is the failure to exercise the care needed by a

45

child, and since such care must vary with the specific facts of the case and the context of the surrounding circumstances,[17] the word "neglect" can have no fixed or measured meaning, and each case must be judged on its particular facts.[18] In effect, these courts are saying that although they cannot define child maltreatment, they know it when they see it.[19] Because of the potential for arbitrary application and the evidence of frequent injustice, existing definitions have been harshly criticized.[20]

Researchers do not have the luxury of claiming that case-by-case decision making is beneficial. If a study's definition cannot specifically describe the types of child-rearing situations that should be labeled "child abuse" and "child neglect," data coders must make individual assessments of each case in the study. The unpredictability of their decisions undermines the reliability of study's measurements. Thus many studies use the existence of an official report of child abuse or child neglect to determine whether a case falls within the scope of the study.[21]

The plight of program evaluations illustrates the problems caused by measurement unreliability. To determine whether a program improves a family situation, evaluations must compare the family situation before the onset of services with the family condition afterward. Because existing definitions cannot reliably determine when maltreatment is present, however, they cannot tell when it has been removed. Like the initial determination that a case falls within the scope of the study, recidivism is often judged by the existence of a subsequent official report concerning the family. Unfortunately, a subsequent report may not have been made for many extraneous reasons—even though the parents continue to abuse or neglect their child.

Even a definition that could discern if the maltreatment had ended would not be sufficient. To be useful in evaluation studies, a definition must identify relative improvements in the quality of child care. The alternative, treating successful intervention as an either/or issue, can be unfair to the program and to the parents because it may understate the ability of parents, with the program's help, to improve their child-rearing practices.

To fill this gap in outcome measures, program evaluations often turn to proxy measures that seek to gauge the improvement in child care by assessing changes in parental attitudes and behaviors deemed related to child maltreatment. Elaborate scales have been developed to assess parental attitudes about children and child rearing, parental knowledge of good child-rearing practices, parental expectations of the child, parental self-esteem, and the willingness to keep appointments.[22] Unfortunately, the validity of such proxy measures has been widely questioned.[23] An evaluation of the Parents Anonymous program found that maltreatment was reduced even though parental attitudes toward children did not change.[24]

Lack of Taxonomic Delineation. Contrary to popular usage, there is no single behavioral entity called "child maltreatment" or "child abuse" or "child neglect." Society uses these general terms to encompass various forms of parental conduct that are harmful to children. Hence, maltreating parents are not a uniform group; many different behavioral patterns are involved—each with its characteristic psychosocial dynamics. Factors leading one parent to rape a child forcibly, for example, differ from those causing another to neglect needed vaccinations for a child. As Zigler points out:

> The nature of child abuse is . . . in need of a more differentiated and conceptually based classificatory system. Child abuse is a phenotypic event having a variety of expressions and causes, and we will make little headway so long as we insist on viewing every act of child abuse as the equivalent of every other.[25]

While some researchers attempt to identify and isolate the particular form or forms of child maltreatment they are studying,[26] most do not. Instead, they tend to use a generalized definition of "child abuse and neglect" that lumps together the caseload of the particular agency being studied.[27] With a population that has similar behavioral dynamics—for example, battering parents as defined by the battered child syndrome[28]—the findings are not necessarily invalid. In most cases, however, assuming that the population being studied is somehow representative of all maltreating families and generalizing the study's findings to all forms of child maltreatment is a prescription for strikingly conflicting conclusions.

> An example of conflicting findings stemming from differences in population definitions concerns two studies done in different settings, a hospital and a public department of social services. Findings from the hospital-based study were that high levels of maternal stress, measured by family mobility, broken homes, and a history of violence or neglect, differentiated children admitted to a hospital for "failure to thrive" or for "abuse" from the children admitted because of an accident (Newberger et al. 1975). The social services department study, which included no "failure to thrive" children and no abused children, only those identified by the department as "neglected," found that the social and family background factors did not differentiate neglectful mothers from adequate mothers. (Giovannoni and Billingsley 1970).[29]

Similarly, the evaluators of the first major federal demonstration treatment program for child abuse and neglect reported that lay therapy was the most successful method of treating child abuse and neglect.[30] Unfortunately, as Giovannoni and Becerra describe:

> Although ten different programs were compared by the researchers, no uniform definition was used, save admission to the program, of the mistreatment involved that brought the cases into the program in the first place. How, then, is it possible to compare treatment outcomes when this crucial datum on treatment inputs has been omitted?[31]

Consequently, neither the field nor the evaluators themselves were able to tell whether the finding about lay therapy applied to all forms of child maltreatment or to a few. Yet the difference is crucial.

The Federal Child Abuse Prevention and Treatment Act (P.L.93–247), first passed in 1974, has accentuated the problems caused by definitional inadequacy. Before its passage, most major research studies were performed by experienced clinicians studying families within their own treatment programs, families with whom they were intensely familiar. Distinctions among the relative and diverse forms of child maltreatment came naturally to these clinicians. Thus much of this work was done on and identified specific syndromes such as the battered child syndrome,[32] the child maltreatment syndrome,[33] and the apathy futility syndrome.[34]

P.L.93–247, with its expansive and undifferentiated definition of "child abuse and neglect," broadened research concerns to include all forms of child maltreatment.[35] With the law's additional funding for research, more researchers became involved in child abuse and neglect studies. Unlike many of the earlier researchers, however, most of the later researchers were not clinically associated with the treatment programs of the clients being studied. Although being outsiders offered many advantages, it also decreased the researchers' ability to reflect the relativity and diversity of child maltreatment in study designs. In this respect, the problems caused by inadequate definitions have worsened.

Child abuse and neglect is not the only area of social research plagued by inadequate definitions. Few writers, however, have commented on the problems caused by definitional inadequacy.[36] Most discussions of research findings briefly mention such problems, if at all. Instead, the discussion quickly turns to the incidence, the causes, the effects, the prevention, and the treatment of child abuse and neglect—ignoring the lack of agreement about the nature of the underlying condition. Research reviews, for example, often begin by complaining that inadequate definitions undermine all research findings but then describe and compare the findings of various studies as if there were no problem with existing definitions.[37] This apparent indifference to the harmful effects of definitional inadequacy makes them all the more serious.

Recommendations

Partly because definitions of "child abuse" and "child neglect" have been considered preeminently legal concepts, there has been a tendency to believe that better research definitions must await better legal definitions. As a result, efforts to improve definitions have been dominated by lawyers, and researchers have not been deeply involved. In 1978, for example, the National Center on Child Abuse and Neglect announced that it would support taxonomic studies of child abuse and neglect.[38] Although 436 applications were submitted to the center, no one applied to perform this kind of research, despite the explicit invitation. Several researchers have argued that no attempt should be made to define the terms "child abuse" and "child neglect." Gelles described why he did not attempt the "impossible task" of defining "child abuse" for his study of family violence:

> The term "child abuse" is a political concept which is designed to attract attention to a phenonomenon which is considered undesirable or deviant. As a political term, "child abuse" defies logical and precise scientific definition. Malnourishment, sexual abuse, failure to feed and clothe a child, beating a child, torturing a child, withholding medical care from a child, allowing a child to live in a "deprived or depraved" environment, and helping a child stay out of school have all been defined at various times and in various laws as "child abuse." The definitional of child abuse varies over time, across cultures, and between different social and cultural groups.[39]

Definitional weaknesses can no longer be ignored. Research studies must use more widely accepted, more precise, and more taxonomically delineated definitions if they are to describe, count, compare, and understand the various forms of child maltreatment. Researchers not only have an important stake in better definitions but also can make an indispensable contribution to improve definitions. Only with their skills can a definition be fashioned to reflect the complexity of the harmful child-rearing situations that society labels as "child abuse" and "child neglect."

Achieving wide agreement over comprehensive definitions of "child abuse" and "child neglect" that are both precise and taxonomically delineated will take a long time, if it is even possible. Governmental and academic pressures for immediately useful research[40] make it unrealistic to suggest that all research in child abuse and neglect be suspended while the field waits for such optimal definitions. Nevertheless, research studies should not be planned and conducted as if inadequate definitions do not strike at the heart of a project's purpose. Many of the problems described in this chapter can be mitigated if definitional inadequacy is acknowledged as a major obstacle to more successful research and if steps are taken to limit the damage.

A good model for the development of definitions is found in the National Study of the Incidence and Severity of Child Abuse and Neglect mandated by the Federal Child Abuse Prevention and Treatment Act. The work statement for the project characterizes the development of operational definitions as "one of the major tasks." The work statement went on: "It shall be essential to develop these definitions as clearly as possible to indicate what is and what is not included."[41] Thus a major goal of the first phase was to develop operational definitions, such as the forty-eight-hour rule, that could decisively identify cases of child maltreatment. The resulting 145-page report on operational definitions systematically described the role of definitions in the incidence study, the consequent characteristics of such definitions, the advantages and disadvantages of the various alternate definitional approaches, the particular approach selected, and a reiteration of its limits as well as its advantages.[42] The study's procedures were then designed within the constraints imposed by the definition adopted. These definitions are far from perfect; many observers will have cause to take issue with them. They exemplify, however, the degree to which definitional questions must become an explicit methodological concern.

To maximize its utility, research on child abuse and neglect should include (1) a careful determination of definitional needs, (2) the development of operational definitions to meet those needs, and (3) the circumspect statement of findings based on the limitations imposed by such definitions.

Determination of Definitional Needs. Not all research studies need precise and delineated definitions of "child abuse" and "child neglect." Research on agency operations, for example, can use the organization's internal definitions. On the other hand, careful attention to definitional issues is required in most studies of incidence, effects (sequelae), causation (etiology), and program effectiveness. Therefore, before research begins, a specific assessment should be made of the study's definitional needs and the practicality of developing a definition to meet such needs.

Development of Operational Definitions. If the study requires an operational definition of "child abuse" or "child neglect," its development (or adoption from another study) should be an early project task. The specificity of the definition, as well as its comprehensiveness, depends on the study's needs. The study, for example, may focus on only one form of child abuse or child neglect, thereby obviating the need for an exhaustive definition of all other forms of child maltreatment. Most studies, though, require a definition that systematically describes specific parental conduct and consequent harm to the child.

To operationalize these two fundamental elements, each must be placed in a verbal formulation that allows its reasonably objective assessment. Parental conduct might require description in terms of the specific act or omission, the parent's state of mind, and the immediate or chronic cause of the parent's conduct. Gil's catalogue of behavioral circumstances in cases of child abuse illustrates how the effort should be approached.[43] Similarly, the harm to the child might require description in terms of its form (physical, emotional, or cognitive) and its degree. Describing the form and degree of consequent harm to the child may well be the most difficult aspect of the necessary definitional work. Elmer's research in assessing the effect of child abuse exemplifies the difficulties involved.[44]

Unless definitional issues are of minor importance, all of the above information should be presented in a separate or easily identifiable section of the study's final report, which also explains and justifies the definition selected. Such a section on definitional issues would resemble, and could be incorporated within, the usual section on methodology.

Circumspect Statement of Findings. No matter how promising a study's definitions seem, the study should be planned to highlight and limit the consequences of possible definitional inadequacy. In addition, the study's findings should be described as a function of the definitions adopted by the study. It is not sufficient to add a caveat about the possible weaknesses in the findings caused by definitional inadequacy. Whenever findings are discussed, they should be clearly, unmistakably, and repeatedly stated in terms of the study's definitions. Thus, a finding should not be stated as "the effects of child abuse were found to be" but as "when defined as x, y, but not z, child abuse was found to cause."

51

Conclusion

If real progress is to be made in understanding child abuse and neglect, research studies must use more widely accepted, more precise, and more delineated definitions of this serious social problem. By describing the harmful effects of definitional inadequacy on research, this chapter argues that definitional issues should be an explicit methodological concern of research.

5

Contributions of Research to Criminal Justice Policy on Wife Assault

Jeffrey Fagan

In the 1960s and 1970s profound changes in family economic policy were gradually accompanied by closer attention to family social policy.[1] The growth of social services in the 1960s, designed primarily to wrestle with extramarital social problems such as crime among strangers or substance abuse, not only focused public policy on the economic behavior of families but also opened up the family as a social institution amenable to public scrutiny. Thus family behavior and social roles became issues of public policy. What had been condoned because it was "private" was now defined in a social context and placed in the public domain. Accordingly, family social interactions were more subject to social intervention and sanction.[2]

Until this time, when public policy began to examine the private realm of family life, few people considered the home—especially marriage—to be other than "a compassionate, egalitarian, peaceful affair in which violence played no part."[3] Three major trends in this era raised doubts about this tranquil view of American family life. First, the "discovery" of child abuse in the mid-1960s focused public attention on violence in the home. Medical and sociological research confirmed the existence of a "battered child syndrome" while other research documented the incidence, severity, and frequency of violence toward children.[4] Second, the reemergence of the women's movement at that time helped make visible the use of physical force as a conflict resolution tactic within the family and elevated it to prominence as a social concern.[5] Public attention turned to battered wives as part of a growing concern with rape, physical and sexual abuse of children, and violent crime toward strangers. By the early 1970s numerous studies of wife beating and other forms of spouse abuse had been published.[6] Third, the emphasis on victimization in criminal justice research in the 1970s identified family violence as an important and complex phenomenon confronting the police and courts.[7] A new social knowledge of family violence had emerged and for the first time brought underlying issues of violence and power in the family to public view, while political pressure was exerted on the criminal justice system by feminists to fulfill its mandate to treat violence toward women as a serious crime.[8]

With growing awareness among policy makers and legislators of the seriousness of family violence, concerns arose about the response of the criminal justice system. Early writings on police responses to family violence were critical, citing the refusal of police to get involved in family disputes, their avoidance of arrest and other criminal sanctions, and their inappropriate use of nonlegal remedies such as mediation.[9] Police viewed family disturbance calls as dangerous to responding officers and otherwise viewed family disturbances as problematic and intractable interpersonal conflicts that were inappropriate for police attention.[10] Nevertheless, the new social knowledge of family violence led to recognition that domestic disputes were a major problem facing law enforcement.[11] Increased awareness of the seriousness of family violence confronted the police and the criminal justice system more generally with demands for greater protection of victims and more vigorous enforcement of criminal law in family violence and prompted changes in laws dealing with wife battering and efforts to strengthen the criminal justice response.[12]

These developments have been informed by political activism as well as theory and research from several perspectives, including emerging empirical evidence on violence in the home and other research on violence among strangers. Criminal justice policy toward family violence has been informed by major studies of alternative police responses and criminal sanctions.[13] Critical research on violence toward wives, however, has remained outside the knowledge base that has informed criminal justice policy. Other than homicide, criminologists have only recently and infrequently focused their attention on crimes between family members and criminal justice responses.[14] Researchers continue to study separately violence toward "strangers" and toward "intimates." As will become apparent in the reviews of major criminal justice reforms, the use of knowledge in developing policy is based on independent bodies of empirical research and theoretical traditions. Arguably, policy has reflected research paradigms and theories of criminal or violent behavior toward strangers, rather than either an integrated perspective or the unique contributions of family violence research. Few efforts have been made to integrate the emerging knowledge on violence in the home with other violence research.

This chapter examines the contributions of family violence and other criminological research to criminal justice policy in the public response to family violence. It begins with a brief history of the recent emergence of family violence as a social concern and the divergent perspectives that led to its "discovery" and the resulting criminal justice reforms. Then it reviews the major developments in police, prosecution, and dispositional policies. The relative contributions of family violence research and other perspectives and paradigms are analyzed. The third section offers three alternative explanations for the limited contributions of family violence research to criminal justice policy on wife assault. The chapter concludes with a brief agenda to integrate family violence theory and research with contemporary criminological study of violence in the home.

For this essay the discussion of family violence research and criminal justice policy is limited to forms of violence and abuse committed, threatened, or attempted by male spouses, former spouses, common-law spouses, or cohabitants against female partners. Obviously, violence toward children, siblings, and parents is also *family violence* and has generated both theory and extensive empirical knowledge in the past two decades. In assessing the link between research and policy, however, research on responses of the justice system to abuse of children or the elderly may not be generalizable to assault on wives. The differences in jurisprudential issues regarding children and elderly dependents and the variations in administrative response systems require a broader and more complex analysis. Accordingly, the terms "wife battering," "spouse assault," "domestic violence," and "family violence" in this chapter are used interchangeably to describe the phenomenon of assaults and abuse by men against women in current or former intimate relationships where they are or were cohabiting or emotionally involved.

Alternative Perspectives on Social Knowledge of Family Violence

The new social knowledge of family violence developed during an era when social intervention in family life had gained widespread support and created a context for defining family violence as an urgent social problem. A series of processes ensued that shaped and influenced both knowledge of family violence and public responses. The nature of the problem and its etiological roots were subjected to varying interpretations and definitions. As expected, definitions, research traditions, and policy development all varied according to the interests and perspectives of the definer. Thus the perspectives that were influential in the development of criminal justice responses to family violence reflected larger concerns over the definition, etiology, and social "ownership" of family violence as a social problem.

Emergence of Domestic Violence as a Policy Issue. The emergence of family violence as a social problem reflected the events and forces that led to its recognition as a social issue.[15] The "discovery" of wife abuse was due in large part to the work of feminist organizations and scholars who documented and publicized the issue.[16] Battered women presented themselves to feminist grass-roots organizations through rape hotlines started by these groups, as well as victim assistance agencies and rape crisis centers. These grass-roots organizations quickly defined the range of services needed by victims of family violence: shelter, transportation, counseling, legal assistance, and child care.[17] They also defined the limitations of existing legal remedies available to battered women. Accordingly, they took the lead in initiating legislative change, altering police and court procedures, and working as advocates for victims within traditional social service agencies. They were critical in defining family violence as a multifaceted public policy issue whose solutions spanned the organizational boundaries of specific social or legal institutions.

As family violence became a public policy issue, the criminal justice system was obliged to respond in new ways. Traditionally, family violence was perceived as an ever-present and perhaps intractable problem, creating dangerous situations for the police and cases difficult to resolve for the courts. Within criminal justice agencies, however, several movements created favorable conditions for developing responses to family violence. Police training in crisis intervention implicitly acknowledged the responsibility of the police to respond effectively to violent situations.[18] Victim-witness services also proliferated in the early 1970s and were magnets within the criminal justice system for victims of family violence, who quickly became a major portion of the caseloads of victim advocate programs. In Philadelphia a women's group started a voluntary program of legal counseling in the district attorney's office to inform victims of their options. Class action law suits in New York (*Bruno v. McGuire*) and California (*Scott v. Hart*) set the groundwork for later legislation that strengthened legal options and mandated police response to family violence.[19]

Although the feminists' interest in domestic violence and the victims' services trends coincided in time, distinctions remained between the way they viewed the problem and their solutions to family violence. Their early origins—feminist grass-roots organizations on the one hand and criminal justice system auspices on the other—led to differing approaches to stopping violence and are reflected in the service emphases of programs sponsored in these divergent milieux, their interpretation of the role of the criminal law, and ultimately the kinds of organizations involved in social intervention. The result was distinctly different approaches to family violence intervention. Jeffrey Fagan et al. identified three kinds of approaches: feminist, social control, and legalistic.[20]

Feminist approaches focused their attention on the woman victim. Little attention was paid to the family unit as a whole, apart from children who were at risk of injury. In fact, some family violence projects believed there was a conflict of interest in serving both the victim and a "family" unit that included her victimizer. Feminism was an explicit part of the conceptualization of the project and informed the kinds of interventions and the approach to working with victims. The emphasis was on protecting the woman from further harm, providing options and means for women to take concrete steps to end the abuse. Within the justice system feminist approaches were illustrated by the victim assistance programs, which extended their services to include the concept of "victim empowerment": they actively encouraged victims to pursue not only legal remedies but also those social supports that would enable them to make life-style and economic choices.

Social control approaches generally emphasized the family unit. They viewed the family unit as the client and the victim as a contributor to the problem. The theoretical position of programs with this approach was often a family systems model, in which all family members were part of a system of violence and its solution required treating all family members. Early intervention was thought to be able to head off severe violence before criminal justice sanctions were necessary. The interventions, though often quasi-legal methods such as mediation or diversion services, were predicated on the notion that the authority of the legal system would exercise control over the "disputants" and coerce or influence them to obtain help to stop the violence. Unfortunately, this approach ignored the fact that violence may have been a constant pattern in the relationship and that invoking legal sanctions may have occurred long after the violence was in an early stage in the relationship.

Legalistic approaches focused on the victim and the assailant in the context of the laws that were being broken and were rooted in assumptions of specific deterrence. Deterrence approaches emphasized the application of legal sanctions through arrest and prosecution of assailants or invoking the threat of legal sanction through civil remedies that carried criminal penalties if violated. Mandatory arrest policies in several states reflect this approach to family violence.[21] Innovations included special prosecutors to improve prosecution services and make them more accessible to victims of family violence, though little else. A small number of these programs linked extralegal services such as shelter, counseling, and civil legal representation to the special prosecution units.[22]

These differences began the process of the disaggregation of interventions for family violence and laid the foundation for separate but parallel response systems. Each approach was informed and conditioned by different assumptions about family violence and definitions of it, which developed from separate bodies of knowledge. Naturally, they developed within divergent institutional bases consistent with their definition of the problem, their approach to working with victims, their philosophy of organizational administration, and their theory about why violence occurs and how it stops.[23] Feminist approaches were most often expressed in shelters or crisis intervention programs. They originated in grass-roots organizations and later in private (usually nonprofit) organizations. Issues such as the relationship between battering and sex roles in the family or sexism in society are part of the fundamental assumptions underlying this approach and are incorporated explicitly into the services offered. Social control approaches gravitated to social service agencies, either with formal ties to the courts (such as diversion or mediation programs) or under the auspices of agencies with access to legal intervention (such as protective service agencies). Legalistic approaches tended to be sponsored by and affiliated with criminal justice agencies. Though often linked by referral networks with other systems, these processes contributed to parallel approaches to stopping family violence, based on unique understandings of its etiology and methods to stop it. These approaches relied on different research traditions and bodies of knowledge.

Defining and Explaining Family Violence. What one does to stop family violence depends on how it is explained or thought to be caused.[24] Once family violence rose to the status of social problem, several definitions emerged that varied with the interests and perspectives of the definer. Definitions varied on several dimensions: victim-offender relationships, the kind of abusive or violent behavior, the nature of the harm or injury to the victim, and the motivation or situational context of violent events. The explanatory models of family violence also varied, particularly in the location of its etiology.

Early definitions were rooted in the experiences and activities of public and private agencies that saw victims of family violence. Child welfare agencies saw battered children in increasing numbers as hospital staff and social workers identified and reported children as suspected victims of abuse. They saw family violence primarily as a problem affecting children and broadened its definition to include sexual and emotional abuse and physical neglect.[25] The emergence of grass-roots programs for rape victims and soon after the development of shelter services for battered women identified significant numbers of adult victims of domestic violence. Victim assistance programs and police crisis intervention programs identified a wide range of victims, from children to the elderly.

Government activity in family violence in the 1970s not only legitimated family violence as a social problem but also subtly redefined it to shape its acceptance as a valid area of state intervention. The definitions of the nature and cause of family violence were influenced by the mission and interest of each agency trying to stake a claim to the new social problem.[26] For nearly a century the problem of child maltreatment had been placed squarely in the domain of child welfare and social service agencies, with the support of the criminal justice system and the medical profession.[27] Thus the 1974 reauthorization hearings for the National Center for Child Abuse and Neglect (NCCAN) gave rise to a popular definition that child abuse was a problem whose roots lie in social factors (such as unemployment, housing, health) and systemic family dysfunction.

While a consensus on a definition of child abuse was reached fairly quickly, this was not true of violence by male spouses against women. Definitions varied with their purposes. Nearly all those concerned with family violence agreed on the importance of operational definitions of physically harmful behavior. Gelles and Straus distinguished violence from aggression: violence includes acts perceived or intended as physically harmful; aggression includes any malevolent behavior regardless of the severity of physical injury.[28] The social and legal meanings of aggression and violence differed, depending on the victim-offender relationship and the presence or absence of injury. There was disagreement on the importance of nonphysical injury resulting from emotional maltreatment, harassment, or persistent denigration and on the accrual of harm from isolated and relatively inconsequential acts that nevertheless occurred in regular episodes and that were often precursors of serious physical violence.[29] These other harmful acts escaped narrow definitions of violence since little or no physical injury resulted. Though important to the well-being of victims, definitions that included nonphysical injury had little relevance to the codified behavior of concern to the criminal court.

Accordingly, the utility of discrepant definitions varied according to their application and the social milieu in which they were considered. Nonphysical injuries either were not useful in criminal prosecution or were simply dismissed as part of the complex dynamics of family life. Instead, criminal justice policy and research relied on definitions that stressed codified behavior to inform legal policy or response. For family violence researchers, concerned with measurement of harm and explanation of behavior, definitions of physical and nonphysical harm (and the corresponding measures) were both critical. At the simplest level the possible escalation of minor violence or nonphysical aggression to physical violence was critical to identification of victims at risk of serious injury. Fagan and Sandra Wexler, for example, found that the explanatory power of competing theories varied according to the definition of aggression or violence used.[30] The same study found that the comparative effectiveness of intervention also varied according to the measure of violence or accrued harm. Empirical knowledge of family violence was quite sensitive to subtle changes in definition and measurement.

With the discovery of wife battering in the 1970s came several competing explanations of its causes and cures. Each new paradigm spawned controversy, which some attributed to claim staking by various federal agencies. Several studies have noted four kinds of explanation of the sources of family violence: family dysfunction or individual pathology; situational factors external to the assailant or family; societal or cultural norms supportive of violence *in general;* and ideological supports for male supremacy and patriarchy.[31] These themes vary in the locus of etiological influence, ranging from the individual to societal structures and belief systems. They also differ in their implications for policy and intervention, suggesting policies from control of individual offenders to resocialization or macrosocial changes in behavioral and attitudinal norms and ultimately in the distribution of social and economic power between men and women. Obviously, these competing explanations will draw empirical support from quite different research paradigms.

In sum, the divergent views of family violence and discrepant definitions of services and policy development fostered the separation of research paradigms according to the *milieux* where they were applied. Research on family violence conducted in one paradigm had limited utility in another social arena. Measurement of the situation and context of violence, critical to theory development and testing, adds much to explanations of the motivational component of violence but contributes little substantively to policy on arrest and prosecution. As a result, the study of violence in the family and against strangers proceeded separately. Family violence was defined as a separate kind of crime, the result of processes unique to families and not ripe for study within the larger contexts of deviance, violence, and other crimes. Independent bodies of theory and empirical knowledge on violence against family and against strangers now exist. Rarely is family violence research integrated into the study of aggression or "criminal careers." Arguably, theories of interpersonal violence are incomplete without an integration of family violence research.

The Social "Ownership" of Family Violence. The debate over the definition and nature of family violence spilled over from researchers and practitioners into government attempts to define it for social policy. Four congressional hearings on family violence were held within an eighteen-month period starting in 1978, providing forums for conflicting claims about the causes of family violence and possible responses.[32] No consensus on definition, cause, or solution emerged; instead the hearings clarified the positions of several government agencies. Each went on independently to pursue a course of action consistent with its legislative mandate and agency mission.[33] By 1979 seven federal agencies had developed programs or become associated with family violence.[34] Each had developed its own definition of the problem and response to it.

The interest of the legislative and executive branches of federal government and the competing definitions of family violence made it "available" to several federal agencies. No single agency took a leadership role, nor did any agency's view prevail. A series of bills that would have augmented funding for these programs were introduced but defeated. Wexler attributed the defeat to growing opposition at that time to federal involvement in family violence—in effect, an attempt to reprivatize family matters despite almost a decade of federal involvement.[35]

During this era, the program of the Law Enforcement Assistance Administration (LEAA) in the Department of Justice was the most extensive federal response. In addition to state and local block grants, federal discretionary funds totaling over $8.2 million were spent in four fiscal years through 1980. The LEAA's definition of family violence gained attention and acceptance in policy-making arenas, in large part because the LEAA program was the largest and most visible federal program. In effect, the withdrawal of federal support from other agencies left the LEAA to inherit the family violence issue, which accordingly was defined as a criminal justice problem. The appropriate theory was deterrence, and the corresponding policy response was crime control through legal sanctions. Despite the broader interpretation and responses that had emerged across the country from feminist organizations and social agencies, dollars for services, accordingly, followed this definition of the problem and this policy.

Parallel Policies. Family violence policy emerged from social problem to public policy in parallel paths. The separate evolution of definitions, assumptions about etiological and appropriate interventions, programmatic responses, and research models was specific to diverse interest groups. Although violence in the home was widely recognized as a serious problem, there was no unifying approach to research, programs, or policy. Research on family violence[36] remained separate from the study of violence toward strangers, and criminologists made few attempts to integrate the emerging knowledge of violence in the home with other research or policy on violence. Despite agreement on the importance of the criminal justice system in a comprehensive response to family violence, intervention services, too, remained largely separate among criminal justice, social service, and private (usually feminist) organizations. These separate systems were unified only through referral networks and reciprocal contributions to helping victims or prosecuting offenders. Responses of the criminal justice system were advanced both by the system's own interests in responding to a large and difficult police problem and by political activism from groups seeking better protection of victims through criminal justice sanction and control.

Criminal justice policy, however, reflected the prevalent assumptions about the causes of crime and effective forms of sanctions and control. In the historical era in which family violence emerged as a social problem, the conceptual frameworks that drove crime control policy were concerned with deterrence-based policies emphasizing sanction through arrest and punishment. General deterrence of the occurrence of wife abuse or specific deterrence of its reincidence through aggressive response and sanctions became the policy emphasis in the criminal justice system.[37] The efficacy of deterrence requires that criminal sanctions be swift, sure, and serious.[38] Criminal justice policy makers were selective in using the new social knowledge of family violence, adapting those perspectives that were compatible with this theoretical framework. The contributions of family violence research to these policies are described in the next section.

The Development of Criminal Justice Policy

The changes in criminal justice policy that have occurred over the past fifteen years were predicated on criticisms of the police and the criminal justice system more generally for failing to respond effectively to family violence. Specifically, critics claimed that sanctions for violence against family members were rare or weak, that criminal justice agencies often did not regard and process family violence cases with the seriousness accorded to violence against strangers, that victims of family violence were not afforded the protection given to victims in other violence cases through punishment and control of offenders, and that the lack of severe sanctions might contribute to or reinforce the underlying causes of family violence.[39] The social and political processes described in the previous section gave rise to significant reforms and experiments in criminal justice processing of family violence cases, particularly wife battering. This section reviews the major developments in this period, noting the contributions of family violence research in each area. The section also notes examples of critical research on wife battering that is not reflected in these reforms and the perspectives on family violence that are thus not reflected in contemporary criminal justice policy.

Police Intervention. Early criticisms of police handling of family violence cases, coupled with litigation and growing awareness of the seriousness of family violence, have led to significant changes in policy and practice in many jurisdictions. These efforts focused more on sanction and control of offenders than on the protection of victims. In general, such efforts were designed to make the police response to family violence more aggressive and to increase the likelihood that sanctions would be forthcoming for incidents of wife battering. Specifically, policy changes were intended to increase the probability of arrest in reported cases of wife assault. Delbert Elliott concludes that one-third of all domestic disturbance calls involve some form of family violence and the majority of these involve violence between "intimate" cohabitants or former cohabitants.[40] Based on observational studies of police intervention in domestic disturbances, Donald Dutton found that arrest occurs in only 21.2 percent of wife assault cases where *prima facie* evidence exists for arrest.[41] Elliott estimated the probability of arrest to vary from 12 to 50 percent but found mixed support for the claim that arrest is less likely to occur for family violence than for violence against strangers.[42] Nevertheless, the arrest option appears underused in wife assault, given evidence that arrest may reduce repeated assaults, at least for a short-term (six-month) interval.[43]

Both research and litigation have led to mandatory arrest policies in some jurisdictions for incidents where there is probable cause to suspect wife assault.[44] The premise is that strict and swift application of criminal sanctions in wife assault cases will better protect victims and reduce the likelihood of repeated violence. Class action law suits in Oakland, California (*Scott* v. *Hart*) and New York City (*Bruno* v. *McGuire*) established a legal basis for mandatory arrest policies. The empirical basis for these policies derives both from accumulated evidence of the ineffectiveness of nonarrest or informal police dispositions of family violence calls and from experimental evidence of the deterrent effects of arrest compared with nonarrest dispositions.[45]

The Minneapolis domestic violence experiment has been the most influential study in the development of policies to increase the likelihood of arrest for wife assault. It was designed as a test of the specific deterrent effects of arrest on the recurrence of wife assault and was intended to provide a critical test of the effectiveness of legal sanctions compared with nonlegal, informal police responses. Lawrence Sherman and Richard Berk used an experimental design in two Minneapolis police precincts to assign violent family disputes randomly to one of three police responses: arrest, separation of victim and assailant, and advice/mediation.[46] The study excluded felony cases and was limited to situations where the assailant was present when the police arrived. During the six-month follow-up period, biweekly interviews with victims and reviews of official reports of family violence were collected. Despite the repeated measures on subsequent violence, dichotomous measures of recidivism were used. The severity, incidence, and time to reincidence were not reported.

The study found that arrest was more effective in reducing subsequent violence in misdemeanor wife assault cases than other police responses. Those arrested had the lowest recidivism rate based on official reports (10 percent) and victims' reports (19 percent). There was no evidence of differential effects among conditions based on the characteristics of offenders, though within-group differences were found.[47] A subsequent reanalysis offered more qualified support for the deterrent effects of arrest.[48] Despite a number of internal and external validity threats, these results provide compelling evidence that has informed police policy and legislation nationwide.[49] A replication of the Minneapolis experiment is currently under way in six cities, supported by the National Institute of Justice. Thus the Minneapolis study has provided critical, determining evidence in the development of criminal justice policy on wife assault.

Prosecution of Family Violence. Major developments in prosecution of family violence cases have centered on increasing the percentage of cases formally prosecuted and improving the quality and aggressiveness of prosecution. Prosecutors receive family violence cases in two ways. In many jurisdictions police refer nearly all arrests to prosecutors for screening, evaluation, and formal charging. In other jurisdictions police screen out many cases before formal charging by prosecutors. In these cases, as well as those where the police have declined to arrest, victims can sign complaints directly with prosecutors. Regardless of how the case is obtained, prosecutors then decide to decline or accept the charges and pursue a conviction in the courts on the original or modified charges.

Historically, prosecutors were accused of a lack of interest in family violence similar to that of police. Specific criticisms suggested that they either failed to file charges (that is, dismissed charges) or aggressively pursued a conviction and sanction against the offender.[50] Elliott suggests that the high dismissal rate by prosecutors in wife assault cases offered police further disincentives to make arrests or to investigate carefully and gather evidence for successful prosecution.[51] Others suggest that prosecutors often find an unreceptive judicial audience for wife assault cases, especially in sentencing deliberations.[52] With serious sanctions not forthcoming, prosecutors find little incentive to pursue a wife assault case aggressively through conviction and sentencing. Although there was clear evidence that the majority of wife assault cases were dismissed, Elliott found little evidence that different factors were involved in the decision to prosecute *family* violence cases from those involved in violence toward *strangers*.[53] Differences were attributed in part to the quality of evidence but primarily to differences in cooperation from victims and witnesses, a complex issue in the prosecution of family violence cases.

The problems of the cooperation of victims have been attributed to prosecutors themselves, creating a form of self-fulfilling prophecy.[54] Although problems of cooperation by victims may also be found in violence cases where there is a nonstranger but nonfamilial or impersonal involvement, the specific criticisms of prosecutors in family violence cases center on the lack of response to the complainant-victim as a "client" of the prosecutor, prosecutors' minimal efforts to ease victims' fears of retaliation, and limited advocacy throughout the complicated legal process.

The major developments in prosecution responses to wife assault have evolved from two primary sources: research on victim-witness programs in the 1970s and successful experiments with special prosecution programs for targeted offender types (for example, organized crime, career criminals). Victim-witness programs established the special circumstances that vulnerable victims faced in the prosecution process: intimidation and fear of reprisal, a possibly lengthy adjudication process, and cutoff from basic social supports such as cash or housing. Special prosecution units were established to accommodate the qualitative uniqueness of wife assault prosecutions within a social organization geared to cases involving strangers: often willing victim/ witnesses, clients who were not placed at risk of social deprivation by proceeding against an assailant, fewer evidentiary complications, and a more receptive judiciary.[55]

Victim-witness models established the need for ancillary services for family violence victims during the prosecution interval. They provided counsel for victims, legal advocacy to expedite hearings and notification of appearances whenever possible, links to critical social services (such as shelter, counseling, social service advocacy), and legal advocacy for protective legal intervention (such as restraining orders). These programs also fostered significant legislative changes regarding evidence to simplify proceedings and minimize the emotional difficulty of confronting a hostile court setting: for example, elimination of the requirement that divorce or dissolution proceedings be initiated before issuance of protective (restraining) order, use of depositions or videotaped testimony in lieu of court hearings, and relaxing of corroborative requirements in misdemeanor cases. Some states have established criminal penalties for violation of restraining orders issued in civil court, while others have created options to obtain protective orders within the criminal justice system.

Special prosecution programs created an atmosphere in prosecutors' offices where family violence cases had high status, providing incentives for vigorous prosecution without competition with other units for scarce investigative or trial resources. They also simplified procedures, so that in some programs prosecutors could sign complaints and serve as plaintiffs. Some programs did not allow victims to withdraw complaints or request dismissal once charges had been filed, thus increasing the likelihood of a complaint's resulting in a conviction while decreasing the negative reaction from judges for consuming court calendars and resources. In effect, these programs established policies of mandatory prosecution of all wife assault cases referred by police. Although larger jurisdictions have adopted these concepts, in many locales family violence cases compete for the attention of prosecutors. Family violence research, which has identified the high likelihood of repeated violence in domestic assaults as well as the special needs of victims, has rarely influenced rural or even suburban counties to improve the prosecution of these cases.

Although family violence research has provided significant, influential information to inform these innovations, its contributions have been limited to establishing the range of supportive services that are critical to sustaining successful prosecutions. Grass-roots feminist organizations identified the range of services necessary to support victims during a crisis period when they sought legal intervention. These services were integrated into the practices of victim-witness programs in particular. Accordingly, the use of community-based services was often made an explicit part of victim support services for wife assault complainants.[56]

The major innovations in prosecution of family violence cases derived from research on victim-witness and special prosecution programs, whose origins only partially addressed the special issues in the jurisprudence of family violence but more often were aimed at improving the efficiency and effectiveness of the prosecution function.[57] The special concerns of battered women in the criminal courts coincide with these innovations, although the impetus for reform may have derived from other interests. What has not occurred, despite strong empirical evidence of the chronic, escalating nature of family violence and its overlap in many cases with other violence, is a reordering of priorities regarding prosecution of family violence cases.[58] With few exceptions, wife assault cases continue to be evaluated and prosecuted with little difference from other violence cases. The organizational, fiscal, and procedural accommodations necessary in prosecutors' offices to pursue sanctions effectively in family violence cases are still not commonplace. In later sections explanations and hypotheses are offered for this state of affairs.

Sanction and Control of Batterers through Treatment. Court-mandated teatment of wife assault is essential to the criminal justice system objective of reducing recidivism.[59] Treatment options support this goal in four ways. First, treatment provides a dispositional option for judges in imposing sanctions. It is an "intermediate" sanction and form of social control that is harsher than probation but less drastic than incarceration. Whether or not incarceration is an appropriate sanction in a particular case, judges are often reluctant to invoke such "last resort" sanctions for family violence. They may fear the consequences to victims of the removal of economic support, and they may still (inappropriately) view domestic violence cases as less serious than violence against strangers and thus less serious in the allocation of scarce jail space. The availability of a dispositional option makes the cases more salient for judges and thus for prosecutors and police.

Second, treatment is seen as a means of protecting women who choose not to dissolve their relationship but whose violent partners will not seek treatment voluntarily. Third, treatment placements provide a form of control that strengthens the traditional probation sanction. Monthly, superficial contacts with probation officers for misdemeanor offenses are replaced by weekly or biweekly therapeutic intervention in a structured milieu. Failure to abide by probation conditions mandating treatment can result in court action and an escalation in the severity of sanctions. Fourth, treatment has specific clinical value in reducing recidivism. Treatment interventions are often specifically designed to reinforce the substantive meaning of the arrest sanction.[60] The format challenges assailants' belief that their arrest and conviction were unjust or that their use of violence was justified. The specific learning components of contemporary treatment models enable offenders both to learn alternative responses for conflict management or anger control and to internalize the negative consequences of violent behavior.[61]

Treatment alternatives and options have a longstanding place in the criminal justice system.[62] Dispositions with treatment components are common for drug offenders, drunk drivers, those diagnosed as mentally ill, and other offenders whose behaviors are presumed to be the result of some underlying behavioral problem or social skills deficit. Also common are options for diversion before prosecution, where the outcome of treatment intervention influences the disposition of the case. These models have also been commonly used for various kinds of offenders, including wife batterers.[63] The prevailing approach today, however, for offenders convicted of wife assault and ordered into treatment involves treatment as part of a court sanction following conviction, in conjunction with probation supervision.

The last decade has seen rapid growth in court-mandated treatment.[64] Treatment options developed in two ways. First, treatment programs were founded in both public and private agencies as a result of public pressure on the criminal justice system to respond more effectively to wife assault. Second, a small number of self-help groups developed among batterers.[65] Today the structure, justice system links, philosophies, and clinical approaches of batterer treatment programs vary widely.[66] Despite extensive evaluation of treatment programs, few experimental studies have been conducted to assess the circumstances under which they are successful.

Family violence research has made significant contributions to the development of treatment programs for batterers. Using an organizational and procedural model that was already in place within the justice system, treatment of batterers created a dispositional option for judges and prosecutors that made viable the concept of criminal sanction in a complex court calendar of heterogeneous offenses and offenders. The diversity of therapeutic models and approaches is beyond this essay. Important distinctions exist between family systems, anger management–assertiveness, and feminist treatment models.[67] It is critical to note that the models that prevail today reflect explanations of wife assault and violence that do not challenge basic assumptions of criminal justice system officials about the causes of crime. The philosophical base, stressing individual responsibility and behavioral control, is compatible with contemporary intervention models in the criminal justice system. This creates a political context where the treatment of batterers can be linked to probation sanctions and is in effect the social control component of the sanction while probation provides the supervision component.

The early treatment models were based on social learning orientations, an outlook especially compatible with the individual explanation mentioned earlier in this essay and described in detail by Fagan and Wexler.[68] Interventions based on other explanations of violence (societal, patriarchical) are incompatible with the social control model of probation supervision and have not found widespread currency in the development of treatment models.[69]

Feminist therapy calls for resocialization of men and, in lieu of anger management, a redirection of their view of women and sex roles and their instrumental use of violence to retain power and domination.[70] The social and cultural supports that reinforce the maintenance of power are critical to this model.[71] These critical perspectives on violence, with substantial empirical evidence to support them, have been less influential in guiding the development of sentencing options and treatment interventions for wife assaulters.[72] Sanction and control continue today to express perspectives that regard violence as an act of individual deviance. In the sections to follow, some explanations for this imbalance are suggested.

The Effect on Policy of Precedent in the Battered Women's Defense in Homicide. The relationship between family violence and homicide has been studied extensively.[73] Wolfgang popularized the concept of "victim-precipitated homicides" to explain the deaths of men who had first assaulted their spouses. Today about one homicide in four involves family members, and half of these involve "intimate" partners.[74] Over 1.5 million women are assaulted by their partners each year, but just over 800 kill their assailants.[75] Angela Browne reports Massachusetts Department of Public Health statistics that show that one woman in that state is murdered by her husband or boyfriend every twenty-two days. Although women are the majority of victims in family violence, it is the woman who kills her husband who gets public attention and who is subject to the full force of the law.

The handling of these cases illustrates the complexity of introducing family violence research into the adjudication process, but it is also an example of a tactical maneuver by defense attorneys to influence sanction policy through case law in family violence cases. Browne compared forty-two women who were charged with a crime in the death or serious injury of their partners with 205 women who had been in abusive relationships but did not kill their partners. Women in this study killed to survive what they believed to be an imminent threat of their own death. These women were neither violent nor criminal offenders, nor were there systematic differences in the women or in the backgrounds of the men they killed. The differences between homicide and nonhomicide cases were found in the men's behavior—the frequency and severity of their violence and the injuries suffered by victims, their violence both inside and outside the home, their use of sexual violence, and their drug and alcohol use. These were men who had lost all empathy, replacing it with the need for absolute control. They had lost all control over their rage and violence, since the absence of empathy eliminates an important inhibitor of the continuing escalation of violence. The frequency and severity of violence became so intense at the time of the fatal incident that the women saw their death as inevitable and acted to avert it by killing the assailant. They had the worst of all Hobbesian choices: stay and be killed, leave and be killed, or kill.

The development of defense strategies for battered women who kill their assailants has provided a unique opportunity to influence criminal justice policy. Unlike the processes that influenced other criminal justice or legislative reforms, the introduction of family violence research into courtroom deliberations and ultimately into case law is the result of tactical maneuvers by defense attorneys to establish the context of extreme violence and to show how the conditions of violence can shape the perceptions and social judgments of victims and their responses to their assailants. The result is a slow but perceptible accumulation of case law that is built on family violence research and reflects the very foundations of its unique paradigms.

To establish *self-defense*, evidence is offered that the justifiable use of a reasonable amount of force is necessary against an adversary when the danger of bodily harm is imminent and the use of such force is necessary to avoid this harm.[76] This perception and the decision on how much force is needed to prevent further assault need only be *reasonable*, even if they later turn out to be erroneous.[77] The defense is viable if the perceptions are reasonable. Components of the self-defense plea, including imminent danger, equal force, accuracy of perceptions, and efforts to retreat, require evidence derived from analyses of the history and context of violence in the relationship. Evidence of these perceptions derives directly from the studies of victims of severe wife assault, the context of violence and its influence on the victims' perceptions and judgments, and the circumstances surrounding the history of the relationship.[78] These factors are central to the tradition of violence research that evolved simultaneously with the feminist origins of services for battered women.

Browne interprets the statutory provisions of self-defense as requiring more than simply a history of physical abuse. Also necessary is a knowledge of the history of the circumstances surrounding both prior violence and the specific fatal incident. These are critical for establishing the woman's perceptions at the time of the homicide, particularly in evaluating the imminent danger to herself based on the escalating history of prior violence and the absence of any means to stop it. The use of this defense does not establish new law but uses family violence research to adjust "existing statutes to account for differences in the experiences of men and women . . . so that the *same* standard can be applied to all victims."[79]

The self-defense strategy acknowledges the danger to women posed by male violence in its extreme and their basic right to defend themselves from imminent harm. The strategy establishes the circumstances that might explain the homicide as a necessary choice to save the woman's life. Research and evidence to support these contentions must draw from perspectives that emphasize more than simply the occurrence of specific behavior. These developments in case law and sanction practices reflect unique contributions of family violence research to criminal justice policy.

Barriers to Use of Family Violence Research in Criminal Justice Policy

The contributions of family violence research to criminal justice policy on wife assault have been selective and limited to those areas that were compatible with prevailing conceptual frameworks on violence and social control. Despite the development of integrated theories in criminology, few social scientists in general or criminologists in particular have integrated the emerging empirical literature on aggression within families with other perspectives on violent behavior.[80] Family violence continues to be defined and studied *by criminologists* as a separate crime, not a form of violence or aggression. Recognition of the seriousness and prevalence of wife assault and child abuse has led to significant developments in criminal justice policy and practice, but the use of family violence research to inform their responses has been selective and limited.[81] Policies reflect aspects of family violence research that fit comfortably within the structure and philosophy of the criminal justice system. As a result, critical perspectives on wife assault are often overlooked in criminal justice policy. This section discusses three sources of explanation for these developments.

Paradigms of Social Science. Earlier, competing explanations of family violence were noted. R. Emerson Dobash and Russell Dobash, Fagan and Wexler, and Dutton, among others, have identified four possible sources of family violence: individual or family pathology; situational factors deriving from social forces; subcultural or societal explanations; and ideological factors that determine social rules and norms.[82] The emphasis on sanction of offenders through arrest and prosecution places a greater premium on individual explanations than on other sources of explanation. Accordingly, family violence research that identifies the causes and remedies within individual assailants has had the strongest currency for the development of criminal justice policy. Research on offenders has greater utility in a system geared toward the sanction and control of offenders. Research that examines the validity of ecological theories or ideological explanations has less value in a jurisprudential setting where the occurrence of codified behavior is the critical issue.

These distinctions are symbolic of deeper divisions in research traditions and paradigms. The virtual separation of research on family violence and on violence against strangers (other than for homicide) reflects important differences in theory, definition, measurement, and research paradigms.[83] There have been numerous criticisms of social scientific efforts to explain family violence, particularly the use of methods derived from the natural sciences and the attempt to develop a "science of man."[84] Such studies have difficulty acknowledging the context and meaning of specific acts. Yet theorists studying drug use, delinquency and violence by gang members, and even drug-related homicide have identified the importance of context in sorting out the motivation of specific acts.[85] Theories and explanations of these behaviors have tried to address the variety of meanings that may underlie identical behavior. These advances in family violence theory have been accompanied by diversity in research design and measurement and generally an accommodation of alternative paradigms in research use for policy development in these areas.

Family violence research emphasizes the importance of non-physical harm or injury as well as explicit measures of violence such as the Conflict Tactics Scales.[86] Certainly, the social and legal meanings of aggression and violence differ, and family violence theory should encompass this distinction. The social meaning of aggression is critical to theory that places these acts in the larger context of violence toward wives. Theory and research in this direction, however, have little bearing on criminal justice policy, since the non-physical dimensions of aggression are irrelevant to codified law and, accordingly, to criminal justice policy. Yet, in the evaluation of legal policy, distinctions between physical injury and nonphysical harm (such as economic retaliation or psychological abuse) can lead to very different conclusions about behavioral change and the effects of law reform.

Family violence research has been concerned with explaining the occurrence of aggression in families, not just violent acts. It focuses on identifying explanations and interventions that will reduce the likelihood of its recurrence for the victim and, by extension, by the assailant.[87] It has often relied on the reports of victims, who are "socially distant" informants in a criminal justice process oriented to the behavior of the offender. Family violence research has often applied a contextual approach to discern the intention and meaning of violent acts as part of theory construction and validation and has used measures that include both physical and nonphysical injury to test theory. Samples have generally been clinical or purposive samples of victims or former victims.[88] Theory has often examined the ecological and societal contributions to aggression, factors again extraneous to the logic of the criminal justice process.

In contrast, the use of research in criminal justice has emphasized studies with several discernible characteristics: offenders as subjects if not respondents; experiments or quasi-experiments rather than descriptive studies with clinical samples; violence measures that operationalize codified law or behavior and that also deemphasize non-physical aggression, injury, or harm; independent variables that operationalize official responses to family violence or the flow of cases through the system, that test explicit formulations of deterrence theory, and, most important, whose policy applications are compatible with the identification and control of offenders as a means of reducing violence. Exceptions to this are the theories and empirical knowledge that have informed the design of treatment programs for batterers. Research *methods* such as the Conflict Tactics Scales have been widely used as evaluative tools for policy assessment and for epidemiological study of family violence.[89]

In this state of affairs important information from other studies or paradigms may not inform criminal justice policy. For example, there is evidence that batterers often assault strangers as well and that the severity of spousal assault is well correlated with assaults on strangers, that domestic assailants may move on from one abusive relationship to another, or that they may generalize their violence from intimates to strangers.[90] Yet there is little evidence that prosecutors use such information to target family violence offenders for high-priority prosecution. Similar research suggests that prior calls to police for domestic violence are a risk factor for serious injury. Yet few law enforcement agencies report routine checks for prior domestic disturbances as a criterion or guideline for decisions about how to respond. Threats in the context of a longstanding violent relationship should be regarded differently from threats to strangers but again rarely inform police response decisions.[91]

The selectivity of the criminal justice system in using family violence research may not be inappropriate, depending on how one views its function in family violence cases. A narrow reading, which emphasizes the detection and punishment of offenders, suggests that the current state of affairs does not merit significant change. Franklin Zimring suggests that a specific jurisprudence of family violence is unnecessary.[92] Once the police role expands to include the protection of victims and the use of criminal sanctions to avert violence, other family violence research may contribute toward this purpose.

The use of family violence research in criminal justice policy should reflect the practical application of policy goals. For example, police may shift from an informal to a formal response knowing that a threat, property damage, or other nonphysical but chronic aggression has occurred as a prelude to a violent episode. The importance of other research paradigms and explanations of violence may increase when criminal justice policies shift from apprehension of offenders to policies that simultaneously consider the protection of victims. This is particularly true in the absence of specific law violations but where other risk factors are acute. Then factors such as the context of violence, noncodified forms of violence, and victims' risk become important policy ingredients.

The Social Organization of the Criminal Courts. The "criminalization" of family violence resulted in a sudden, rapid increase in the number of wife assault defendants arrested and referred to the lower and superior courts. In effect, an entire new class of defendants entered the criminal justice system whose offense and (at times) characteristics were quite different from the former kinds. If the use of family violence research has been selective, one explanation may lie in the uniqueness of family violence cases in the criminal court and the conflicts generated by this new class of defendants both for the social organization of the court and for the established norms within it. Organizational perspectives, which stress the structural context of legal decision making, suggest that holistic and working group processes of decision making will determine case outcomes, leaving little room for the more objective contributions of research.[93] Family violence research has generally not addressed the social organizational issues that influence policy changes in the criminal justice system.

If sanctions are the product of structural factors, the effects of organizational characteristics should prove significant.[94] The "going rate" for an offense is the sanction officials expect an offender to receive for specific offenses and is thought to be influenced by organizational factors independent of specific case variables.[95] Robert Emerson defines the "stream of cases" facing officials as influencing legal decisions in several respects.[96] First, cases are evaluated for prosecution and sentencing in relation to other cases as well as on their merits. Second, the seriousness of cases changes at different stages of processing, so that cases at arrest may seem more serious than at sentencing (when others have been winnowed out). Thus a felony assault against a wife may seem quite serious to the arresting officer faced with less serious domestic incidents but less serious at sentencing in contrast to cases involving offenders with prior criminal records. This may be a process especially sensitive to the differential processes of accumulating a prior record for domestic or other assaults. In sorting cases for prosecution or setting priorities for cases for last resort sanctions, criminal justice officials may look to a going rate for guidance. The relatively short history of wife assault cases has not allowed for such a rate to be developed among the closed social network of court actors involved in plea negotiations.

The ability to invoke last resort solutions, such as imprisonment, is a critical organizational function. Herbert Jacob observed that prosecutors in criminal court possess more information than other courtroom personnel and have a disproportionate influence over the disposition of cases.[97] By introducing a new class of cases into an established stream, prosecutors alter the group dynamics developed over a lengthy period and in response to a shared experience base. Moreover, they have the upper hand traditionally. The traditionally informal documentation and case disposition procedures of wife assaults bred informal routines. The formalization of such cases by prosecutors may introduce changes in the standard operating procedures for cases that routinely involved offenses against strangers. A new set of legal actors (special prosecutors, victim advocates) were introduced into what previously was probably an informal working group whose membership was stable, whose norms were well established, and that was likely to be made up of men. Documentation changed, too, as victim advocates and changes in the presentation of evidence were introduced.

The calculus of sanction severity thus may be questioned by changes in the legal actors, the formality and nature of their roles, the balance of knowledge of case specifics, and the absence of a going rate for punishment. In other words, the kinds of consensus usually present among criminal court actors may not be present when a new class of cases is introduced. In fact, it might produce dissent among legal officials concerning the going rate for wife assault, not only because of the absence of a knowledge base but also because of their own attitudes toward family violence.

These processes have been observed in the introduction of juvenile offenders into criminal courts and more generally in studies of organizational change in criminal courts.[98] Though not a concern easily remedied by family violence research, it is an area where understanding the dynamics of organizational change can be influential. Fagan et al. found that changes in policy and procedure occurred and *lasted* for family violence cases when the political incentives and fiscal resources were provided to accommodate new procedures.[99] Rather than displacing organizational functions or people, systems were expanded to accommodate the new class of cases and people to process them. Judges remained reluctant to incarcerate family violence cases other than the most seriously injurious ones. The creation of dispositional options was especially important in maintaining the calculus of when last resort sanctions such as incarceration were invoked.

This kind of research can address the social, organizational, and political dynamics of change in criminal justice policy. Despite steps toward strengthening criminal justice responses, police and prosecutors are still likely to resist the loss of discretion without broader court changes that advance the personal goals of those in the justice system. Careful research to illustrate the circumstances of organizational accommodation in a complex social system will contribute to the integration of family violence cases in the criminal justice system.

Paradigms of Social Control. The definition of family violence reflected in responses of the criminal justice system is one of individual pathology, and the appropriate remedy has been a strategy of deterrence and control of offenders.[100] Earlier the compatibility of treatment with this core philosophy was seen as facilitating research use of the growing knowledge of batterers. The creation of treatment programs for batterers provided the social and organizational accommodation described to sustain change throughout the systems of social and legal control. For sentenced offenders, those whose offenses might not otherwise provoke a sentence of incarceration, these programs provide a satisfactory dispositional outlet for the courts and accomplish the basic elements of social control of offenders. For pretrial cases or for cases with more serious histories of violence, a clash of control and protection paradigms may occur.

Control of offenders that protects victims, however, may be more difficult to implement and may lead to conflicts in paradigms of control. Specifically, conflicts may arise when risk factors suggest incarceration but the going rate or prevailing policies for control of offenders do not dictate incarceration. That is, victim protection policies may suggest that offender controls be activated that may not otherwise be used in an offender-focused policy. For example, in an overcrowded local jail a policy might be developed to ease overcrowding where those arrested for wife assault can be released on low bail or on their own recognizance. Their crimes may appear to be less serious than those of other violent offenders or alleged drug dealers, which threaten "public safety" and not the relatively "private" matter of family conflict. Exemptions from these release policies are certainly warranted in some (if not all) wife assault cases. Yet this places considerations of victim protection in wife assault cases and attendant strategies for control of offenders in direct conflict with other crime control strategies and broader issues of criminal justice policy.

This example is an actual case, a recent occurrence in a major city whose jail is under a federal court order to depopulate. Family violence research is unequivocal about the danger to victims posed by this policy—the chronic, escalating nature of wife assault poses special danger when retaliation for an arrest becomes a potential trigger for a violent episode.[101] Yet the clash of control paradigms is apparent, when considerations of public danger from street criminals and private safety to battered women compete for priority as factors in decision making and resource assignment.

Research on the differential effects of criminal justice sanctions also suggests that offender control models are most effective for less serious cases but that victim protection models (such as removal of victims to a shelter or mandatory overnight incarceration of offenders) are more appropriate for more serious cases.[102] Such disaggregation

77

and setting of priorities for wife assault cases has not been evident in the development of criminal justice policy. While some setting of priorities of cases for prosecution may occur, the winnowing process following arrest suggests that police responses should consider the severity of violence and consequences of an arrest in subsequent decisions about control of offenders and considerations of the protection of victims.[103] Research suggests that protection of victims should be a basic element in an offender control strategy for more serious cases, based on the potential harm unleashed (through retaliation) for victims in serious cases where arrests have occurred but offender control is uncertain.

While threats of retaliation against victims occur in some cases involving strangers, they are sufficiently infrequent not to merit a policy response. When such threats occur, protection is usually afforded to witnesses in volatile cases such as organized crime or high-level drug dealing. But there is potential interaction between offender control and victim protection in nearly all wife assault cases, especially when the victim and the assailant cohabitate or when prior threats have occurred. If invoking victim protection is associated with offender control, a disincentive may be created for intervention. This conflict in control paradigms is rooted in the larger issues of system capacity, organizational dynamics among system agencies, and the social and organizational "currency" of family violence cases. It clearly is an instance where research has not informed policy but where policy should look to family violence research to determine appropriate responses. It is an opportunity to merge research perspectives to determine empirically the relative danger and severity of wife assault cases in a larger stream of violent crimes.

Promising Opportunities

There are many opportunities for research use to be promoted to improve the quality of justice, as well as to enhance victim protection and offender control. Critical research on family violence can enhance the developments in criminal justice policy. Greater emphasis on research on batterers or general male populations with specific emphasis on family violence is necessary to guide criminal justice policy not only for treatment but for early intervention and sanctions. Perspectives from criminological research can also inform family violence research, with greater sharing of theoretical and methodological advances in the now separate disciplines. Specific hypotheses that integrate theories of family violence and violence toward strangers can form the core of a research agenda to take advantage of the substantial agreement that now exists on many theoretical and empirical issues. Research on strategies for organizational change and research use can also guide dissemination strategies to increase the acceptance of family violence research and the development of policies. Some specific examples are described below.

Applying Paradigms of Crime against Strangers to Family Violence Research. It is apparent that research use will increase when research on batterers becomes more commonplace. Although critical knowledge has been developed from studies of victims' reports, criminal justice agencies faced with broad offender populations and the need to reconcile policies for diverse kinds of offenders may be uncomfortable with policy development based on "distant" informants. To test etiological theory as well as evaluate criminal justice policy, research on wife abusers must increase.

Recent developments in criminological research can inform the study of family violence to promote its utility within criminal justice policy processes. Longitudinal studies using criminal career models have gained prominence in recent years.[104] Capitalizing on measurement and analysis advances in modeling criminal careers, the concept of "battering careers" may be developed through both prospective and retrospective studies of batterers. Alfred Blumstein, David Farrington, and Souymo Moitra have identified specific career types, from "innocents" who have little or no criminal activity, to "desisters" who quit after a very short interval of criminal involvement, to "persisters" who often are high-rate offenders involved in serious crime.[105] They concluded that each type is explained by unique etiological factors and that the social and personal processes that sustain longer patterns also vary for desisters and persisters. The concept of different battering careers is worthy of empirical study and can accommodate etiological questions as well as the development of career patterns. These perspectives can contribute important information to policy as well as to both sanction and intervention practices.

Studies of criminal careers among "stranger" assailants should also be expanded to incorporate crimes in the home against family members, both crimes against property and violent crimes. Fagan et al. showed that severe violence in the home often spills over into violence toward strangers.[106] Nancy Shields and Christine Hannecke suggest that these patterns may be mutable.[107] Unified theoretical perspectives on violence against family members and strangers can be tested to determine if a special theory of family violence is warranted.

Increasing empirical knowledge on violence careers to include both kinds of violence is a critical step toward promoting research use where the danger from offenders can be more thoroughly assessed.

Similarly, desistance has received considerable attention in criminological research, as well as in studies of drug use and other addictive behaviors.[108] Fagan has suggested a desistance model for family violence.[109] Whether desistance models can be identified to promote cessation of family violence and whether they can be captured in intervention services as part of criminal justice policy are critical empirical questions.

Studies of the effects of legal and social sanctions have obvious importance. The current generation of National Institute of Justice replications of the Minneapolis experiment is a critical first step. Sensible policy would recongize the variety of batterers and incorporate these variations in explaining the effects of sanctions. Social disclosure by victims and shelter interventions should also be tested as strategies to determine the combined effects of legal and social sanctions.

Analysis of Organizational Change and Research Use. The study of implementation and organizational accommodation of reform is a potentially fruitful avenue for family violence research. Fagan et al. analyzed the ways in which services for victims were implemented, changed over time, and institutionalized.[110] They also determined the conditions that influenced the process of institutionalization and accommodation. Specific factors included the ability to establish "domain" or an area of acknowledged expertise, leadership, institutional sponsorship, personal and organizational incentives, ideology, and resources.

The role of family violence research in these processes varied. Obviously, research that was compatible with the functions and social processes of the justice system gained wider and faster acceptance. Projects in which the justice system was the gatekeeper were more influential in invoking criminal sanctions than others. Despite recognition of the critical role of shelters and other services, implementation and knowledge use varied with the distance of a project from the justice system. Acceptance was predicated on projects fostering perceptions of their irreplaceable role in the response to family violence. Nevertheless, while other factors such as organizational and political leadership mitigated these processes, the central role of the justice system reflected the dual track of the earlier stages of problem identification and policy development. Organizational studies are necessary to determine the role and characteristics of influential family violence research in systems where significant reform of criminal justice policy on family violence cases has occurred.

Research on attitudes of police officers toward family violence and policy changes is an important start. Further research is needed on the conditions in which family violence or criminological research has informed criminal justice policy toward family violence. Identifying the conditions in which research has been rejected or accepted, both organizationally and in terms of the research itself, can launch a body of knowledge on research use. Other studies are also needed on the extent to which policy changes have been influenced by research. Earlier efforts by the National Academy of Sciences to study the effects of federally sponsored research and development should be specifically replicated for family violence. The results can inform dissemination strategies for family violence research that can guide the translation of empirical knowledge into criminal justice policy and promote its acceptance and implementation.

6

Alternative Analytical Paradigms for Conducting Policy-oriented Research

Charles P. Gershenson

Social issues relating to families and children are affected by past policy decisions, current policies, and their interaction with exogenous factors over time. In essence, policy questions are the result of social issue analysis leading to formal scientific study through the application of appropriate research design. They define the problem in the form of objectives or questions.

Recognition of social issues, a task once done through research studies, is now primarily conducted by the mass media through investigative reporting or by advocacy groups using case studies and purposive sampling surveys. Surveillance systems such as unemployment rates, infant mortality rates, child maltreatment reporting rates, and domestic violence arrests also help define social issues.

Research is usually necessary to move from an ambiguously stated social concern to the formulation of an informed and rational policy decision. Family violence, child maltreatment, and children at risk of developmental delay are real concerns, but the concepts are too vague for either policy analysis or decision making. The manner in which the issue is defined as a problem meriting public attention and action affects the findings.

Responsibility for converting a social issue to a defined problem generally is the responsibility of a skilled research analyst. But there is no generic research analyst. Research is only one aspect of professional training in the social and behavioral sciences. The statistician has generic statistical and data analysis skills but usually lacks the research skills necessary for hypothesis formulation, instrument construction, and data collection and editing or the substantive knowledge necessary for interpreting the analytical findings.

Family violence is viewed differently by the sociologist, the social psychologist, the clinical psychologist, the social worker, the law enforcement officer, and the economist. There is no best theory of family violence, and in the next decade a genetic explanation may lay waste to current theories. Nevertheless, social issues need to be addressed and policy decisions made simultaneous with the search for additional information. The current debate about AIDS illustrates the continuous interaction between social issues, research, and policy questions. Currently, the priorities are research and educating the public in preventive measures.

Definitions

Certain terms having to do with policy need greater specificity or clarity. The following definitions are attributed to David Gil:

> Policies are guiding principles or courses of action adopted and pursued by societies and their governments, as well as by various groups or units within societies. . . .
> The domain of all social policies can be identified as the overall quality of life, and the circumstances of living of individuals and groups in society, and the nature of all intra-societal human relations.
> The interrelated generic processes that affect the domain of social policies are: (1) resource development, (2) division of labor, and task or status allocation, and (3) rights distribution.[1]

The following terms are my own conceptualization of the social change process:

• A social issue is a perceived change, usually negative, in quality of life, circumstances of living, or intrasocietal human relations for a group of individuals or families.
• Problem definition is the specification of the extent, direction, and character of the perceived change and of the principal causes of change.

The Process of Social Change

The formulation of policy questions is done with the belief that some change is called for in a particular domain or that there is a reason not to change. For heuristic purposes, the analyst considers the process of social change to begin with the perceived social issue. The identification of the issue is followed by the research effort leading to the problem definition. Next, the analyst examines tested and untested alternative solutions. If none are available, the analyst may conduct evaluated demonstrations, longitudinal studies, simulation modeling, or other research to find solutions. This is the second opportunity to use research to address social issues, but instead of problem definition the emphasis is problem resolution.

All too often, problem resolution research is initiated before the problem is understood. An example is the federal effort to motivate adolescent parents to relinquish their infants for adoption. Is the perceived social issue an increase in the costs of the Aid to Families with Dependent Children (AFDC) program? Child maltreatment by adolescent parents? Elective abortion? An effort to meet the needs of childless families desiring healthy infants for adoption? Or some combination of these reasons? The policy world is neither neat nor orderly, and ideology may take precedence over rational decision-making processes.

Another example is the large-scale effort to reduce child maltreatment by adolescent parents through comprehensive services including parent education, counseling, respite care, formation of social groups, networking, case management, child care, family planning, school continuation, job training, and housing. There is no conclusive evidence that children of adolescent parents are at greater risk than children of poor families, though there is evidence that children from poor families (earning less than $15,000 per year) are at greater risk of maltreatment than children from higher-income families. A 1986 study by Andrea Sedlak of the national incidence of child abuse and neglect found a maltreatment rate of 32.3 per 1,000 poor families and of 6.1 for higher-income families, using the term "demonstrable harm" to define maltreatment.[2] When the definition is extended to "endangerment and demonstrable harm," the rates increase to 54.0 and 7.9 respectively. That adolescent parenthood is compounded with poverty has been adequately documented. But making a policy decision to allocate resources for either adolescent parents or families living in poverty based on risk indexes alone is questionable and undesirable. It is an example of poor decision making due in part to ambiguous problem definition, faulty research, the incorrect use of valid research findings, and imperfect analytical paradigms.

The next step in the social change process is to examine the costs and likely outcomes of the proposed solutions. To gauge the impact on other social issues one must try to estimate the costs of the resulting change or, as economists describe it, the opportunity costs. The 1988 decision of the Oregon legislature to reduce state support for transplant operations and to use the funds for prenatal and hospital care for poor pregnant women is an example of this stage in the process of social change.

Research is not often used at this stage, though optimization and allocation techniques would assist decision makers who must combine quantitative data with societal values and the political climate in deciding how best to allocate resources. No analytical technique leads to a decision; the findings from research and other quantitative techniques simply inform the decision process. If conflicts in values and political dissension are minimal, the quantitative findings will significantly affect the decision.

Those responsible for making policy use the information from research studies to pursue legislative action, to effect regulation, and to make administrative decisions. Public bodies gather additional information by conducting hearings and use it to formulate and authorize new policy. Their task then shifts to implementing the new policies.

Implementation is the process of translating a policy into a viable, efficient, effective, and valid activity. Although the words viable, efficient, and effective are readily understood, there is increasing evidence that those involved in implementation sometimes introduce program changes that run counter to the policy intent. The result may be that "street-level bureaucrats" have the final say in policy implementation. For example, the policy decision to identify all suspected cases of child maltreatment ultimately is implemented by our neighbors and professional people on the basis of their perception of child maltreatment. The consequence is that there are more than 1 million false-positive reports annually.

Formative or process evaluation is the process of evaluating the goals, objectives, resources, staff, and system that are developed in response to a policy decision. Again, the concern is with viability, efficiency, and validity. The information is used primarily by the program administrator to make decisions that will correct and improve the program's operation. This is a fourth context in which research is used to affect policy.

Process evaluation as policy research is undervalued, has low professional status, and is generally avoided by academicians: it is usually left to contracting firms. The accumulated knowledge of implementation processes is limited, yet it is a critical link between recognizing a social issue, developing policies to deal with it, and ultimately either resolving or improving the problem.

Effectiveness, outcome, and social issue impact are the driving objectives of summative evaluation. Have the goals of the program been achieved? The findings of a summative evaluation inform the program administrator and may lead him or her to examine systemic changes that affect outcomes. The policy analyst re-evaluates the policy alternatives, and the research analyst may redefine the problem. For example, when I initiated the federal program in 1963 to deal with the issue of adolescent pregnancy, I concentrated on defining the problem and testing various alternatives to service delivery. These efforts provided the foundation for the current approach, which has not changed much over the past twenty-five years. Extensive evaluations showed that comprehensive services helped adolescent parents cope with their new roles as parents but did not prevent other adolescents from becoming pregnant. The social issue had changed from a concern about infants to a concern about the breakdown of the two-parent family as the nurturing environment for children, particularly for the black family. The solution contributed to changing the social issue, and what in the short term was an improvement has become a more complex long-term problem. Short-term gain and long-term loss are almost axiomatic to solutions of complex social issues based on open system assumptions and analyses based on classical statistics.

The process of social change is recursive, progressing from social issue, to a definition of the problem, to alternative resolutions, to policy decisions, to implementation, to evaluation, and back to social issue. The analyst plays different roles and uses different analytical paradigms at different points in the cycle.

The World Is Round

Donella H. Meadows succinctly stated my basic premise as follows: "The world is a complex, inter-connected, finite, ecological-social-psychological-economic system. We treat it as if it were not, as if it were divisible, separable, simple, and infinite."[3] The analyst who addresses policy questions is well aware of the interactional nature of social issues. But the analytical paradigms used through the application of classical statistical techniques can misrepresent the real world.

Studying policy questions with different analytical paradigms may result in different policy conclusions. This is not surprising. What is surprising is the lack of recognition that the application of a particular paradigm not only affects the findings but inherently changes the definition of the problem. The research analyst reviews and analyzes a great deal of data: quantitative, descriptive, unbiased, biased, complete, incomplete, reliable, unreliable, valid, and invalid. The resulting perception of reality becomes the analyst's personal "mental model" of the real world.

The analyst who examines reality with the intent of changing it seeks a "good" account of reality that is as accurate as possible. For example, the belief that the world was flat was one perception of reality; the subsequent theory that the world was round was closer to reality. As more data were analyzed, scientists' perceptions of reality became still more accurate; they were able to determine that the Earth's shape changes from a fixed ellipsoid to a changing ellipsoid as the forces of gravity act on its molten core.

Many analysts live in the flat world of exploratory and confirmatory data analysis, correspondence analysis, nonlinear multivariate analysis, and system dynamics. These are but different analytical paradigms, different assumptions and ways of thinking, and different social accounts waiting to be used by those who see the world as round, or more to the point, as a closed system of feedbacks (complex interactions of several factors, people, and policies) that results in uncontrolled growth or decline or instability.

Data Analysis and Statistics

Invariably, the analyst who collects data has recourse to some form of analytical paradigm to facilitate comprehension. The statistical approach begins with a statistical model, usually based on multinormal distribution and linear relationships. These are assumed to represent the real world as expressed in some data base. Although the fit between the model and the real world is assumed to be true, rarely is that assumption made explicit and never is evidence presented to show the fit between the two. There is no evidence, for example, that family violence or child maltreatment is normally distributed, and it would be interesting to know whether studies have used statistics based on these assumptions. Sensitivity to this issue has led to the increasing use of nonparametric and robust statistics—for example, use of log-linear techniques.

In statistics, the difficulty of using continuous and discrete variables simultaneously limits the use of nominal and ordinal variables in multivariate analysis. Converting them to "dummy variables" is a convenience for applying multinormal models.

Assumptions of linearity are difficult to sustain. Saad Nagi's recognition in 1974 that substantiation and reporting rates of child maltreatment were not linear led to his prescient hypothesis that as maltreatment reporting increases the number of false-positives also increases. However, this significant hypothesis failed to consider the recursive impact of increased reporting per se on substantiation incidence.[4]

Data analysis is based on an entirely different analytical paradigm. Data analysis does not start with a model but looks for combinations and transformations of nominal, ordinal, and continuous variables with the explicit intent of reporting the data in a simple, comprehensive, and usually graphic way.[5] In this country John Tukey has been in the forefront in developing alternative analytical paradigms free from the constraints of the English school of statistics. He differentiates statistics and data analysis in his comment:

> The view that "statistics is optimization" is perhaps but a reflection of the view that "data analysis" should not *appear to be* a matter of judgment! Here, "appear to be" is in italics because many who hold to this view would like to suppress these words, even though, when pressed, they would agree that the optimum *does* depend on assumptions and criteria, whose selection may, perhaps, even be admitted to involve judgment. At least three different sorts and sources of judgments are likely to be involved in almost every instance: a1) judgment based upon the experience of the particular field of subject matter from which the data came, a2) judgment based upon broad experience with how particular techniques of data analysis have worked out in a variety of fields of application, and a3) judgments based upon the abstract results about the properties of particular techniques, whether obtained by mathematical proofs or empirical sampling. . . . The most important maxim for data analysis to heed, and one which many statisticians seemed to have shunned, is this: "Far better an approximate answer to the *right* question, which is often vague, than an *exact* answer to the wrong question, which can always be made more precise." Data analysis must progress by approximate answers, at best, since its knowledge of what the problem really is will at best be approximate.[6]

The advances in computer technology make more sophisticated data analysis feasible. Although the probability models upon which current statistics rely may not be applicable to the real world of policy questions. At least data analysis offers another way of looking at the world with fewer assumptions and greater ability to use discrete and continuous data. Others, however, are adamant that the model must follow the data and not the other way around.

System Dynamics

Social issues are dynamic, and they involve complex continuous interactions of people, institutions, and the environment. They also entail positive and negative feedback. This concept and the term "cybernetics" were formulated by Norbert Wiener to study the idea that complex systems operate with internal feedback that causes them to become self-regulating.[7] Jay Forrester applied these concepts to engineering problems related to the development of electro-mechanical computers about thirty years ago.[8] As the concepts were applied to a wider array of problems, the name of the field of study changed first to industrial dynamics and then to system dynamics.

Continuous time, interaction, and feedback are central to system dynamics. Continuous time and interaction are familiar terms used in such statistical measurement techniques as correlation matrixes, mutiple regression, discriminant function, factor analysis, analysis of variance and covariance, and other techniques to examine interactions. Because most of these techniques assume multinormal distributions and linear relationships, they have the limitations mentioned previously. In addition, they have the limitation of being frozen in time and nonrecursive. Even in longitudinal studies data are collected at specified times without any analysis of how a variable changed from one time period to the next. Glen Elder's longitudinal studies in life-course development are based on the premise that "parent-child behavior is shaped over time by the reciprocal interactions of mother, father, and child, and that family interactions are influenced by a changing social and economic order."[9] If he had continued his premise and stated explicitly that changing family interactions also change the social and economic order, he would have been using a system dynamics analytical paradigm. He recognized the feedback cycles within the family but did not extend the concept to feedback cycles encompassing the family and the social and economic order.

What is feedback? As an example, let us examine this conference: Doug Besharov obtained some foundation money to organize a conference and invite participants to write papers for publication. His purpose was to influence future research. If the publication is recognized as constructive and does influence research and policy formulation, Doug will continue to get money to run conferences and publish reports. This is a positive feedback cycle and usually leads to exponential growth. It is similar to putting money in the bank and letting compound interest accrue daily; the balance increases monotonically, assuming supply-side economists have achieved their goal of zero income tax. Positive feedback cycles are destabilizing, as there is no control to check either continued growth or decline.

According to the law of symmetry, if there is positive feedback there must also be negative feedback. For example, an increase in family violence results in increased prevention services. More prevention leads to a reduction in family violence, which results in a reduction in prevention services. Less prevention leads to an upswing in family violence. Similarly the thermostat in a room senses the temperature and tells the furnace to send heat when it gets too cold. When the room warms up the thermostat tells the furnace to stop sending heat until the room cools off again; then the thermostat sends new instructions to heat the room. The negative feedback cycle results in oscillating and self-regulating behavior. Negative feedback cycles are stabilizing.

According to G. P. Richardson and A. L. Pugh, "A feedback loop is a closed sequence of causes and effects, a closed path of action and information. An interconnected set of feedback loops is a feedback system."[10] The development, formulation, and analysis of systems of feedback is the essence of system dynamics. It entails the development of many mathematical equations depicting causal and contingent relationships. These equations represent relationships between level and rate variables, which are similar to stock and flow concepts used in econometrics. Mathematically, level is defined as integration and rates are algebraic equations.

The underlying premise of system dynamics is that the dynamic behavior of social systems is a consequence of a *system structure* that mathematically models the real-world system under study. Outside factors do not affect the behavior of the system. All factors that affect the system are internalized. This mathematical model can readily be transposed to a graphical model for continuous simulation modeling on a computer. Different policy alternatives can be tested on the model to examine system outcomes over time, enabling the analyst to test different policies and obtain both short-term and long-term outcomes.

The concept of time is used repeatedly to sharpen the distinction between the system dynamics approach to policy analysis and the traditional (classical) approach in which the concept of time is seldom discussed. Experience with system dynamics indicates that in many situations the short-term consequences of policy changes may make a situation worse; but in the long run improvement occurs. Mandatory reporting of child abuse and neglect, for example, has overwhelmed the protective care systems with a decreasing prospective of indicated cases. System dynamics studies of complex systems have revealed the existence of multiple time lags that policy analysts never use in their analytical frameworks or procedures. These become apparent in system dynamics conceptualizations. Moving from social issue recognition to problem definition requires time for research and for data and information gathering. The development of alternative solutions may take very little time if the solution is stored "on the shelf." If no solution exists, the necessary research and development may take a great deal of time, such as the search for a AIDS vaccine. A policy decision also take time, and implementation never occurs quickly. These time lags interact with all other factors in complex systems and alter system behavior.

In dealing with family violence, there are also time lags from the initial occurrence and identification to the investigation to the provision of services to changes in family behavior. Each step occurs in real time, and the time lags differ among subgroups of the population. The static aproach that analysts use has too many limitations for continuous use in addressing policy questions.

A simple example illustrates how easily we mislead ourselves and others using descriptive statistics: For the past twenty-five years I have been providing information to Congress and others about the average amount of time children spend in foster care. When I reported, based on a random sample of children still in foster care on one day in 1977, that the median duration of care was thirty-three months it shocked all of us. In fact, it contributed to the Adoption Assistance and Child Welfare Act of 1980, which changed the country's philosophy about placement of children in foster care. More recently I had the opportunity to compare the use of censored data for 1985 based, as in 1977, on how long children still in foster care had been there with the duration of foster care for children who had left foster care. For the former group the median duration was seventeen months, and for the latter group the median was nine months. My conceptual framework in using censored data failed to recognize that I was omitting many children in short-term care. I am consoled by the fact that the legislation was good for children and did change the way states conceived of and practiced foster care. The error was in conceptualizing a static model of a complex foster care system. System dynamics would have directed my attention to the flow of children through the system and thus prevented the mistake.[11]

Alternative Paradigms

As Tukey indicated, the analyst must settle on a perception of the problem and then make underlying assumptions in selecting a methodology. These two judgments affect the analyst's definition of the problem. The analyst's task is awesome. He must choose among varying constructs of the social issues—for example, the medical construct of child maltreatment formulated by Kempe and Helfer and the ecological model of Gil and Newberger.[12] These specification assumptions are based on different sets of assumptions, which the analyst may modify and adjust or discard entirely by substituting another set of assumptions. Another set of assumptions, meta assumptions, is implicit in the methodology used. They include assumptions about the underlying distribution (normal, Poisson), randomness, linearity, etc. These assumptions cannot be readily changed or discarded unless the analytical paradigm is changed or discarded.

These two sets of assumptions are always embedded in policy analysis and affect both the definition of the problem and the conclusions. Consequently, using different meta assumptions will change both the problem definition and the findings and may lead to conflicting policy choices. This has been demonstrated by David F. Andersen in two studies, one relating to retirement policies within the enlisted military force and the other an examination of the Coleman report on the equality of educational opportunity.[13] As Andersen showed in reference to the Coleman report,

> When taken together, the two studies paint a picture of dialectic evolution in social policy. The Coleman study, based on the regression paradigm, arrived at a compelling set of policy conclusions for American educators.
>
> Leucke and McGinn, by attacking Coleman's methodological priors, inferred a substantially different policy picture. . . . Definition of the problem derived from Coleman's paradigmatic perspective appeared to give some resolution. But when viewed from a different perspective, both the definition of the problem and its alleged resolution appeared to weaken and lose validity.

Summary

The task of the analyst is to inform the process that allows policy makers to reach rational decisions. Social issues and policy studies are part of a complex process of social change, and the objectives and methodologies change from discovery to problem definition to problem resolution to allocation to implementation. At each phase, the analyst must cope with both specification and meta assumptions. Policy analysis as a field of activity, not yet a discipline, suffers from time lags: frequently policy decisions need to be made before research results are known. Policy analysis also suffers from too great a reliance on open system paradigms—for example, the use of multiple linear regression—and mathematical assumptions untested in the real word. System dynamics and data analysis are alternative analytical paradigms that have much to contribute to understanding policy issues.

7

Asking the Right Questions about the Future of Marital Violence Research

Sally A. Lloyd

When research on marital violence began in the early 1970s, the assumption was that violence in the home was a relatively rare phenomenon, limited largely to individuals with deep psychological problems.[1] Two decades later it is clear that violence is a family legacy that cuts across social class and educational and income levels.[2] Recent studies of marital aggression indicate that marital violence decreased slightly between 1975 and 1985.[3] The incidence of marital aggression is still relatively high, however; the 1985 survey of 3,250 households indicated that 15.8 percent of the couples surveyed had been maritally violent in the past twelve months. Nearly 6 percent of all couples had engaged in acts of severe violence (violence likely to result in an injury).

The current state of knowledge on marital violence has been summarized in several recent reviews and books.[4] The field has expanded greatly during the 1980s, resulting in increased understanding of the correlates of violence in marriage. Methodologically, however, progress has been much slower. As early as 1980, Richard Gelles called for research emphasizing theory building, longitudinal designs, more nonclinical samples, and methodological triangulation (testing a hypothesis with divergent methodologies). We have made major inroads in some of these areas, for example, observational studies of violent couples by Gayla Margolin, R. S. John, B. Burman, L. Gleberman, and M. O'Brien and K. Daniel O'Leary's longitudinal study of violence before and after marriage.[5] Unfortunately, eight

The author gratefully acknowledges the support of the Harry Frank Guggenheim Foundation in the form of a research grant. The author would like to thank Joe F. Pittman and Cheryl A. Wright for their helpful comments on an earlier draft of this essay.

years later, most of the research needs Gelles mentioned are largely unaddressed.

We are especially lacking in research with direct application to conjugal therapy and the prevention of the development of violence in the first place. As Dennis Bagarozzi and Winter Giddings comment, the demographic study of marital violence does not provide the therapist with guidelines for conjugal therapy.[6] Gelles similarly notes difficulty in applying a decade of his own research to clinical practice.[7] Why, in the wake of fifteen years of research, is there still such a gap between research and practice? This gap results partly because of the questions that have been asked in most research. I believe that the time has come to reformulate our questions about violence in marriage.

My focus on asking new questions is not meant to downplay the contribution of broad sociological studies of violence in the home or the contribution of detailed examinations of the dynamics of the battering syndrome. These studies have been invaluable in documenting the extent and nature of the problem and the need for protective services for battered women and assertive law enforcement policies. Such policies, however, while an important front-line effort, cannot answer all the needs of violent couples. Batterers in intact relationships and spouses who see nothing wrong with violence may benefit from conjugal therapy or skills training programs. It is important to offer multiple options to both the victim and the perpetrator of violence; it is unfair for professionals to decide that the only solution to violence in marriage is termination of the relationship.

Thus this chapter addresses what is sometimes overlooked in the study of the violent marriage: violence does not necessarily herald the demise of the marriage. Indeed, estimates from various shelter programs indicate that over 50 percent of battered wives return to their husbands, even though particularly severe violence and injury might have occurred.[8] While these marriages may eventually dissolve, in the short run they are stable. The statistics compiled by Murray Straus and Richard Gelles are compelling given that they studied only intact marriages.[9] They estimate 1.6 million beaten wives in the United States during 1985, testimony that violence is a continuing problem in many marriages.

How, then, can we recalibrate our questions to address the gap between research and practice? I have identified five broad topics for inquiry: how distressed marriages differ from violent marriages, how multiple patterns of violence may be identified, why some children with violent backgrounds fail to become violent adults, whether the level of violence within a particular couple changes over time, and how the dynamics of the violent marriage may be delineated.

Differentiating Distress and Violence

Research on marital violence has progressed along several parallel lines. On the one hand, numerous studies have examined groups of battered women, or groups of batterers, explicating their childhood histories, self-esteem, personalities, and other characteristics.[10] On the other hand, large-scale surveys of households have emphasized the incidence and correlates of violence. These studies have linked marital violence with socioeconomic status, age, length of marriage, and the cycle of violence.[11]

Detailed qualitative analyses of the ways a battered woman rationalizes her return to the assailant[12] are as important to our understanding of the battering syndrome as are accurate estimates of the incidence and socio-demographic correlates of violence.[13] If we are to untangle the mystery of marital violence, we must recognize the necessity of multiple levels of analysis. Violence cannot be understood outside the broader social context within which it occurs (as Rebecca Emerson Dobash and Russell P. Dobash so eloquently argue in their analysis of patriarchy and violence, *Violence against Wives*), nor can violence be understood outside the actual experience of individuals.[14] Thus far, then, the work of these two approaches can be viewed as complementary and equally necessary to our understanding of marital violence.

Large gaps still exist. Specifically, we need more studies that explicitly compare unhappily-married couples who are violent with unhappily-married couples who are not violent. Such studies will allow us to interpret research results more accurately, for in many cases it is impossible to distinguish whether characteristics attributed to abusive relationships are a result of the physical abuse in the relationship or a result of the distressed nature of the relationship. Take, for example, the association between conflict and the use of violence in marriage.[15] While this association adds to our understanding of marital violence in general, it falls short of explaining why one couple high in conflict resorts to violence while a second couple does not. What is unclear is whether the violence results from uncontrolled conflict or whether high conflict is more characteristic of distress, showing violence to be a result of some other factor.

The importance of such comparisons cannot be overstated, especially when many studies directly comparing violent marriages with distressed marriages have discovered as much similarity as difference. Alan Rosenbaum and K. Daniel O'Leary conducted one of the first studies using comparison groups of distressed (unhappy) and nondistressed (happy) marriages.[16] They discovered that abused wives were not different from distressed wives on any of the measures used in the study. Abusive husbands were no different from distressed husbands in degree of marital distress, attitudes toward women, or self-reported alcohol use. Abusive husbands did differ from distressed husbands on cycle-of-family-violence variables and assertiveness. The latter finding on the lower level of assertion of abusive husbands was not replicated, however, in a second study comparing abusive and distressed couples.[17]

In my comparison of marital conflict in distressed and violent couples,[18] I found that these groups did not differ in their tendency to escalate conflict, in their ability to resolve conflict, or in the hostility of the wife. Violent couples were significantly different from distressed couples in hostility of the husband and the frequency of negative marital interaction.

Christy Telch and Carol Lindquist examined differences between abusive and distressed couples on alcohol use, sex-role stereotypes, jealousy, self-concept, marital anger, communication skills, assertion, marital adjustment, and cycle of violence.[19] Differences between abusive and distressed couples surfaced only in alcohol use and cycle of family violence. Karen Coleman, Maxine Weinman, and Bartholomew Hsi found abusive and distressed couples to differ on alcohol and drug use, frequency of marital arguments, and level of education.[20] Julian Barling and Alan Rosenbaum studied the relationship between work stress and wife abuse; abusive husbands did not differ from the comparison groups on job satisfaction, commitment to their jobs, positive stress, or job involvement.[21] Similarly, Randall Morrison, Vincent Van Hasselt, and Alan Bellack found few differences between maritally violent and distressed couples.[22]

The use of distressed and nondistressed comparison groups is vital to the growth of the field as it can help us understand why some distressed couples are violent, whereas others are nonviolent. The policy implications of such knowledge are great, for our ability to delineate the factors that differentiate distress-violence and distressed-nonviolent couples will affect prevention as well as remediation efforts. Thus, if as several studies suggest, the cycle of violence is the key to unlocking the differences between the distressed and the violent, we may need to try to break the cycle of violence before marriage occurs. If, however, distressed-violent and distressed-nonviolent marriages are characterized by different patterns of conflict negotiation, then intervention may need to be aimed at developing skills to manage anger and to negotiate conflict (as outlined by Gayla Margolin).[23] The point here is that we do not yet have a clear understanding of how distressed-violent and distressed-nonviolent marriages differ. We need to expand this area of research to distinguish the characteristics that define a distressed marriage from those that define an abusive marriage.

In addition, we must expand the types of comparison groups used. Thus far, researchers have relied heavily on self-referred and community-identified abusive and distressed couples (that is, most abusive couples studied were involved in therapy programs, either self-initiated or court referred). Such comparison groups should also include nonidentified, nontherapy-seeking abusive couples. Couples who are referred for help or who voluntarily seek help may be different from couples who are experiencing violence and have not been identified by outside agencies. This is an important distinction, for the type of comparison group used may lead to very different conclusions about the differences between distressed-nonviolent and distressed-violent marriages.

Multiple Patterns of Violence in Marriage

Perhaps one of the most important needs in research on marital violence is divergence in description: that is, we must move away from a uniform view of the violent marriage, the male batterer, or the battered woman toward a view of violence as a very diverse phenomenon. Not all violent marriages are alike, and, more important, the methods of intervention and need for services will vary considerably based on which type of violent marriage one is attempting to address. Margolin notes that several violence researchers have alluded to the idea that multiple types of marital violence exist.[24] A few authors have formalized this line of thinking by constructing typologies of violence, most notably Suzanne Steinmetz; Douglas Snyder and Lisa Fruchtman; M. Penfold, S. Morrow, and C. D. Webster; and J. P. Deschner.[25]

Very early in the development of marital violence research, Steinmetz differentiated between two types of violent couples: "Saturday night brawlers" and "chronic battered syndrome."[26] The brawlers experienced intense conflict that escalated to reciprocal violence; husbands and wives were both as likely to be the aggressor as the victim of a particular brawl. The chronic syndrome resembled what Lenore Walker would later call the battered woman syndrome: intense fear on the part of the wife and repeated severe battering by the husband.[27]

97

Snyder and Fruchtman constructed a data-based typology of women who had been admitted to a shelter.[28] What makes this piece of research unique is the authors' conscious effort to examine how the women who had come to the shelter varied in background characteristics, extent of abuse, and other factors. Their analysis yielded some patterns of wife abuse. In type 1, the relationship between assailant and victim is stable, abuse is infrequent and often attributed to alcohol or external pressures, and the woman is likely to have acted aggressively toward her husband as well. These women are the most likely to return to the assailant. Type 2 is characterized by highly unstable and explosive relationships, many marital separations, and severe and injury-producing violence. Type 3 women receive the most chronic and severe abuse; their children are frequently abused by the assailant as well, and these women do not report a history of violence in their families of origin. In type 4, most of the abuse is directed toward children and little toward wives; these women seek shelter to protect their children. Type 5 women report an extensive history of violence in their families of origin, including parental neglect and physical abuse; often, their husbands began to abuse them before marriage. These women are also more likely to return to the assailant than are type 2, 3, or 4 women.

M. Penfold and others present a typology of marital conflict and violence.[29] Their typology is based on clinical work with relatively serious cases of marital violence. The constant high pattern is characterized by frequent conflict that erupts from time to time into violence. The partners rarely withdraw from a conflict; rather, they may even enjoy their combativeness. The physical fighting is usually not extremely serious. The unpredictable volatile pattern, in contrast, is characterized by very little overt conflict. Partners frequently withdraw from conflict. Penfold hypothesizes that these couples nurture grievances and anger for long periods of time; when disagreements finally begin they are likely to be highly violent.[30] The steady escalation pattern is characterized by a slow yet steady buildup of discord over time. This buildup eventually reaches dangerous proportions; over time, violence becomes a common feature of conflict negotiation.

Jeanne Deschner offers a typology similarly based on clinical work.[31] She describes the batterer specifically, emphasizing different backgrounds and personalities as the keys to understanding various types of batterers. Her typology includes the following groups: socially chaotic and deprived, "child-parent" (batterer dependence), obsessive-compulsive, responding abnormally to loud complaining, pathologically jealous, mentally ill (psychotic), and mentally disturbed (personality disorder).

Although these typologies emphasize different aspects of marital violence (that is, the victim, the aggressor, or the relationship), they share in common an emphasis on the variability of marital aggression. The formation of such typologies is important for several reasons. First, an emphasis on different patterns of aggression contributes something qualitatively unique to our understanding of violence in marriage. Violence may interact with background factors, the current state of the marriage, and the like to produce different consequences, meanings, and reactions for different couples. Second, typologies demonstrate that violence varies widely in degree of frequency and severity. Third, typologies demonstrate that the cycle of family violence is a significant precursor for some, but not all, battering relationships. In fact, individuals who grew up within a violent household and who are currently involved in a violent marital relationship may represent only one of several types of battering dynamics.

Most important, typologies point out that violent relationships require a wide variety of treatment and intervention options. Shelter and protection for the battered woman who fears for her life remain the most important options that a community can provide. Help for the violent relationship must begin with protection but cannot stop there. In addition, some battered women desperately need assistance with housing, employment, and the like. Such assistance may be irrelevant, however, to the women who intend to return to their spouses. The latter group may benefit more from joint counseling that emphasizes anger management and conflict control skills.[32]

A typological approach can also help in classifying couples into types of violent versus nonviolent relationships. Given that spouses' reports of the frequency and types of violence in their marriage are not always congruent,[33] classifying a particular relationship as violent or nonviolent may be a difficult task. In addition, it may be hard to identify cutoff points that accurately reflect the state of the relationship; for example, is one incident of "minor" violence (such as a push) equal in relevance to one incident of "severe" violence (such as a beating)? For practical reasons, we must often rely on artificially precise definitions of violence in our attempts to compare relationships.

This point can best be illustrated with a comparison of an a priori classification scheme (based on predetermined cutoffs) with the natural grouping of partners (based on cluster analysis). Table 7–1 presents an a priori breakdown of 100 couples into "nondistressed," "distressed," "minor violence," and "severe violence" groups (these data are part of a larger study of marital violence being conducted by

TABLE 7–1
A Priori Groupings of Couples

	Nondistressed[a]	Distressed[b]	Minor Violence[c]	Severe Violence[d]
Number of couples	17	12	17	54
Dyadic adjustment[e]				
Husband	117.53	99.92	106.59	99.37
Wife	119.12	93.08	110.53	97.31
Minor violence[f]				
Husband-initiated	0.00	0.00	0.94	3.57
Wife-initiated	0.00	0.00	0.82	5.02
Severe violence[f]				
Husband-initiated	0.00	0.00	0.00	1.63
Wife-initiated	0.00	0.00	0.00	2.67

a. Couples with neither the wife nor the husband reporting any incident of violence within the past twelve months.
b. Couples with either husband or wife reporting marital distress but neither reporting violence.
c. Couples with either husband or wife reporlting at least one incident of minor violence, such as pushing, shoving, slapping, or throwing objects at the spouse.
d. Couples with either husband or wife reporting at least one incident of major violence such as kicking, hitting, or beating.
e. Scale scores range from 0 to 151; the higher the score, the greater the satisfaction. A cut of 100 is used clinically to establish distress.
f. These numbers indicate frequency of violence during the past 12 months.
SOURCE: Author.

the author).[34] The nondistressed group consists of couples wherein both husband and wife report Dyadic Adjustment Scale (DAS—a measure of marital happiness) scores of greater than 100 and neither husband or wife reports any incident of violence in the past twelve months (measured with the Conflict Tactics Scale).[35] The distressed group represents couples wherein either husband or wife reports marital distress (under 100 on the DAS) and neither partner reports violence. The minor violence group includes couples wherein either husband or wife reports at least one incident of minor violence (throwing objects at the spouse, pushing or shoving, or slapping) but no severe violence (kicking, biting, hitting with a fist or object, beating, or threatened or actual use of a weapon). The severe violence group includes couples wherein either partner reports one or more incidents of severe violence in the past twelve months. This breakdown was based entirely on standard definitions of distress, minor violence, and severe violence.

A somewhat different picture emerges when these same couples are classified on the basis of a cluster analysis. Such an analysis allows the interrelationships among the variables to determine which relationships naturally "group" together. Results of a cluster analysis of the 100 couples are presented in table 7–2.[36]

There were eight groups of couples identified by the cluster analysis. Group 1 is a nondistressed, relatively violence-free group and appears to be similar to the nondistressed group in the a priori classification. Group 3 is quite similar to the distressed group in the a priori classification (note, however, that the cluster analysis produced no types that were completely violence free). Surprisingly, a nondistressed-violent group appears (group 2); this group is characterized by the presence of both minor and severe violence. There are two types of distressed–minor violence couples (groups 4 and 8) and three types of distressed–severe violence couples (groups 5, 6, and 7).[37]

This typology illustrates that a priori definition of group membership may actually mask important differences from couple to couple. Cluster analysis produces several types of couples that predetermined cutoffs would have ignored, most notably a nondistressed violent group and multiple types of severe violence groups. This typology is not intended to downplay wives' greater risk of injury or the differential bases of power in a marriage. It is important to acknowledge, however, that violence in some marriages may be best understood as a destructive negotiation pattern whereas violence in other marriages may be understood as the husband's assaultive personality. Such different dynamics call for different methods of intervention and remediation.

Some of these types may actually represent different stages in the development of violent relationships. For instance, the nondistressed-violent group could represent an early stage wherein violence has not yet affected satisfaction with the marriage. To the extent that negative marital interaction seems to erode satisfaction in marriage[38] and negative interaction is associated with the use of violence in marriage,[39] such nondistressed-violent relationships may eventually evolve into one of the distressed-violent types. Such speculation can be supported, however, only with longitudinal study.

Typologies of distressed, nondistressed, and violent marriages could be expanded to include other relevant characteristics, such as the cycle of family violence or characteristics of conflict. Such ty-

TABLE 7-2

Typology Based on Cluster Analysis

	Group 1[a]	Group 2[b]	Group 3[c]	Group 4[d]	Group 5[e]	Group 6[f]	Group 7[g]	Group 8[h]
Number of couples	27	12	27	13	6	1	2	8
Dyadic adjustment[i]								
Husband	115.59	113.92	101.11	98.77	96.83	95.00	91.00	74.13
Wife	121.15	110.50	95.70	93.69	95.00	96.00	92.50	79.25
Minor violence[j]								
Husband-initiated	0.19	3.58	0.48	2.31	6.50	1.00	6.50	3.88
Wife-initiated	0.26	2.92	0.44	7.00	8.33	17.00	12.50	3.25
Severe violence[k]								
Husband-initiated	0.00	1.67	0.11	0.23	2.33	4.00	12.50	1.75
Wife-initiated	0.07	1.00	0.22	1.85	7.00	20.00	9.50	1.00

a. Nondistressed, relatively violence-free couples.
b. Nondistressed, violent couples.
c. Distressed, relatively nonviolent couples.
d. Distressed couples, who engage in minor violence.
e. Distressed couples, low frequency fo severe violence.
f. Distressed couple, wife reporting high frequency of severe violence.
g. Distressed couples, high frequency of severe violence.
h. Extremely distressed couples, who engage in minor violence.
i. A score of 100 or greater indicates satisfaction with the marriage; score below 100 indicates dissatisfaction.
j. Frequency of objects thrown at spouse, shoving and slapping during the past twelve months.
k. Frequency of kicking, biting, hitting with a fist or object, beating, and threat or use of a weapon during the past twelve
    months.

Source: Author.

pologies may help elucidate how background factors and internal dynamics interact with the use of violence in marriage. In addition, such typologies may identify a key group that has gone unstudied: partners who experienced or witnessed violence in their family of origin but who have not repeated the cycle in their own marriages.

Do All Children Exposed to Violence Become Violent Adults?

One of the most widely heralded factors associated with marital violence has been the cycle of family violence. Being abused as a child, observing parental marital violence, or both have been related to being an abusive husband or an abused wife.[40] Although the results of these studies are not entirely consistent, it appears that the observation of parental marital violence is the more salient characteristic,[41] a transmission that may operate more strongly for husbands than for wives.[42]

To understand the cycle of family violence better, we must broaden our concept of the intergenerational transmission of violence. Thus far, the emphasis has been on examining whether similar aggressive behavior is transmitted from the family of origin to the family of procreation. Such specific behavior, however, is probably only a small part of what is transmitted across the generations. In addition, children may learn patterns of conflict negotiation that also increase the likelihood that violence may occur in the families they form as adults. For example, the use of persistence (keeping after the partner until he or she gives in) as a conflict negotiation tactic is associated with the use of violence in premarital relationships.[43] Persistence may also be transmitted intergenerationally, so that the learned predisposition to behave violently in close relationships has both direct and indirect components. The direct component is the modeling of violent behavior, and the indirect component is the modeling of negotiation tactics that may lead to violence. Thus, studies of the cycle of family violence may need to conceptualize the transmission of violence in broader terms, recognizing how destructive communication patterns and the lack of constructive models of conflict negotiation affect the process.[44]

My second point raises two questions about the cycle of family violence. First, do children exposed to violence grow up to be violent adults? The answer to this question seems to be an equivocal yes, in that observation of parental marital violence is typically associated with reports of husbands' use of violence.[45] This issue, of course, has been studied retrospectively, so that we have little notion of how likely a child exposed to parental marital violence is to become a violent adult. Second, do all children exposed to violence become violent adults? The answer to this question is an unequivocal no, despite the popular notion that the cycle of family violence often assumes so. The most important question then becomes, If not all children exposed to family violence grow up to be violent adults, then what differentiates those who do from those who don't? It is quite surprising that this question has rarely been asked. What we are left with is strong evidence of an association between violence in the family of origin and violence in the family of procreation, with no idea why some fulfill the predisposition whereas others avoid the destiny. Basically, then, we do not know how the cycle works or what mechanism serves to pass violent behavior from generation to generation.

Because studies indicate that the cycle of family violence is one of the more consistent differences between distressed and violent husbands, our need to understand better the intergenerational transmission of violence seems paramount. I believe that studies on individuals who had violent childhoods and yet who are not maritally violent are among the most important for future research. If we can indeed identify factors that set apart those who become violent from those who do not, given similar childhood experiences with violence in the home, we may be able to design more effective strategies that will help break the cycle of violence.

The retrospective answer to this question may already exist, for it mainly requires answering the cycle of violence question in a backwards manner: What factors are associated with the nontransmission of family violence? Eventually the question must be addressed in a prospective manner, however. This could be accomplished in two different ways: either by following individuals from early childhood on through marriage or through longitudinal study of marriage, with extensive retrospective interviewing on family background. Clarifying the role of the cycle of family violence in the development of a violent marriage can best be done in the context of longitudinal, prospective studies.

How Do Violent Relationships Develop?

Longitudinal study is needed in all areas of research on violence. Two questions in particular need to be addressed through this study. First, how does a violent relationship develop? Such study would ideally start with courtship, since patterns of both conflict negotiation and violence may be formed long before the couple marries.[46] We actually know very little about how violence develops; for example, does marital distress occur before, after, or concurrently with marital violence? Just as violence appears in varying patterns in marriage, violence probably develops in a variety of ways. In some cases, a pattern of escalated conflict may eventually erupt into violence, whereas in other cases violence may suddenly appear without warning. It is possible that many currently violent relationships began with a period of nonviolence; bringing couples back to such a nonviolent phase may best be accomplished through an understanding of how the violence developed in the first place. Understanding how a violent relationship develops (whether the nature of the violence is battered wife/abusive husband or severe reciprocal violence) will have important implications for prevention and intervention.

We must also begin to address the question of what factors predict a change in the frequency of violence in the marriage? Often violence is viewed exclusively as a pattern that increases in frequency and severity over time. As Gayla Margolin and V. Fernandez demonstrate, however, in some cases the aggression actually subsides over time.[47] While much is known about the correlates of violence in marriage, little is known about the factors that produce a change in violence. Prevention and remediation efforts have been hampered by the lack of knowledge in this area. If we could predict the conditions under which violence is likely to increase in severity or frequency, then we may be able to offer protection to the battered wife or crisis intervention to the couple. If in addition we can delineate the conditions leading to decreased violence in a marriage, then we may be able to counsel couples toward that goal successfully.

Do Violent Couples Display Unique Interaction Patterns?

In attempting to bridge the gap between research and practice, we must strive to understand the dynamics of violence in marriage. We need to place increased emphasis on a conflict model of marital violence.[48] In its simplest form, such a model views violence as a strategy of conflict negotiation. In its expanded form, issues of sex and dominance cannot be ignored. This conflict model uses conflict theory and studies of marital conflict negotiation as conceptual bases. It calls for a change in the content of studies of marital violence, emphasizing patterns of marital interaction and conflict dynamics. Two examples of this orientation stand out: research by Margolin and others on interaction patterns and marital violence, and Rebecca Emerson Dobash and Russell P. Dobash's analyses of the early years of marriage and the development of the violent marriage.[49]

While conflict is a facet of any relationship, be it collegial or romantic,[50] closely knit groups, such as the family, may be prone to particularly intense conflict.[51] Because close relationships are characterized by interdependence, frequent interaction, and the implicit right of influence, opportunities for disagreement abound.[52] These very characteristics may increase the likelihood of violence in relationships.[53]

Conflict is so woven into the fabric of family life that Jetse Sprey argues for a theory of the family as a system in conflict rather than as a system in harmony.[54] Within the family, frequent occasions for hostility arise; however, such hostility is more often suppressed than expressed.[55] As a result, when conflict does occur, it may cover accumulated grievances as well as the issue at hand.[56] The negative affect associated with a buildup of hostility may be particularly potent in maintaining relationship distress[57] and, I would argue, aggression between partners. Recent evidence from Margolin and others supports this idea;[58] partners in aggressive marriages display more hostile behavior toward each other and may have developed a more structured pattern of conflict interaction.

Within a framework of conflict, violence is viewed primarily as a negotiation strategy. Violence may be a particularly potent strategy for two reasons. First, it quickly brings the partner under one's control,[59] and, second, violence may be reinforced to the extent that it stops perceived aversive behavior on the part of the partner.[60] Indeed, David Finkelhor emphasizes that violence is a response to perceived powerlessness and, therefore, a means to reestablish power.[61]

When is violence used in lieu of other negotiation strategies? The evidence accumulated thus far suggests that violence is used as an attempt to get one's partner to act according to one's own desires or, more succinctly, as an attempt to control the partner.[62] John Scanzoni argues that conflict is inseparable from issues of power and authority in the relationship;[63] similarly, violence may be difficult to separate from issues of conflict and control.[64]

Violence also appears to be a tactic that is used when other means of conflict negotiation break down.[65] Interestingly, the use of physical aggression in close relationships does not preclude the use of more constructive tactics such as negotiation or reasoning.[66] Rather, the occurrence of violence may be an indication of faulty conflict management. In fact, Straus and others conclude that ongoing, severe conflict is almost sure to end in violence. The framework of conflict emphasizes that violence is a particularly powerful means to maintain authority or get what one wants when other methods have failed.[67] Violence is, after all, the "ultimate resource."[68]

Using conflict theory as a conceptual base for the study of marital violence suffers from a major limitation, however, to the extent that issues of gender are often overlooked.[69] Males and females not only use different strategies to get what they want from relationships,[70] they also may experience conflict on different levels. What is perceived as the "pursuit of resolution" by the female partner may be interpreted as "rehashing the same old issue" by the male partner.[71] In studies of violence in relationships, gender is a key issue, for females are far more likely to be injured in a marital assault than are males.[72] In addition, gender is particularly important when violence reflects males' attempts to maintain power and authority in the marriage.[73] Dobash and Dobash emphasize that violence cannot be understood outside the social context of patriarchy and male domination.[74] This idea can be expanded to include violence as an issue of the overall "social relations between the sexes,"[75] which brings this discussion full circle. Issues of male dominance and authority in society may be inseparable from issues of male dominance and authority at home, for these two processes reflect and reinforce each other. My basic thesis here is that many times we need to intervene in a couple's relationship. Unfortunately, the dynamics of a couple's use of violence have not been extensively studied, which impedes the development of effective intervention.

Conclusions

This chapter began with a tautological question about research on marital violence, Are we asking the right questions? Five areas for future inquiry were outlined: specifically, how do violent and distressed marriages differ, can we identify multiple patterns of violence in marriage, what keeps the cycle of family violence from being transmitted, what predicts changes in violence over time, and how can we better understand the dynamics of the violent marriage?

All these questions were meant to address issues in the gap between research and practice. Without knowledge of how a violent relationship develops or why violence increases over time, our efforts to prevent violence or to remediate in the context of conjugal therapy are sorely hampered. In order to enhance our ability to intervene effectively in a violent marriage, which may indeed be a stable marriage for some time, we must turn our efforts more strongly toward understanding the dynamics of husbands' and wives' use of marital violence. Such understanding may provide an important, yet largely overlooked, option for partners in a violent marriage: that of working toward halting violent behavior without dissolving the marriage. Ultimately, this chapter calls for researchers in marital violence to recalibrate the questions they have been asking in order to increase the applicability of their research to practice with intact, violent marriages.

8

How Theoretical Definitions and Perspectives Affect Research and Policy

R. Emerson Dobash and Russell P. Dobash

The object of this essay is to demonstrate how different theoretical perspectives generate different policies and solutions. Language and concepts are extremely important in establishing initial perceptions of the problem to be explained, and we begin by considering various interpretations of the terms "violence" and "abuse." We then sketch the major features of approaches that have been used in describing and explaining violence against women, including biological, individual, interactional, cultural, institutional, and contextual perspectives. These have not been used to address the same theoretical issues. Some have focused on explaining the violence or why women stay in violent relationships, others on what role institutions of the state play in the continuation or reduction of violence, and still others on how beliefs and ideologies support and justify or reject violent behavior. Each approach has emerged from a different point of departure and uses different assumptions, concepts, language, and explanatory traditions. These diverse points of departure lead to different definitions and explanations of the problem that have important implications for what are seen as its causes and for policy and possible solutions. Throughout, we consider the benefits and limitations of the attempts to implement policies and practices implied in each of these approaches. The focus is on violence used by men against their wives or cohabitants.

The Scientific Process

The contenders for the explanation and the solution of the various forms of violence in the family have been numerous. The social sciences that produce these alternative questions and explanations do not exist in an academic or scientific vacuum. Each arises out of the political, economic, and social climate of its time and adds to or changes that climate. Science is a production of knowledge involving three equally important facets: ideas, which are always a product of their time and of their academic disciplines; the information or data deemed to be a substantiation or test of those ideas (and there are debates about which kind of information is best, most scientific, most informative, most useful, and the like); and the social functions or uses of the ideas and information.[1] These may be thought of as theory, data, and social policy or social action.

The process of science reflects a dynamic tension among the ideas, the tests of truth or validity, and the tests of social function. We should ask three questions of all scientific descriptions and explanations: (1) What are the ideas or definitions of the problem? (2) Are they valid? (3) What functions do they serve? where do they lead? what can or may be done with them? Here we wish to focus on the ideas and solutions, leaving the second question for the paper on research methodology.

When we consider how the scientific process relates to explanations of violence in the family, we see that every piece of research contains at least three facets: some definition of the problem, including its name and some description or explanation; some general idea about its causes; and some general or specific notions about the kinds of solutions to be sought. This process is multifaceted and cannot be distilled down to any one of these elements. It cannot, for example, be reduced to the famous request of Jack Webb in the 1950s television crime series, "Dragnet," "Just give me the facts, ma'am. All I want is the facts."

Naming and Defining the Problem. All work on violence begins with some working definition of the problem, including its name. The name begins to create an image of the problem, and employing a language of description further enhances that image. The problem we have studied since the early 1970s has been given many names: violence against women, wife or woman abuse, male violence, marital violence, spouse assault, domestic violence. Each conveys a different idea about the nature of the problem, its likely causes, and possible solutions. If the issue being addressed is violence by men against their wives or cohabitants, that should be made clear by naming it wife or woman abuse. If it is violence between marital partners, implying an equal occurrence and importance of women who are violent to their male partners, it should be named marital violence or spouse abuse. If it is violence between any persons in the

109

family setting without concern for who is involved, perhaps because each form is assumed to be identical with or indistinguishable from the others, it should be named family violence.

While these and other kinds of violence are all possible areas of study, each may include very different forms of violent relationships and provide a different image of the problem from the outset. Thus each may lead to very different kinds of descriptions or explanations and serve very different social and political functions. What is certain is that "family violence," "marital violence," and "spouse abuse" are misleading and inaccurate when they are meant to apply to male abuse of women in their position as wives. Such gender-blind terms not only are inaccurate but also neutralize, sanitize, and provide euphemisms for wife abuse. Try adding the words "he" and "she" in an interchangable fashion throughout any such discussion, and the gender-linked nature of this behavior, as well as the inaccuracy of gender-blind terminology, immediately becomes clear.

Describing and Explaining. The second part of defining the problem is to provide a perspective from which to view it, including the level at which it is analyzed. This helps us begin to describe what is thought to be its fundamental nature and to try to explain it. Descriptions and explanations are usually shaped by some preexisting perspective, or general world view. We may begin by naming the problem wife abuse, child abuse, or elder abuse and proceed to describe or explain it at the level of history, biology, individual characteristics, interaction or relationships between individuals, responses of institutions such as the law, social work, medicine, or the family, ideological or belief systems, or some combination of these.

Setting Boundaries. In the process of defining the problem, boundaries are set around what we believe to be its nature or, at the very least, the most important facets to study. This means that either explicitly or more often tacitly we establish a domain of inquiry that includes certain issues and problems and excludes others. If a social issue can be thought of as having a past, a present, and a future, specifying a domain establishes the present. Once its present has been set within certain limits, our vision is restricted within the confines of those limits. At the same time two additional restrictions of our vision or action are set. They include those factors that might be seen as antecedents or possible causes of the problem, what we might call its past, and the possible solutions that might be sought, or its future.

Research that defines the problem as an individual one and

focuses on individual descriptions and explanations inevitably leads in two directions: backward to a consideration of antecedents, explanations of causes, which can only be attributed to the individual, and forward to solutions that can only reside in the individual. Similarly, research that focuses on institutions or ideologies can only find antecedents and solutions within the limits set by the starting point. Only by combining the perspectives can the limits be broadened.

Here we want to consider a number of significant perspectives to tease out the alternative ways the problem has been defined and what causes and solutions can be proposed from each. Our goal is to consider ways of moving toward knowledge and understanding that can be used for meaningful forms of social change, that is, change oriented to protecting the victim, eliminating violence, and changing the conditions that support the violence. Although lesser goals are certainly possible, nothing less than these can, in the long term, be truly meaningful.

We want to concentrate on some of the questions that have been asked and others that have not yet been fully explored. Thus we examine theoretical ideas that have already entered into the political arenas of policy, practice, and efforts to effect change and some of those that are emerging.

There are very few general theories about wife abuse, child abuse, or elder abuse. Mostly there are limited theories, ideas, and speculations about some particular aspect of the problem, such as how frequently it occurs, its nature and severity, who are the victims and abusers, why women stay, whether violence is learned in a violent home or elsewhere, how the legal system responds, and when and how women seek help. We sketch the significant features of the major perspectives that have shaped the questions, explanations, policies, and practices of the 1970s and 1980s and will shape those yet to be asked in the 1990s.

Perspectives

Biological Explanations. Biological explanations of violent behavior have played a minor role in efforts to define the abuse of women, explain its causes, and formulate solutions. But they have not been entirely absent and so deserve some attention. Biological explanations of social behavior have several assumptions in common. First, all human behavior, including social behavior, is seen as ultimately caused by biological traits or attributes, such as hormones or genes. Second, since biology cannot be changed, any social behavior that is said to be biologically determined is usually defined both as natural and desirable and as unchangeable and inevitable. Thus biological explanations often assert the inevitability and usually the desirability of a "natural" state. Eugenics, sociobiology, and ethology adopt such a perspective.

One common style of argument within this reductionist tradition is to note the behavior of some animal and then assert that the corresponding behavior prevails in human beings. One often hears reference to male dominance as a consequence of strength and bread-winning; the lion is a common image of this. This style of argument is an attempt, sometimes without evidence, sometimes with limited or erroneous evidence, to justify a given set of social relationships by maintaining that they are biological or natural.[2] It also serves to stop or inhibit efforts to bring about change in human social relationships by maintaining that they are biologically fixed and thus socially inevitable.

Inevitability of the patriarchy. Some ethologists and sociobiologists have posited that hormone balance, brain masculinization or feminization, and ultimately genetic factors explain the origins of patriarchal relations between men and women in the evolution of mankind and account for their continued existence.[3] Steven Goldberg attempts to use biology to explain and justify male violence, aggression, and superiority in this book *The Inevitability of the Patriarchy.*[4] He, like Eysenck and Jensen, was influenced by the now discredited researches of Sir Cyril Burt; among them they have tried to prove and to justify superiority by class, race, and gender.[5] According to this way of thinking, men are naturally violent and aggressive, and this cannot be changed. Indeed, it is deemed desirable because men's aggressiveness leads them to do all or at least the most important work necessary for survival. For Goldberg the key is hormones.[6]

Rose, Lewontin, and Kamin offer a detailed and convincing challenge to the theory of biological determinism and the evidence used in its support.[7] By referring to Goldberg as "the propagandist of patriarchy," they emphasize that the power of his ideas lies in their ideological acceptance while noting the weakness of the supporting evidence.[8] Such biological arguments about gender differences and inferiority were among those used against the Equal Rights Amendment in the United States.

Violent-Prone Woman. Another biologically based notion is that of the "violent-prone woman." Erin Pizzey, one of the cofounders of the first refuge for battered women in Britain, along with two psychiatrists, John Gayford and James McKeith, claims that battered women fail to leave their violent partners because they seek physical attacks "or offer themselves as victims for male violence" or "find pleasure in pain" because they have become "prone to violence" or addicted to it through early exposure.[9] They cite an episode supposedly witnessed by Pizzey in which a mother jabbed her baby girl with a safety pin but the baby, "although in pain, saw that her mother was still smiling and smiled back." This episode provided them with what they defined as a "major clue to understanding women who seem hooked on violent relationships."[10] No other evidence was offered for this extraordinary speculation, which, was based on a mixture of notions about human learning and addiction to adrenalin produced during violent attacks. Later versions became even more biological.[11]

This idea was strongly criticized at the time by us and others both because it lacked supporting evidence and because it was a dangerous and detrimental variant of blaming the victim.[12] The various versions have now been criticized by biologists for the inadequacy of evidence and explanation.[13]

No evidence has been offered in response, but this has not deterred even further biological speculations, extending to the notion that infant brains require regular doses of hormones that can only be obtained through violent and pain-giving activities that somehow result in behavior in later life whereby adult men inflict the pain and women seek it. It is not clear why there is a difference between the sexes. This argument poses an intergenerational link and (without convincing evidence) traces complex human social interactions to simple biological causes, rendering them inevitable or irredeemable and placing them beyond present forms of intervention. "The fault of male violence lies, in this view, . . . in a biological victimization dependent on . . . hormonal interactions with the brain in or around birth."[14]

The fault leading to the desire to be physically abused is assumed to reside in the mother and to be transferred only to female children. No direct attempt is made to explain why the male acts violently, except to infer that the violent-prone female somehow makes him behave so. This biological argument sounds amazingly like a variant of the psychoanalytic theory of female masochism. In both the circle is closed completely around women, both for causing male violence and for becoming its victims. Apart from the negative effect on the victims, explaining men's violence by blaming their victims absolves them of responsibility and of any need to change. If the biology or behavior of women is the cause of the problem, then change in their biology (not deemed possible) or their behavior—the focus of much current attention—must also be the solution.

What are the consequences or social functions of using this idea?

Provision of housing, police protection, and other forms of assistance or material resources need not be of concern if battered women are viewed as seeking violence and thus creating and continuing it through their own efforts.[15] According to the authors of this idea, such battered women need to be taken into care with their children and to "de-escalate," which could take years. Thus victims, like any other drug addicts, are to be institutionalized, presumably for their own good. This preposterous solution is obviously a retrograde step in attempting to assist the victims of any social problem. Evidence and experience indicate that confinement does not work for the guilty; yet this approach leads to the wonderfully ingenuous proposal that we lock up the victims. Such a proposal is so extraordinarily dangerous that we doubt that it would be given serious consideration.[16]

Before leaving this discussion, let us be reminded of the two tests of any description or explanation, the validity of the information and its social function. For those who are not convinced by the negative social function or consequences of this work and wish to cling to this explanation, let us end by reflecting on how we might all test the truth of the evidence used to support this idea. The believers in it might repeat this experiment with their own children—smile warmly, jab them with a needle, and note the response. Not only does this defy common sense, it also contradicts well-established tenets of the physiology of pain.[17] Unfortunately, similar ideas, with a similar lack of convincing evidence, have often prevailed in popular mythology and in the ideas and practices of some policy makers. The evidence for Pizzey's thesis is so extraordinarily weak or conspicuous by its absence that it is unlikely to pass into the annals of science or policy—or is it?

Biological explanations of crime are now being widely promulgated in the United States. The ideological support for these ideas is such that we may see more attempts to describe, explain, and respond to male violence in this way. Perhaps, therefore, we should leave this discussion with a cautionary note sounded by biologists:

> Biological determinism is a powerful and flexible form of "blaming the victim." As such, we must expect it to become more prominent and diversified as the consciousness of victimization grows while the possibility of accommodating to demands [for resources, assistance, reduction in violence] shrinks.[18]

About the social functions or consequences of this form of explanation, they state that "all of these recent political manifestations of biological determinism have in common that they are directly opposed to the political and social demands of those without power."[19]

114

Individual Descriptions and Explanations. We now turn to those descriptions and explanations that concentrate on the individual. The work at this level of analysis can be characterized as concentrating almost solely on describing characteristics of individuals who are known to experience a particular problem, such as violent men, abused women, abusing parents, victimized children, or abused elderly persons. This approach is often very narrow, focusing only on one person in the dyad and frequently excluding questions about what actually happens or why it happens. Since individual characteristics or traits are seen as central to describing or defining the problem in its present form, we are also set on the course of viewing them as the causes and as the arena for seeking solutions.

The individual characteristics focused on can usually be categorized as either sociodemographic characteristics, such as age, sex, race, class, and level of education, psychological or personality traits, usually thought to be abnormal or pathological. In either case the theoretical underpinning of the individual approach is causality rooted in "the logic of difference." That is, it is a search for how the individual who is involved in violence, either as abuser or as abused, is somehow different from everyone else. The normal is usually juxtaposed to this deviance, though this is rarely articulated. Without saying so, the research usually means by "everyone else" the white, Anglo-Saxon, middle-class male with a "normal" personality or background.

One may ask whether blacks are more violent than whites, whether women are more violent than men or equally violent, whether the less educated are more violent than those with more education. You will notice that all these questions have been asked in a form that casts the less powerful or less dominant group in the role of the abuser, even though we could have asked the question the other way round and created a different image of the problem.

There is an unstated idea about who is normal and who is different. It may be that since the more dominant groups are usually the ones asking the questions, they are more likely to see the groups they represent as normal and others as different or deviant. For whatever reason, the shape of the questions is fairly common and, if we think about it, should not be surprising. After all, if what is being sought is some sort of characteristic that makes a person different from everyone else, that is, the "normal" population, then those groups that are themselves not the norm (blacks, the poor, women) easily, almost thoughtlessly, come in for immediate attention and speculation. Questions about personality characteristics are similarly shaped. Because of their respective disciplines, many sociologists almost automatically seek the answers to their questions in the demographic traits of individuals while psychologists pursue a similar line with personality traits. Let us consider these in turn.

Sociodemographic characteristics. Race, age, class, gender, and education are the easy, almost automatic, hunting ground for sociologists who, when confronted with a social problem, respond by asking the demographic questions, Who experience it? and, implicitly, How do they differ from the norm, that is, from everyone else? Some journals, particularly in the social sciences of North America, are filled with articles describing the class, age, gender, and racial characteristics of those who have experienced practically everything on earth, including the "unearthly act" of going to the moon. These data not only are omnipresent in describing the nature of the phenomenon but also are meant to do double duty by serving as its explanation. Explanation, however, is much more than simple correlation. Explanation entails an analytical consideration of the antecedents of violence and an account of causal connections that encompasses more than simple post hoc speculation based on observed correlations.

Most frequently the demographic characteristics of the victims of wife abuse rather than those of abusers are described. Consider a hypothetical example from a survey showing that thirteen-year-old black girls who were beaten as children are more likely to grow up to be beaten by their male partners. What would this correlation mean? And what might be done with it? We might simply be left to draw our own conclusions about this finding, including formulating ideas about causes and possible solutions. Could this mean that black women with such experiences as adolescents choose men who are violent or that because of their early experience they "make men violent" or that they just accidentally seem to end up in violent relationships? Perhaps we are not meant to draw anything from the information; if so, why report it? What if this pattern is not found in other studies? What if it is the result of poor measurement techniques or some other flaw in method or measurement? If researchers do not reflect carefully on the possible meaning and validity of their findings or, better still, study potentially controversial or detrimental ones such as this in greater depth and detail, the public and policy makers are left to act as they will in what could easily become a racialist response.

If the cause of the problem is seen as lying in demographic characteristics, what, then, is the solution? Following the logic of difference dictates that the persons involved will eliminate the problem if they become like the norm. For this example, does it mean that the black woman should become white? that her family history

116

should be changed or overcome? Even if this were possible, how would it stop male violence?

At best this sort of work can provide a description of some selected set of characteristics of those persons known to be violent, and policies can be developed to allocate resources such as education, material assistance, and advice to such populations. At worst it has no implications for policy or may be used to identify a population for forced intervention if that is the intention of policy makers. Such research provides only a description, or a list, of individual characteristics. It does not provide information about how the observed characteristics operate to produce violence. That would require a different kind of study explicitly designed to examine the means by which demographic characteristics such as age, education, family background, and unemployment are linked to violence or generate it. Such links may or may not exist, but this cannot be known unless they are explicitly and carefully studied in relation to the emergence and continuation of violence. This has not been done.

Unfortunately, what often happens with these inventories of individual characteristics is a tendency simply to assume that because something has been shown to coexist with violence, it somehow causes the violence to occur. Solutions may be based on these false assumptions about cause. But there is a long way between charting the characteristics of a population known to be violent and developing explanations.

Personality traits. The focus on psychological or personality traits, again, seeks to describe some set of individual characteristics of those known to experience violence. Once described, these characteristics are then assumed, almost always without further analysis, to be the major component of the cause of the violence and, of course, as we have repeatedly said, its solution.

One of the better-known examples of this approach is the theory of learned helplessness.[20] This is not a general theory about male violence or why it occurs. It is an idea about only one facet of the problem, why women stay in violent relationships. The focus is on the woman victim and some element of her personality that, it is theorized, explains why she does not leave a violent man. The concept leads to a focus on the woman's psychological state and her motives for leaving or staying. It is not about the woman's actual ability to escape in light of real life circumstances and material conditions. It does not attempt to explain or address the man's violent behavior except to claim that the woman "contributes" to the man's continued violence through a process of collusion in a "cycle of violence"; that is, she continues in the relationship rather than leaving it. As in the violent-prone thesis, the causal net is thrown around women victims while male abusers swim through virtually unnoticed.

The notion of learned helplessness was borrowed directly from existing work on laboratory animals in which rats and dogs were placed on electrified pads, in tubs of water, and in other difficult situations from which they could not escape. Once they had learned that there was no way out, they ceased to try even when a route was finally provided. According to this account, battered women, like the dogs and rats used in experimental settings, also learn to be helpless and do not escape from a violent relationship even though the escape route is there. "Battered women are all the same, . . . they are suffering from a psychological disability and . . . this disability prevents them from acting normally."[21] When this trait is combined with other features of the predicament of battered women, they lead to "psychological sequelae that can constitute the battered woman syndrome."[22] Since it is primarily learned behavior that creates this syndrome and keeps a woman with a violent man, she can learn new behavior and will then be able to escape. Once again, the woman's behavior and not the man's is the focus of attention and deemed in need of change.

Apart from this problem of focus is a problem of the solution that is posited. Once we have "established" that women suffer from a syndrome, there is only one solution. Adherents of the ideas of learned helplessness and the battered woman syndrome propose that a battered woman should receive "intensive and extensive" therapy to establish the "depth of her learned helplessness" as the first step in changing her "maladjustive attributional system."[23] Ideas such as these have had a profound and far-reaching effect on American conceptions of the problem of violence in the home. They are apparently deeply enshrined in the procedures of the American legal system as an allowable defense when women use violence against their partners.[24] Although we might accept the utility of such a defense for individual women while arguing that other concepts might have been developed and employed, we should be very concerned about the implications of these ideas for the conceptions of all women and battered women in particular.

Recent analysis has shown that expert testimony and judicial officials focus almost exclusively on the attributes of the helpless, passive, emotional female victim, reproducing the "familiar stereotypes of female incapcity."[25] The concepts of learned helplessness and of a battered woman syndrome reinforce the traditional legal stereotypes of female victims, stereotypes that have long been apparent in the legal systems of Britain and especially the United States.[26] These ideas and conceptions have now become a part of the everyday discourse and professional lexicon of the United States. Such thinking ignores or slights the significance of women's low pay and poor employment prospects, the increasing feminization of poverty for women living on their own, the social pressures to remain married, problems of loneliness, and the increasing difficulties facing women seeking a violence-free life. Indeed, even the findings from Walker's own research on this issue indicate that material factors, such as employment, number of children, the woman's educational level, and others, are more important than the psychological characteristic of learned helplessness in accounting for why women stay with violent men.[27]

It may be that women have few viable alternatives to violent relationships. The woman may not be helpless, but her situation may be fairly hopeless. Indeed, given the poor material circumstances faced by women on their own, they may lose either way. The decision to go or to stay may equally be defined in negative or positive terms. As for the helplessness of battered women, it seems that the women are, in fact, quite able. They hold responsible jobs, manage households, rear children, do the shopping and domestic work under conditions that might crack lesser mortals.

One of the negative consequences common to this argument and the violent-prone woman thesis is that the pressure is placed on the woman to change her own personality and behavior to deal with the man's violence. If she is unable to use available resources, it is solely her responsibility because such women "are generally indecisive and frequently unable to utilize available resources."[28] If she does not escape, it is she once again, who fails, she who feels guilty, she who is responsible. We must seriously ask, Is this really the cause of the problem of male violence? Is this the locus of its solution?

Rather than seeing the individual woman as suffering from learned helplessness, perhaps we should consider how she is located in a context of situational hopelessness. The first theoretical conception tries to explain why a woman does not leave a violent man by using a notion of personal inadequacy described as a syndrome, an illness, a psychological or an emotional condition. The second tries to explain why the victim responds to her predicament in a certain way (staying, leaving and returning) by the circumstances in which it occurs and the viable alternatives available.[29] The first produces an image of the passive victim, incapable of action (leaving) or capable only of blind action (homicide) when suffering from a mental condition (learned helplessness) resulting in diminished responsibility.

The second offers an image of an actor in a difficult situation, actively making decisions and trying out solutions, all of which are more or less difficult to achieve. Certainly, "having a psychological term to explain a state of mind" may make us all feel better and absolve us of responsibility, but it provides no explanation of the predicament of women in violent relationships, nor does it help us to find solutions.[30]

Interaction. Focusing on interaction usually involves roles, relationships, and behaviors of two or more persons as they relate to one another. This perspective is sensitive to the dynamics of social interaction. It may have more or less breadth depending on whether the roles and behavior are placed in a wider social or historical context, but a narrow focus is usually adopted. We have identified four starting points for this kind of analysis: dysfunctional personalities and family systems that lead to dysfunctional interaction; a cycle of violent interaction that "bonds" women to violent men; a cycle of violence that transmits violence across generations; and an analysis of violent exchanges.

Dysfunctional personalities. The dysfunctional personality approach is rooted in psychological or psychopathological perspectives. Its adherents propose that two flawed persons come together to produce dysfunctional interaction (violence) and a dysfunctional system (a violent family). Violence in the family is mainly conceptualized as a sequence of events between partners. "It was found that wife beating could be best understood as a significant component of interactional behavior sequences between the partners."[31]

Weitzman and Dreen provide a good example of the sick-individuals-equal-sick-interaction thesis, concentrating on notions of dependency, stress, and inadequate coping, "which increases dependency on already dependent phobia partners."[32] The batterers are seen to have psychological profiles filled with repression, intimacy fears, and the need for control that lead to a hunger for power. Battered women are said to lack self-assertion, maturity, and self-identity and to have an internalized helplessness, shyness, and reserve—all of which contribute to marital disputes. According to Weitzman and Dreen, battered women tend to be more "verbally assaultive than clinging and withdrawn" and engage in not entirely innocuous behavior—"passive reactions to stress can themselves be precipitants to violence," and such women "tend to attack their partners at any hint of inadequacy."[33] For these commentators the imagery is of emotional immaturity that results in abnormal interaction and

120

ends in violence. A "violence-prone system" emerges in these relationships and, once abuse or violence occurs, "a battering system."

Systems theory offers a variant of this approach, in which the entire family becomes the object of attention and intervention. Systems perspectives are now much in vogue in the social sciences and the helping professions. The principles of this approach have emerged from cybernetics, and it is claimed that they can be applied to any sort of system, mechanical, electric, or human. According to its adherents, systems theory conceptualizes the family as an equilibrium-seeking system of interrelated elements open to external forces. The notion that family members constitute an interacting group is, of course, not exceptional. But systems theory treats these relationships as abstractions and is thus concerned with properties of systems and gives little if any attention to individual motives, intentions, and interpretations. Using this theory to analyze violence in the family results in a failure to consider individual and interactional factors. Violence becomes a property of the system, all members of the family are components of the system, and therefore husband and wife are seen as "equally culpable and victimized."[34] As system properties, "the dynamics of violence are similar regardless of who is the victim."[35]

The policy and practice directives flowing from these sick interaction and family systems perspectives are very similar. Therapy is the answer, usually family therapy or conjoint therapy in which each participant examines how his or her behavior causes the problem and can be changed to eliminate it. It is advisable, according to those who adopt this position, to meet "with several family members rather than one individual" to ensure an "objective and impartial perspective."[36] The system, not individuals, is treated; responsibility, guilt, and motivation are apparently not a part of this form of intervention. A failure to consider the phenomenological level of personal and interpersonal experience means that these approaches usually fail to consider the direction of violence and its consequences for the usual victims, women.

The cycle of violence. The second interactional approach is the cycle-of-violence thesis. Here it is believed that the behavior throughout the violent event, from tension to making up, produces a bond between the woman and her violent abuser and that the woman makes a tacit agreement to future violence when she accepts the man's apology or responds positively to his pleas for forgiveness. The initial cause of the violence is not discussed, but attention is focused on how it is the women who is responsible for its continuation. Again, this is a variant of blaming the victim. She is also held responsible for its solution, largely by leaving the violent man. It might be reasonable to assume that this does not change the man's violent behavior but simply leaves him to transfer it to the next woman with whom he establishes a relationship.

The intergenerational cycle of violence. The third interactional approach is the intergenerational cycle of violence, in which members of one generation learn violent behavior and attitudes through direct experience in their families of orientation and later act similarly in their families of procreation. This endless chain of violent families begetting violent families is based on several theoretical notions: that violent behavior and attitudes are learned through direct tuition; that children who witness violence between their parents learn only to imitate, rather than to avoid, such behavior; and that girls learn to be victims and boys learn to be abusers, rather than some other combination. These questions have not been studied but merely asserted by referring to the history of those known to be violent.

This approach suffers from several problems. First, what is defined as violence in the family of orientation often extends to almost any form of physical punishment. This is particularly problematic in a society in which most children receive some form of physical punishment during childhood. Careful attention needs to be paid to exactly what kind of violence, by whom, and directed at whom before it is possible to draw conclusions about an intergenerational connection. In addition, it would be necessary to study the siblings of violent adults to ascertain whether all of them "inherit" the affliction. If not, this would raise serious reservations about an intergenerational link.

Violent exchanges. The final variant of interaction to be discussed is the analysis of violent exchanges. This approach has generally been used to examine violent encounters between males in a public setting, not between men and women in a family setting. We discuss it here largely to show how its gender blindness, which implicitly places a veneer of male culture, orientation, and values over the encounter, renders it ineffective for explaining the violence men direct at women and also to show how it is based on a presumption of two equals, usually males, involved in an encounter in which the victim supposedly agrees to violence and precipitates his own demise.

This approach views a violent encounter as a face-to-face interaction between aggressor and victim, who are assumed to be fairly evenly matched socially and physically.[37] The encounter begins with verbal conflict, which is followed by threats and evasive action and

122

then by physical attack. Often these are witnessed by a third party who encourages physical attack or even initiates it. The immediate interaction is a face game with six stages. It begins when the victim does something that is an offense to the "face" of the other and ends with a "working agreement" that the situation is one suited to violence.[38] It is an image of two male egos squaring off in an adolescent contest defending male pride and prowess. From the outset it is not clear who will become the victor, who the victim, as each challenges and counterchallenges the other to a contest that may seem very like the gunfight at the OK Corral.

This is a gender-blind explanation of the processes leading to a violent event; it is only about men and male culture. Its gender exclusivity may not be a problem as long it is used only to describe violence between males. It cannot, however, simply be expanded to include women. That would require an explanation that is sensitive to the very different dynamics involved when men are violent and women are the victims.

The Sociocultural Perspective. The sociocultural perspective views violence as a part of the wider culture. The broadest view adopts notions such as "we live in a violent society." Narrower approaches conceptualize violence as forming an accepted part of certain sections or subcultures, where violence is socialized into the young and practiced throughout the group. Attention focuses on belief systems, ideas, and attitudes that characterize entire societies and the individuals within them. Ideologies are examined for their effects on institutional practices and individual attitudes. There is belief in some kind of rough fit between and across these broad arenas.

A narrower approach focuses on subcultures rather than on the whole society. Subcultural approaches have been prominent, especially in sociology, for some time. Violence is seen as normative in certain groups, and this view is meant to explain apparent differences in the use of violence among ethnic, class, or regional groups. Working-class men and women, for example, may be thought to be more violent because they are the products of a distinct culture that reinforces and glorifies violence or at least defines it as an inevitable part of daily life. Again, this perspective also adopts, at the group rather than the individual level, the "logic of difference" between us and them. The focus is on the different culture of a group rather than the psychology of the individual. Once again, the dominant group escapes unnoticed while the less powerful become the focus of attention.

To substantiate this explanation, more information than is now

available would be needed. It could not be obtained through surveys because of their inability to provide in-depth information about complex social processes. Rather, research findings and forms of explanation would need to focus explicitly on specific communities and identifiable subcultures and to demonstrate clearly the connections between culture and violent behavior. These would need to be compared with the dominant culture to examine similarities and differences.

If groups could be identified with violent values and patterns of behavior that differ from those of nonviolent groups, the policy implications would point to direct community action oriented to changing these patterns. Clearly, community and group work on the streets, work sites, recreational and educational centers, and the family would be crucial if this interpretation were adopted.

Institutions. Here research findings and accounts focus on the responses of agencies to the problem of violence in the home. They describe the nature of such responses and attempt to explain why they occur, primarily by focusing on the attitudes and perceptions of participants in institutions. Though often reductionist, at its best this approach considers the operation of organizations, including policies, practices, priorities, professional or bureaucratic demands, influential personnel, communication within and between agencies, and legacies relating to previous responses to the problem of wife abuse. Medical and psychiatric professions, the criminal justice system, and social and personal services have all come under examination for inaction or inappropriate action. Although medical and social service agencies have been studied, the bulk of the work has focused on the police and criminal justice. This research tends to be extremely empiricist, with little theoretical guidance, although the conclusions reached are, of course, based on a number of presuppositions about agencies and their personnel.

Apart from simply describing institutional behavior, this work would have greater explanatory powers and clearer policy implications if it were to include an explicit treatment of several levels of institutional response: the nature of the organization and its focus (or responsibility); its historical development; professional or organizational ideologies or beliefs about this violence and its participants; explicit policies, practices, and priorities concerning the problem; the difficulties confronting those working in institutions, such as heavy workloads and procedures that facilitate or impede effective responses; and the attitudes and beliefs of individual practitioners.

Despite some of the important work in this area, much of it characterizes institutional responses solely through the use of aggregate data, focuses only on particular acts or outcomes such as arrest, and ignores context.[39] Most important, as researchers in this area have themselves pointed out, it fails to provide meaningful explanations of attitudes, outcomes, and institutional actions.

The Contextual Approach. The contextual approach tries to describe and explain a phenomenon by placing it within the numerous contexts in which it occurs. This requires a combination of historical, individual, interactive, institutional, and cultural perspectives. Since every social issue exists within each of these contexts, it is thought necessary to study it accordingly if we are to develop realistic explanations and understandings. We would argue that only through this approach will we be able to develop sensitive and effective policies. For the most part, this approach to explanation has had a feminist orientation.

Placing the problem of wife abuse in its historical context makes it possible to consider the legacy of violent behavior and toleration of it within our social institutions and belief systems. This highlights the inheritance that may be continued or transcended. It also points most clearly to the ways in which this violence has been an accepted, even revered, aspect of social life rather than a manifestation of individuals or groups who somehow differ from the norm. Carefully picking through the myriad of objects stored in this historical attic is not an easy task, but neither is it merely an academic, futile, or self-indulgent one. It provides a vision of what our ancestors were like and what forgotten social baggage they have left us. This is an indispensable part of the puzzle of explaining the causes of violence against women.

Women have been subjected to cruel, systematic, and severe violence throughout recorded history. From the early Roman period violence against wives was condoned and even praised for its beneficial effects on domestic order.[40] While excesses were condemned and some critics even rejected the use of violence to control women, objections generally went unheeded in the context of legitimate patriarchal control.[41]

In the nineteenth century new institutions of the state, especially the modern criminal justice system and social services, emerged to challenge the family and community as the locus of social life and legitimate control. They did little, however, to challenge male control of women within the home. Indeed, patriarchal conceptions of women and hierarchical relations between the sexes were enshrined in the developing organizations and their responses to the family. Violence against wives was usually ignored or trivialized and deemed unworthy of institutional concern or official response.

Historical work has shown how patriarchal patterns, values, and ideologies have penetrated most, if not all, social institutions and provided a rationale for and an endorsement of violence against wives. Institutional responses have provided an inseparable link in the continuation of violence. When joined with contemporary research on institutional patterns of criminal justice agencies, historical work enables us to go beyond the particular circumstances of single encounters to overall patterns. This helps us understand the professional ideals and organizational patterns that shape and determine responses from institutions.

History also takes us beyond explanations that focus on individual pathology. Most scholars would accept that a small number of men who use violence against their wives are suffering from some sort of emotional or psychological malady, but historical and contemporary evidence showing the widespread existence and social toleration of such behavior militates against the simple view that the majority of these men somehow differ from a norm that is absolutely intolerant of violence. Violence is learned, but its sources go well beyond individuals, their personal interactions, and families or subcultural groups and into a wider culture that is clearly and firmly embedded in the institutions and belief systems of the entire society.

Throughout their lives all men, not just certain men, learn the locations, situations, and contexts in which violence can legitimately be used. It is primarily males, usually at a very early age, who learn the benefits of aggression and violence and the suitability of females as victims. Violence becomes a resource to be employed to enforce and reinforce male domination, and one of the most important locations for its use is in the family. Violence is not a property of a system, it is a technique men learn to use in certain settings and against certain persons. Men are not merely compelled to use violence by internal or external factors, pathology, or stress. Violence against wives is primarily purposeful behavior intended to bring about a desired state and conducted in a context of social tolerance or acceptance.

An analysis of the sequences of events leading to the onset and continuation of violence in a relationship may focus on the context of interaction but then place it within the wider context of the institutions of marriage and the family as well as other social institutions, such as criminal justice or the economy, and wider ideological beliefs about men, women, and the family.[42] Such an approach shows how

126

the onset of violence is associated with marriage or the formation of permanent relationships through which men's sense of possession and rightful domination are heightened and how wives become 'legitimate victims' of violence and are isolated from external forms of intervention to support them and constrain abusers.

A closer analysis of violent events in these relationships reveals that the sequelae of events are very like those associated with other kinds of violence, verbal confrontations, and escalation leading to violence, except they are not gender blind. The contextual approach focuses on the violent event in a way that is gender aware. Findings from this perspective have provided information about the contents of verbal confrontations, reexamined earlier interpretations of victims' actions, motives, and supposed culpability, and shown how specific violent events are inextricably linked to subsequent violence through continuing male demands. This goes beyond the mere interactional level by interpreting such events with regard to other, wider contexts in which they occur.[43]

This approach stresses the importance of male domination in the use of violence. Encounters leading to violence are shaped in the larger patriarchal cauldron containing male power, privilege, and legitimate demands for service. These are mixed with the necessity that wives negotiate with husbands for the means to manage their daily lives, for money, resources, and time.[44] Rather than stressing pathological individuals or relationships, this perspective makes it possible to show how violence is an integral part of male domination, not necessarily used by all men but always there to be employed if necessary. Instead of employing a logic of difference, the contextual approach employs a logic of similarity, or continuity, stressing the links between persistent patriarchal patterns and the use of violence. Thus violence against wives is not a result of aberrant individuals or sick marriages but is an extension of some of our most respected traditions, beliefs, and institutional responses as they are encapsulated in patterns of male domination.

Challenges, Policies, and Practices

Contextual analysis has brought interpretations of the position of the victim that challenge those of female masochism or learned helplessness as explanations of why women stay. Examining the effects of such factors as continuing threats by men, women's initial ambivalence and continued hope, pressures to remain married, and the bleak social and economic future of single parenthood that penalize women if they leave any relationship, even a violent one, shows that

127

numerous contexts are involved, including individual, cultural, and institutional issues, not simply personalities or interaction.

This form of explanation leads to new directions for policy and action directed at confronting male violence and supporting individual women. In contrast to the existing institutional policy that had neglected the problem and diverted it to counselors and others who merely provided palliatives or even blamed the victim, the battered women's movement rejected the violence unequivocally and aided the women and their children. In so doing they challenged male power, began to return the problem to the community, and raised a multiplicity of questions about the nature and extent of the problem and its causes and solutions.

Adopting a more individualist and therapy-based approach means that women who suffer violence become the objects of hierarchical evaluation, discussion, judgment, and therapy. These tendencies are more likely in the context of a society dominated by an individualistic view of social problems that is easily translated into mental health responses rather than community-based orientations and approaches.[45]

If agency response and perspectives are integral to the problem, it surely follows that they should be changed. A great deal of institutional change has been accomplished, primarily because of the translation of feminist interpretations into policy. In the United States the criminal justice system is the institution that has received the greatest amount of effort directed at changing responses. New legislation and practices have been aimed at providing additional protection for victims, more meaningful responses to offenders, better processing of cases, and training of agency personnel in more effective responses. We should remember, however, that these changes are far from universal and did not come about because agency representatives readily accepted the criticism emerging from feminist interpretations or willingly agreed to change. In the criminal justice system most change, especially the most far reaching, came about through political action, class-action lawsuits, and active monitoring of enforcement. Despite the successes, much evasion and backsliding toward the traditional approach persist. The lesson here is that persistent vigilance, pressure, and political action must continue if change is to be secured. Other agencies have not seen as much change as the criminal justice system, so that a great deal remains to be done.

This perspective has also brought new orientations to the offender. Traditional efforts rarely entailed meaningful responses: the violent man was often ignored, the violence went unchecked and was sometimes even reinforced, and the woman was left alone in her struggle or often blamed for his violence. New approaches and programs are based on evidence of man's denial, deflection of responsibility, and minimization of the importance and severity of violence.[46] As a consequence, these new approaches emphasize male responsibility, focus on intentions, and seek to eliminate the violence and to alter men's sense of rightful control and patterns of domination. These programs explicitly reject couple counseling in favour of concentrating on the man, his violence, and his responsibility for his past behavior and for changing his future behavior. Some of them build on feminist-inspired work revealing the nature of the violent event, the violent relationship, the unequal positions of men and women in the family and society, and the role of other agencies and the community. Their emphasis is on the unacceptability of violence and the need to change. This provides strong signals to the individuals and the community at large.

Since the contextual approach uses multiple levels in conceptualizing the nature of the problem and its explanation, solutions or responses would follow accordingly. Multilevel analyses and multiagency approaches more closely fit this perspective. The first multilevel analysis and multilevel response came out of the battered women's movement. The problem was viewed as one involving the individual, the institution of the family, the responses of agencies (including the criminal justice system, education, and social services), women's economic and political position, and general beliefs or ideologies about women, violence, marriage, and male domination. Shelters and refuges formed the central response and provided the symbolic heart of action and the physical location for change-oriented activity. The media, education, criminal justice, and social and medical services all became arenas for seeking change. At times efforts became fragmented rather than integrated as the enormous task of taking on even one institution, much less several at once, became apparent. This task, however, provided the ground-breaking work necessary at each level before attempting a multiagency response, which must conceive of the problem as one relating to the position of women in society and adopt the goal of eliminating the violence.

9
Judging the Success of Interventions with Men Who Batter

Jeffrey L. Edleson

Interventions with men who batter their women partners have rapidly increased in number and type over the past fifteen years. They now range from individual treatments to attempts to change the workings of social institutions. Evaluations of intervention success have only recently begun to appear in the literature, and the ways they define success vary greatly.

This chapter critically examines three major groups of program evaluations. The evaluations are summarized and discussed according to current definitions of success and the measurements used to define success. Finally, the public policy implications of current evaluation practice are discussed.

Evaluations of Interventions with Men Who Batter

Only a few authors have reported on one-to-one counseling with batterers or on intervention in social institutions outside the criminal justice system.[1] The major focus of social intervention and, in turn, of program evaluation has been on couple or couple group treatment, group treatment of batterers, and the response of the criminal justice system with emphasis on police actions. The three subsections that follow present the current state of knowledge about the success of intervention in these three areas.

Couple and Couple Group Therapy. Little systematic research has been done on intervention with couples. Although several have written about couple counseling programs few report outcome data.[2] The few who have presented data are reviewed here.

Lindquist, Telch, and Taylor reported six-week and six-month follow-ups with couples who had received therapy for the man's violence. They found that 50 percent of the couples treated experienced at least one incident of violence during the six weeks after completing the program and that six months after treatment all couples interviewed had experienced violent incidents. No comparison data were supplied for untreated couples.[3]

Other researchers report more postive outcomes. Harris contacted thirty couples from two months to three years after treatment and found 73 percent of them "successful," though she does not state what makes a couple successful.[4] Taylor briefly states that of the fifty couples with whom he has worked, 65 percent reported no new violence in the six months after treatment. He does not state, however, how he collected the data or who reported them to him. For example, were interviews conducted by telephone or in person, and was the person interviewed the perpetrator, the victim, or another family member?[5] Considering the significant differences in couples' reporting of violence, such vague reporting casts some doubt on his claims.[6]

A 1984 study of twenty-four court-ordered male batterers found statistically significant improvement between pre-treatment and post-treatment scores on subscales of the Minnesota Multiphasic Personality Inventory (MMPI) and a marital satisfaction scale. At one point the study discusses conjoint couple counseling and at another group treatment for "defendants," leaving the reader unclear about the treatment procedures.[7]

Vague reporting is also evident in the work of Neidig, Friedman, and Collins.[8] In the final two paragraphs of their article they report all of their outcome data. They found the 100 couples with whom they worked to exhibit "typically significant positive change" on the Nowicki-Strickland Locus of Control Scale and the Dyadic Adjustment Scale (DAS). They also report that at four months after treatment about 87 percent of the participants were free of violence. They do not state, however, whether this figure includes the women participants who were probably not violent in the first place; nor do they say who—perpetrator or victim—reported the data they include in their results.

In a more recent article, Neidig provides some greater detail in reporting the results of a batterers' treatment program offered by the military. In data from a sample of forty men and nineteen of their partners, Neidig found significant improvement in marital satisfaction and greater internalized control from pre-treatment to post-treatment, again using the DAS and a locus of control scale. Neidig mentions reviewing post-treatment, military police reports of domestic violence and also interviewing participants at six-month intervals after treatment but only partially reports these data in the following comment: "The majority of those contacted indicated no additional violence since completion of the program."[9]

Three reports by Deschner also do not report results clearly.[10] In her two recent articles she reports an array of sometimes overlapping data. In Deschner et al. she states that forty-seven persons who completed training reported significantly fewer arguments, less anger, and higher relationship satisfaction. She also states that although violence decreased, the change was not statisically significant. In an eight-month follow-up of fifteen couples, eight were violence-free and five reported "minor" incidents of violence. Since she does not define minor incidents of violence as battering, Deschner considers all thirteen couples (87 percent) to be free of battering. In a 1986 study Deschner and McNeil state that for forty-seven persons violence decreased by 50 percent but that this change was found to be statistically nonsignificant. These separate reports seem to be of the same sample and data. Deschner and McNeil also report an "earlier group" of twenty-two people who were "less inclined" toward anger, depression, and aggression after treatment. In an appendix to her 1984 book, Deschner reports similar results for what appears to be the same group of twenty-two program participants—twelve men and ten women. Again, it is unclear whether these results include nonviolent women victims as part of the success rates.

Finally, Deschner cites an evaluation of several Texas programs—including her own—as support for the effectiveness of her program.[11] She and her colleagues state that after a one-year or longer follow-up 85 percent were refraining from violence.[12] Deschner and McNeil cite the same study but with a four-month to one-year follow-up.[13] Concerning Deschner's program, Shupe et al. report having "obtained the case files on twenty men counseled during the two years, 1981 and 1983–4, that the program was in operation." Shupe et al. performed their follow-up in the summer of 1984 but unfortunately combined the Deschner sample with those of two men's programs, leaving the effect of the couple program unclear. In short, the impact of the Deschner couple group program is left unclear by these confusing reports.

As a group, the reported evaluations of couple and couple group treatment appear to be very weak. They seem to suffer from serious problems concerning the definition and reporting of success and from severe methodological weaknesses.

Group Treatment of Batterers. Very few evaluations of treatments for men who batter appeared earlier than 1985. More recent evaluations, though, include qualitative, single-subject, cross-sectional, and none-quivalent control group studies. No experimental evaluations have been completed, although several are in process.

The major criteria for judging success has most often been the degree to which violence is reported after treatment. Feazell, Mayers, and Deschner surveyed ninety programs across North America, finding that from 66 percent to 75 percent of the couples reported that violence had ceased one year after the batterer completed treatment.[14] In a similar survey, Pirog-Good and Stets-Kealey found an average recidivism rate of 16 percent four months after treatment among the programs (sixteen of seventy-two) that conducted follow-ups with clients.[15] Neither article, however, documents the way each program generated follow-up data, whether the victim or abuser reported, or how the programs computed success rates. It is also unclear whether their figures are the products of systematic outcome evaluations or the estimates of program managers completing a survey.

In one of the first published evaluations of group treatment for men who batter, Edleson, Miller, Stone, and Chapman reported the outcome of a three-group multiple-baseline study.[16] Seven of nine batterers who completed twelve sessions of cognitive-behavioral group counseling reported no violent incidents during follow-ups ranging from seven to twenty-one weeks. A limitation of this early study was the use of short, retrospective baseline measurements and the fact that the data were drawn solely from men's self-reports.

In a similar study, Rosenbaum reported on batterers who had completed at least five of six behavioral-educational workshop sessions.[17] Follow-ups of six or more months indicated that eight of the nine men were not violent after receiving treatment. The one client who was violent reported what Rosenbaum termed "one incidence of slapping."[18] Rosenbaum also appeared to rely on men's self-reports and did not provide data on comparison or control subjects against which to judge his clients' progress. The importance of relying on reports other than the man's self-report, as mentioned earlier, lies in the fact that women victims report much higher levels of violence than do their male partners. Thus, both my study and Rosenbaum's may be reporting inflated success rates.

More recently, several authors have reported evaluations that involve larger numbers of subjects and, at times, a greater degree of experimental control. Shupe, Stacey, and Hazelwood report a large-scale follow-up of men who completed, dropped-out of, or were terminated from participation in three Texas treatment programs, two of which offered men's group treatment.[19] In their article they report one-month to three-year follow-up data for 102 men who completed

one of the three treatment programs and forty of their female partners. Eighty percent of the men and 75 percent of their partners
reported that the men had not been violent since completing treatment. The authors state that the abuse reported at follow-up was
likely to be much less severe. Unfortunately, follow-up data from a
comparison group of clients who dropped out or were terminated
from treatment were not reported and, as stated earlier, twenty of the
men also participated in a couple-based program, thus mixing results
for the men's and couple's programs.

Tolman, Beeman, and Mendoza have also reported the initial
results of a study of men's group treatment.[20] Unique aspects of the
study include its examination of a men's program administered by a
battered women's shelter with groups led by male-female teams. The
sample examined includes 149 men and their partners; however, to
date results have been reported for interviews with only forty-eight of
the women partners. Just over half (53 percent) of the men completing
treatment were found not violent at follow-ups up to four years later.
The majority of men (60 percent) were reported to be continuing to
threaten and emotionally abuse their partners at follow-up. These
results are similar to findings in other studies.[21]

Dutton, Edleson and Grusznski, Shepard, and Hamberger and
Hastings have reported evaluations that employ some type of quasi-
experimental control.[22] Shepard conducted a cross-sectional study of
ninety-two men who were receiving group treatment or had recently
completed it. She found that both men and their partners reported
the most dramatic decreases in violence during the first three months
of treatment and that progressively lower rates of abuse were reported
as the program continued. She contacted thirty-nine of the men's
partners one year after the men had completed treatment and found
that 70 percent of the women reported they were no longer being
battered.

Dutton compared the police reports for fifty men who had completed a sixteen-week treatment program with similar reports for a
matched group of batterers who had not received treatment. He
examined police reports for a period averaging two years after treatment and found that the rate of recidivism for treated batterers was
only 4 percent compared with 40 percent for the untreated batterers.
Dutton also examined wives' follow-up reports for treated batterers
who were married throughout treatment and follow-up. He found
that 84 percent of the men were reported not violent since the end of
treatment.

Using a slightly different comparison group, a colleague and I
have reported three studies comparing the effects of treatment on 156

134

batterers who completed a six-month program with sixty-seven other men who had either dropped out of or been asked to leave treatment. In all three studies men who completed treatment were reported by their partners six months later to be less violent than those who did not complete the program. Nonviolence rates were 67 percent, 68 percent, and 59 percent among completers in the three studies, compared with 54 percent and 52 percent among noncompleters at follow-up in the first and third studies. The differences between completers and noncompleters in the first study were statistically significant (P<.03) but not in the third study. The second study did not include a comparison group. The relatively high rate of nonviolence among noncompleters may, in part, be attributed to the fact that some in this group received substantial services before dropping out. Thus, the comparison group used in this set of studies makes it difficult to draw conclusions. Also noted in these studies were continuing high levels of threats of violence made to partners by both completers and noncompleters.

In still another, more recent study, Hamberger and Hastings found that a group of thirty-two batterers who completed a fifteen-session program were less likely than thirty-six program drop-outs to be reported violent one year after treatment.[23] These differences were not, however, significant at the p<.05 level. They did find highly significant changes in the expected direction between pre- and post-treatment reports of violence for program completers. They also found that the men significantly changed on measures of depression and anger but not on a personality profile; many men continued to abuse their partners psychologically. Hamberger and Hastings mention that the data on completers was actively collected while data on drop-outs was mostly the result of abuser or victim initiated reports or police records, thus indicating the possibility of serious measurement problems in this study. As in many other studies, these authors also fail to identify who specifically supplied data used in the statistical analyses.

Finally, several authors have looked beyond rates of violence and threats of violence. Saunders and Hanusa reported pre- to post-treatment changes for ninety-two men who completed twelve sessions of cognitive-behavioral treatment and eight sessions of supplemental self-help group treatment.[24] As a group, these men showed significant desirable changes in anger level, jealousy, depression, and attitudes about women's roles. The study adjusted self-reports for men's tendencies to give socially acceptable responses. Unfortunately, it did not use a comparison or control group. In examining women's reports of violence, Saunders and Hanusa found that reductions in violence reports were significantly correlated with reductions in anger. Not all measures were available for comparison, so it is difficult to assess what other changes might be associated with drops in violence levels.

Gondolf and Hanneken, in attempting to look beyond simple reports of violence and scores on scales, have applied qualitative methods in their research.[25] They have reported findings from qualitative interviews with twelve men who completed twenty-four weeks of batterers' group treatment and remained nonviolent for ten months to two-and-a-half years. The men viewed group treatment as a reinforcement of changes they were struggling to make and greatly valued the open discussions and closeness that they shared with group members. When discussing the group process, the men did not focus on the specific techniques used in the group as much as they did on the discovery of feelings and how to express them. This emotional education, as Gondolf and Hanneken call it, appeared to be an important part of the group process. Qualitative methods do not require the large numbers of subjects necessary for large group experimental designs. It is, however, unclear what qualitative method Gondolf and Hanneken followed, if any. It is unlikely that so few men (twelve) could supply sufficient data to satisfy the requirements of qualitative research designs.

The number and sophistication of evaluations of men's group treatment appear to be growing. Most of the studies cited here have reported nonviolence levels ranging from 59 percent to 75 percent as reported by victims at follow-up. As Gondolf has stated, however, we have little information about other changes that have resulted from group treatment, how those changes contribute to a man's remaining nonviolent, and what processes in group treatment enhance change. He also notes that few studies have used strong comparison groups.[26] Progress in this area may be forthcoming in studies soon to be completed in Minnesota and Wisconsin.[27]

Criminal Justice Intervention. Within the criminal justice system, the greatest emphasis on changing institutional responses has been in police departments. Homant has categorized police response beyond inaction into two groups: counseling-oriented and arrest-oriented actions.[28] In the 1970s and early 1980s a great deal of attention was given to training police in counseling and family crisis intervention skills, and several empirical evaluations resulted. Some have reported success in training police in crisis intervention skills but mixed success when examining the effects of crisis intervention on domestic disputes. For example, in a telephone survey of citizens, Driscoll et al.

136

found that trained teams of police were rated as no more or less helpful than untrained police and that people served by trained teams were no more or less likely to call the police again than were those served by untrained police.[29] Similarly, Mulvey and Reppucci found that citizens interviewed about officers' field performance perceived no differences between trained and untrained police.[30] Although Pearce and Snortum document short-term improvement in citizens evaluations of trained compared with untrained officers, these differences disappeared two weeks after initial contact.[31]

In the mid-1980s a change occurred in police responses to domestic violence calls. The change was in the direction of more frequent arrest and prosecution of men who batter. The poor results of police crisis intervention studies and similar findings from large surveys of police actions, combined with social pressures from battered women's advocates, forced the change in police response.[32] The most important research contributing to the shift away from crisis intervention and toward arrest is the well-known study performed by Sherman and Berk in Minneapolis.[33] They found that the arrest of batterers reduced by about half the likelihood of repeat violence when compared with mediation or asking the man to leave the house for eight hours. Because felony level crimes were not included in the experiment, the effect of police response on the most severe cases of abuse is not known.

In addition to Sherman and Berk's original study, several subsequent empirical articles pertaining to police responses have been published. As a group, these studies have found that when the police arrest a man, and the community, rather than the woman presses charges, the number of withdrawn or dismissed cases dramatically decreases, victims are more often satisfied and less often exposed to violence at follow-up, and fewer homicides take place.[34]

Sherman and Berk's Minneapolis data also show that offenders with histories of severe violence are 15 percent more likely to repeat violent acts after arrest than those with histories of less severe violence.[35] Thus, one might argue that deterrence through police arrest is differentially effective and may be less so with offenders who have histories of severe violence. Victim assistance provided by police tended to be as effective as police arrest in deterring future abuse for both high- and low-injury groups. But batterers who reoffended after their partners received victim assistance were much more violent than men who reoffended after arrest.

Once an arrest has occurred, the prosecutor is next in line to deal with the case. In the Sherman and Berk study, only a few offenders were ever prosecuted after arrest. The low rates of prosecution observed by Sherman and Berk and others have generated interest in how these cases are handled by prosecutors. The reasons for the low rates of prosecution have been highlighted in several studies.[36] Ford's examination of 325 battered women in Indiana found that prosecution occurred "as much by chance as by rational procedures." Errors, chance timing, and the discretion of people working in the criminal justice system contributed to only 30 of the original 325 complaints ever reaching court despite repeated efforts by battered women to see the perpetrators prosecuted. Rauma's examination of 199 cases forwarded to the Santa Barbara, California, prosecutor's office found the likelihood that a complaint would be prosecuted was determined using a combination of legal and extralegal criteria to evaluate the likely success of prosecution. Extralegal considerations included the characteristics of the arrest, the perpetrator and the victim, as well as the number of cases currently being processed by the prosecutor. Rauma labels prosecutors' utilitarian approach of working with cases most likely to be successful as "going for the gold."

Ford's 1984 analysis of complaints voluntarily dropped by battered women presents a very different view of successful prosecution. The decision whether to drop a case was seen as an important "power resource" for the battered woman. While prosecutors "go for the gold," battered women appear to have a very different goal. They take a utilitarian approach, one that uses the threat of prosecution as a power resource to aid in changing the man's violent behavior. Once the threat of prosecution achieves the woman's utilitarian goals, she frequently withdraws her complaint voluntarily. Thus, while prosecutors may see dropped charges as a failure or lost opportunity, battered women see dropped charges as part of a rational strategy for ending the violence in their lives.

These analyses of prosecutor and victim decision making shed light on the processes involved in prosecuting and dropping criminal charges. They do not, however, indicate the success of prosecution efforts to improve victim security. Only a few recent studies have examined the success of prosecution. Grau, Fagan, and Wexler found restraining orders that were seldom enforced by the courts to be generally ineffective in reducing the rates of physical and non-physical abuse.[37] Fagan's reexamination of Sherman and Berk's data found men with more severe histories of abuse to be less responsive not only to arrest but also to prosecution and court sentencing. The differentiation between histories of low and high abuse were also found in the study by Grau et al.

Following a small sample of twelve battered women whose abusers were prosecuted, Ford found that three-and-a-half years later most were no longer exposed to violence. He hypothesized that filing charges offers a short-term power resource and indirectly starts women toward long-term security. Since most women studied had since separated from their partners, it was impossible to distinguish the effect of prosecution from that of leaving the man. In 1988 Steinman completed an evaluation of a coordinated community intervention in Nebraska.[38] His study of 183 victims and their partners found that post-arrest sanctions had little influence on recidivism independent of the arrest. Recidivism was determined using police and county attorney files. Interestingly, most men who reoffended were not charged with domestic crimes.

The studies by Ford and Steinman are small and contain methodological weaknesses. At this point, it is not known whether prosecuting men who batter contributes to the goal of ending violence. Also unknown are the relative contributions of sentencing and probation monitoring.

Increasingly, communities around the country have established interventions that bring together police, prosecutors, judges, probation officers, social workers, and battered women's advocates in a coordinated response to the battering of women.[39] To date, very few evaluations of the coordinated interventions have been completed. In Gamache, Edleson, and Schock we reported an evaluation of three communities that showed significant increases in arrests, convictions, and mandated treatment concurrent with the start of intervention but did not report data concerning violence.[40] Measuring the effect on violence, Pence, Novack, and Galaway reported that at a six-month follow-up 51 percent of victims whose partners received intervention reported no subsequent violence compared with 41 percent of a comparison group of victims from the same community. The contributions of the various criminal justice and social service components were not analyzed. As reported above, Steinman's initial analyses have not shown that post-arrest intervention contributes substantially to reducing recidivism rates.

Taken together, these evaluations offer little promise for the effectiveness of police crisis intervention but do show a degree of promise for police use of arrest. The combination of arrest and men's group treatment may be as Dutton has suggested, the most promising.[41] The relative contributions of post-arrest sanctions, advocacy, and monitoring to ending violence are presently unknown.

Definitions of Successful Intervention

Battering would appear, at first glance, to be an overt, discrete behavior that is relatively easy to define and measure. In fact, there is a consensus in the field that violence rates are the central criterion for judging success of interventions. This consensus breaks down very quickly, however, when one goes beyond simple measures of violence. In this section, the studies cited are examined in terms of the various applied or proposed criteria used to judge the success of intervention.

Different Degrees of Physical Violence. Several measures have been developed to monitor the abuse of women.[42] The most common measure of violence rates is Straus's conflict tactics scale.[43] The CTS consists of nineteen conflict tactics that may be used in high-stress situations. The respondent is required to indicate his or her frequency of using each tactic over the past year. The respondent also answers for his or her partner for the same period on the same scale.

One major criticism of the CTS is that it does not measure the effect of the tactic upon the victim. Instead, the CTS defines severity by groups of tactics. Thus, although a slap may cause greater injury than a hit with the fist, the hit is considered more severe. Straus has answered this and other criticisms by arguing that legal definitions of assault focus on the act of violence rather than its effects.[44] Because both tactics and injuries are important types of data to be collected, Daniel Saunders of the University of Wisconsin, with funding from the Centers for Disease Control, is examining the effects of intervention on rates of violence and resulting injury and has developed an injury questionnaire for measuring the physical effects of battering.

The question of injury aside, most researchers consider any tactic that involves physical contact as battering. Deschner et al. stand out as exceptions. Five couples who participated in their program later experienced up to four "minor physical incidents such as grabbing or slapping the partner."[45] The five couples were included in the 87 percent they reported to be free of battering at follow-up. It is not, however, common practice at any level of intervention evaluation to exclude "minor" violent behavior from the larger category of battering.

Another difference among researchers is the level of violence they find acceptable for judging intervention successful. Some, such as Deschner and McNeil, have evaluated success based on statistical analyses of decreases in violence between the start of intervention and some point after intervention. Most have, however, established zero violence at follow-up as the criterion for judging success. As Grusznski and I have pointed out elsewhere:

> This criterion is a somewhat conservative measure of success. . . . While some investigators might argue that statistically significant decreases in violence would be an impor-

tant indicator of success . . . such decreases would not be clinically significant. Even one violent event in a year may be enough to terrorize a victim and her family.[46]

The question of using decreases in violence or abstinence as a criterion for success mirrors the larger debate over statistical versus clinical significance of outcomes. In short, the debate is about "meaningful" change. How best is such change reported? Is a statistical change the goal, or is the goal better stated as a benchmark that should be achieved regardless of pre-intervention levels? The question probably should not be posed in either-or format. The answer is probably that a combination of measures is important. On the one hand, dramatic decreases in violence resulting from intervention may be a valid indicator that change is taking place. Fewer reports of violence along with abstinence data, would provide a more complete picture of intervention effects.

Expanding the Boundaries of Abuse. Many have begun to question whether the numbers of violence reports should be the only measure of a program's success. Hart questions whether simply ending violence should be judged as success in such programs, pointing out that removing the violence from a woman's life may not remove the terror she is experiencing.[47] Women may, in fact, be constantly living in violence, as Eisikovits, Guttmann and I point out:

> The woman in a terror-filled environment seems continually to live the moment before a violent event. Sudden movements by the man who is 'just reaching for something on a shelf' may cause her to move to protect herself. For the battered woman, the border between what happened and what might happen is likely to become blurred. Given what she experienced in the past, she may no longer distinguish between violence and danger. She may live in constant violence by experiencing the expectation of it.[48]

The importance of looking beyond reports of physical violence is empirically supported in several of the cited studies.[49] Generally it has been found that, although violence may be eliminated, in many cases women victims reported continued threats of violence by their partners. As Fagan has hypothesized, perpetrators may engage in a "displacement" process. This process may involve directing violence toward others or substituting nonphysical threats and manipulation for physical violence. It would therefore seem important to measure more carefully several classes of behaviors including (1) threats of violence; (2) manipulation of resources and children; and (3) harassment of the victim. Within the context of past physical violence, the

141

effects of these behaviors may be as severe as the violence itself and should be central considerations in judging the success of intervention.

As a field, we have yet to systematically develop measures of either these behaviors or their effect on victims. Some have applied existing measures to expand their study of batterers; for example, Saunders and Hanusa examined anger, jealousy, depression and attitudes about women using existing standardized measures.[50] Saunders has reviewed a variety of these existing measures.[51] Such measures may tap factors that seem important to preventing further violence but they should not be substitutes for more accurately measuring behaviors directly relevant to battering. Although new instruments exist and others are being developed, the field is a long way from reliably measuring the critical factors in woman battering.[52]

Other Markers of Success. Gondolf and Russell have argued that "anger control" interventions with men who batter focus too narrowly on ending physically and emotionally abusive behaviors. They believe that major changes in a man's perspective and life style are equally important intervention goals for men who batter. This resocialization or personal transformation involves a man's "taking responsibility" for his actions and the harm it has caused his victim, performing community service to help stop abuse by others, and undergoing a process Gondolf has called "self-concept restructuring." Setting such changes as a goal of intervention implies measurement of a broad set of cognitive processes and behaviors.[53]

Hart has argued that a major criterion for success is whether or not the abuser becomes an "accountable person." She defines an accountable person as one who "must compensate the victim he has wronged in an effort to restore the injured party to the condition or situation prior to the wrongful action."[54] The behaviors in which an accountable man would engage include those suggested by Gondolf and Russell and others—voluntarily limiting contact with his victim and her social network; discontinuing the collection of information from family and friends on the woman; and paying child support and ceasing manipulation of the children.[55] If he remains in the relationship, the man's accountability might include sharing power and control within the relationship; working to restore his partner's dignity, and ensuring an environment where the partner and children may safely express themselves and act according to their own wishes.

The criteria suggested by Gondolf and Russell and by Hart reflect feminist and profeminist analyses of woman battering. The goals of accountability, resocialization, and personal trnsformation reflect the belief that this problem is the outcome of a social structure and requires both men and society at large to change the way they view and act toward women. As Hart concedes, regardless of the intervention applied, very few batterers achieve personal accountability. In evaluating the success of intervention with men who batter, one must ask if standards such as those proposed by Gondolf and Russell and by Hart are achievable with available or even greatly increased resources. Although the goal of accountability is admirable, it may not be realistic for judging the success of societal interventions.

The above goals contrast sharply with the goals of some couple and couple group therapy programs that seek to repair relationships in addition to ending violence. Neidig et al. for example, briefly reported data on the dyadic adjustment scale. Although many couple interventions do not explicitly aim to repair the relationship, the use of marital satisfaction ratings and data on both improved communication and decreased arguments in some cases indicate that an improved relationship is considered a criterion of success. The context in which such measures are presented and the importance they are given often seem out of place. As stated, changes on such measures should be considered important but not substitutes for more direct measurement of violence and other forms of abuse.

Criminal justice interventions appear to value the consumer's satisfaction with the intervention. Numerous studies have been conducted of victim satisfaction with a variety of system interventions. In addition, the outcome of filed complaints appears to be a major concern among prosecutors. Rauma, as discussed earlier, points out that prosecutors "go for the gold" and judge a case's success according to whether charges are finally prosecuted. In contrast, Ford points out that battered women see prosecution and prosecutors as "power resources"; a woman may drop the case when she achieves her personal goals and may consider a dropped case to be as successful as, or more successful than, one carried to court.[56]

Road Signs along the Way to Final Goals. The consensus on measuring violence points to a distinction that should be made between types of goals. Depending on one's view of domestic violence, goals can range from raising men's consciousness to rebuilding couples' relationships to satisfying consumers. All these goals appear to be instrumental in achieving the ultimate goal of ending violence. If one views violence primarily as the outgrowth of relationship difficulties, then fixing the relationship is important. If, however, one views woman battering primarily as a social-structural problem, then one focuses both on men's resocialization and on altering the response of

143

social systems to both victims and abusers. Of course, this distinction is simplistic and, in reality there appears to be a great deal of overlap among researchers, practitioners, and activists in their ranking of various goals.

The debate about goals of intervention with men who batter will not be resolved in the near term because of basic differences in the analysis of battering. There is a need for greater consensus on the methods for measuring and reporting victim injury histories and the several classes of nonphysical abuse that usually accompany violence. These variables are not road signs on the way to ending violence. Rather, they are part of an expanded definition of battering that must be considered criteria for evaluating success in the future.

Implications for Public Policy Efforts

The problem of woman battering has been recorded throughout history, but research on intervention, particularly with men who batter, is in its infancy. In part this is because many of the interventions themselves are relatively new to the social service and criminal justice systems. Except for a few exemplary and well-funded studies, most have been small, low-cost evaluations. This situation is likely to improve as the network of interventions grows larger and more researchers collaborate with program staffs to conduct systematic evaluations. It will only be accelerated, however, if policy makers, government funding agencies, and private foundations adequately fund larger, more controlled experiments.

Finkelhor, Hotaling, and Yllo summarized the major research and funding needs in the area of intervention in domestic violence. Their nationwide interviews with key researchers, practitioners, activists, and policy makers identified a wide range of research and evaluative studies that should be funded over the next decade. In the area of research on wife abuse, they identified eleven high-priority research projects, three of which are particularly relevant to this chapter. The highest priority is a four-year, $400,000 study of both men and women who had successfully "beaten wife beating," to use Bowker's play on words. Another priority is a four-year, $3 million study comparing community approaches to the handling of wife abuse. The completion of these two studies would, if conducted carefully, vastly improve our knowledge about what works in intervention with men who batter.[57]

A third priority is a project to improve our ability to identify spouse abuse. Several issues related to identifying abuse stand out as being in need of further attention. Additional measures not only of violence and nonphysical abuse but of the "secondary" goals that many have recently advocated are in need of development. There is also a need to design evaluations that in a systematic and controlled manner examine the relative inputs of arrest, legal advocacy, prosecution, sentencing, probation, and social service components in coordinated interventions.

Very little is known about the success of intervention with men who batter. The effect of couple and couple group treatment remains unknown; men's group treatment shows some promise, but many questions remain unanswered. Studies of the criminal justice system have focused mostly on police actions. Even with the results of the Sherman and Berk study and the six replications being funded by the National Institute of Justice, we will have adequately studied only a narrow band of police responses to domestic dispute calls.[58] The only other area in which significant controlled studies are under way is in the area of men's group treatment, where studies in Minnesota and Wisconsin promise a degree of experimental control. No other area of intervention with men who batter has been or is being studied adequately.

Finally, what beyond decreasing violence, nonphysical abuse, and injury does intervention with men who batter seek to achieve? Although researchers may disagree about what additional outcomes are desirable, it is important to enlarge the set of outcomes to be studied before undertaking additional large-scale studies. This issue requires an open debate in many sectors. If a larger consensus cannot be reached systematically and openly, large segments of the research, practice, activist, and policy-making communities may discount some of the findings from new studies as insignificant or meaningless.

10
Issues in Developing
a Research Agenda
for Child Abuse

Betty Stewart

One of the things that we are engaged in doing in the National Center on Child Abuse and Neglect is listening to other people, particularly researchers and others in the field. We are making a concerted effort to talk with groups of researchers about the major issues in the field and how we should go about examining those issues.

I assume that most of you know something about the Children's Bureau and the National Center on Child Abuse and Neglect. The Children's Bureau is just ending its seventy-fifth year, having started in the Department of Labor. During its seventy-five years of existence the bureau has gone through many changes, many shifts in its program direction, for better or for worse. But any federal agency that lasts for seventy-five years has shown some ability to roll with the punches and to have meaningful programs that meet a perceived need on the part of the public and the politicians. It is my hope that the Children's Bureau will continue to have a long history as it starts its second seventy-five years.

The National Center on Child Abuse and Neglect is much younger; it was established by an act of Congress at a time when we were just beginning to realize that we had some serious problems of child abuse. The national center was one way of addressing those issues.

The center has also gone through a number of changes in its years of existence, as it has matured and as the field has changed. At the time of the first national conference in Atlanta in 1975, there were no conferences around the country on child abuse and neglect; that was a landmark conference. Next month we will have a special conference with Children's Hospital in Anaheim on child victimization that will be the eighth or ninth national conference we have been involved in, and every day I get announcements about conferences all over the country; so a lot has happened.

We at the national center strongly recognize the importance of research. We have clear understanding that if we do not combine our programmatic responsibilities with research development, we are going to be bankrupt; we have to put those pieces together.

Social workers have been criticized as not being very astute about research or very interested in it. In my career in child welfare I worked at an agency that was involved in research throughout its history. That gave me an appreciation. But when you are out there in a program with all its day-to-day hassles, you lose track of the research perspective. You need somebody to jerk you back and say: Sit down and think about what you are doing; get some perspective on this. At the Children's Bureau and the National Center we have to do the same thing. This year we have planned several research symposia on child abuse, to which we are inviting small groups of national researchers to talk about the issues and about how we should be addressing them—what we know, what we don't know, and where we should be going.

The National Center is not a primary research agency. While we have some discretionary money for research, most of our research is done by people who wear several hats. Our financial resources are limited, and research costs a lot of money; so we have to think carefully to make the best use of our resources. We also have to look at ways in which we can get ideas and knowledge from a wide arena, including how we can combine our efforts with those of other federal agencies and the private sector to understand what is going on in the system.

One of the major activities we are hoping to undertake in the future is a longitudinal study. We will be asking for feasibility studies this year. This is clearly a major effort that we would be unable to undertake alone, and we will be looking to others to work with us on funding. About a month ago we held a seminar to which we invited grant experts on longitudinal studies from various federal departments. We learned that there was a lot that we did not know when we published the priority for longitudinal studies, but we are going to persevere. We are looking forward to seeing what kind of applications we get in that priority area.

In the relationship between research and policy, we are still struggling with a number of areas. One is the area of child fatalities and serious physical child abuse. It was mentioned earlier that child fatalities have been reduced, but we do not have a good handle on how many children die because of child abuse, because we do not have the protocols that would give us that kind of information. We have not yet developed good ways of determining which child abusers will be the kind who will kill children. We do not have the capacity to make those kinds of decisions. These are decisions that child protective services workers are making every day, whether to leave a child at home or remove a child: which is more of a risk to the child? We are making one more effort to understand the characteristics of those who abuse children fatally. From a policy perspective we need to look more critically at ways to prevent this kind of abuse.

The issue of neglect is a major one because it involves the largest number of children. Many children are neglected not because their parents are abusers but because the parents do not have the wherewithal to care for the children. There is a risk to children in removing them from their parents because the parents cannot give them proper housing and clothing and food and shelter. That is an issue that social work has struggled with for a long time—not struggled with it so much as just removed the children and then paid the price later.

Researchers tell us that neglect is something that we cannot afford to ignore, because of the significance of what we know of child development and what children need at certain points in their lives to develop into reasonably healthy, mature, well-functioning adults. We need to understand better the long-range effect versus the short-term solutions.

We do not know what happens or how to break the cycle of abuse. We hear that people who are abused become abusers and that we perpetuate this. But we also do not know why some people who are abused do not end up as abusers.

I am becoming more concerned about the issue of ritualistic abuse. Much of what we have learned about sexual abuse has come from adults in treatment who have been sexually abused. That has led us to begin looking at children who are sexually abused differently.

We are seeing the same thing with adults in therapeutic situations who are talking about having been abused ritualistically. Is this fantasy? Is this reality?

The people that I have talked to who are interested in this kind of abuse tell me that nobody has yet been able really to document a case. People are trying very hard to do so, but it has created some problems.

I just heard about a therapist who is seeing many children who have been sexually abused; she is finding a very high rate of multiple personalities in those children. We have long talked about adult sexual abuse victims developing this kind of constellation, but it is the first time I have heard of it in children. I said I would like to talk with her, and my informant said, "I don't know if she will talk with you. She doesn't really want to make it public." That is the kind of answer that I get. We need to move our understanding to a greater level because we know the kind of toll that such abuse takes on adults. Until we understand the treatment needs better, we are going to perpetuate this with children.

One of our major problems with research is developing good ways to disseminate findings so that they are useful both to researchers and to practitioners. We will be publishing the results of our research symposia. And we will make a concerted effort to see that our child abuse clearinghouse and our family violence clearinghouse get all our research reports and products so that information is readily and quickly available. We are looking at the possibility of publishing some literature reviews and a synthesis of studies that have been done at the national center. We are trying to find ways to bridge the gap between research and practice. One thing we have given some thought to is developing a consortium that would bring together research and demonstration grants and give us an opportunity to test some of these issues in real life.

The researchers who come to our meetings have all stressed that we need to have research on research; we need to understand the methods, instruments, and theoretical frameworks and which ones worked in which situations. Although we at the national center are not primarily a research organization, we do appreciate the need for us to be involved in furthering research to help us know where we should be moving.

11
Differences among States in Child Abuse Rates and Programs

Murray A. Straus and David W. Moore

The purpose of this chapter is to outline a broad program of research on child abuse using state-by-state data and to present the design of one of the projects that might be part of such a research program.

The policies and funding provided by each of the states constitute the main efforts to treat and prevent child abuse in the United States. Although systematic data are not available, it is likely that there are large differences among states in the kinds of programs implemented and in the funding provided for them. Assuming that such differences exist, it is extremely important to know what each state is doing and to have some means of investigating whether the differences in programs and funding make a difference in the rate of child abuse. Studies using this kind of data can provide information that is needed to formulate and implement policies to treat or prevent child abuse. For example, it may be helpful to know how the number of child protective services (CPS) workers per 100,000 children in a state compares with the number in other somewhat similar states. Such information, however, is not now available.

Also not available are any studies that analyze whether differences among states in programs and funding are related to rates of child abuse or to the rate at which child abuse is reported to CPS. The two rates are different because the CPS data constitute an *intervention* rate rather than an *incidence* rate. Under some circumstances, as when

This research is part of the Family Violence Research Program of the Family Research Laboratory, University of New Hampshire, Durham. This research has been funded by National Institute of Mental Health grant R01MH40027 (Richard J. Gelles and Murray A. Straus, coinvestigators). The work of David Moore was supported by a grant for family violence research training from the National Institute of Mental Health (grant T32MH15161).

extensive intervention reduces the incidence of a problem, there is a negative correlation between intervention and incidence.

This essay is intended to start the process of filling in this major gap in research on child abuse. We suggest a program of research that includes obtaining state-by-state data on the rate of child abuse and comparative state research to investigate both theoretical and policy aspects of state-to-state differences in the rate.

Possible Contributions of State Research on Child Abuse

In designing the research program we made certain assumptions; some of these can be tested by the research, and others will remain assumptions. Perhaps the most important assumption is that there are large differences among states in the incidence of child abuse, just as there are large differences in practically every other sociocultural variable.[1] If this assumption is correct, it will permit research on factors that might account for the differences. These factors include differences in the sociocultural characteristics of the states, such as the level of urbanization and the extent to which other kinds of violence are prevalent, and differences in child abuse programs and funding.

The issues that might ultimately be investigated include the following:

• *Differences in incidence.* How do the states differ in the incidence of physical and psychological abuse of children? If the large differences among states assumed to be present are found, the variation will provide the basis for research to determine factors that could account for the differences.

• *Reported differences and their antecedents.* The number of cases reported to CPS is the one aspect of state-to-state differences in child abuse that is well documented. Such data are available for each year since 1976. Factors associated with the differences in reported rates do not seem to have been investigated, however, not even such simple questions as whether the number of reported cases is a function of the number of caseworkers available to receive and investigate such reports.

• *Differences in program and funding.* How much do the states differ in respect to the kinds of programs and their funding (that is, their "program effort")? These data would provide valuable descriptive information and might provide a framework for states to evaluate their own program efforts.

• *Relation between program effort and incidence.* Is there a relation between program effort and the incidence of child abuse as measured

151

by epidemiological surveys of a random sample of parents? The findings will provide information on whether the amount of money spent on child abuse programs is related to a reduction in the incidence of child abuse and whether certain kinds of programs are more effective than others in reducing the incidence.

• *Relation between program effort and reported rates.* Are state-to-state differences in program effort related to the rate of cases reported to and confirmed by CPS? Since data on reported cases of child abuse are a measure of the extent of intervention in child abuse cases, the findings will provide information on the extent to which programmatic effort is translated into intervention.

• *Relation between sociocultural characteristics of states and program effort.* Are differences in program effort a function of sociocultural and economic characteristics of the states, such as urbanization, region, income, and racial composition, and such political characteristics as the degree of party competition and the nature and extent of interest group activities? This information can be helpful in understanding why some states adopt certain policies and others do not.

• *Change in incidence.* Murray Straus and Richard Gelles report a decrease in the national rate of child abuse for the period 1975 to 1985.[2] Some important questions need to be addressed: (1) Has this decrease continued since 1985? (2) Is this decrease found in all states? (3) What characteristics of the states are related to a greater or lesser change in the incidence of child abuse?

• *Relation of changes in program and funding to changes in incidence and reported rates.* To what extent does program effort change over time, and are the changes related to change in the rates of reported child abuse and to the incidence of child abuse? These data will measure the amount and kind of investment in child abuse prevention and treatment and provide information on the results of that investment.

• *Relation between incidence and reported rate.* What is the relation between the rate of child abuse as reported to or confirmed by state CPS and the incidence as measured by the proposed state surveys? Straus and Gelles argue that there is a negative correlation over time, that is, the higher the reported rate, the lower the incidence, because the former is a measure of intervention to control child abuse.

• *Theoretical questions.* In addition to these immediately practical questions, state-by-state comparative research can be used to investigate many important theoretical questions concerning the causes and consequences of child abuse, such as whether the incidence is related to urbanization, the frequency of other kinds of violence such as homicide, the infant mortality rate, the percentage of parents who endorse physical punishment, the extent of interest group participation in the political process, or the relative influence of the Democratic and Republican parties and the degree of party competition.

Availability of State Data

Investigations designed to provide information on the issues listed require a variety of state-by-state data. Some of the needed data are available, but most are not.

Official Child Abuse and Neglect Reported Rate. State-by-state data on the number of child abuse cases known to the CPS in each state have been gathered since 1976, but these statistics show the rate of intervention rather than incidence. The difference can be illustrated by the fact that the rate of sexually abused children known to CPS doubled from 1976 to 1977 and by 1985 was twenty-one times as great as in 1976.[3] It is extremely unlikely that American children suddenly became so much more vulnerable to sexual abuse. The underlying incidence may even have decreased.[4] Why then has the CPS rate increased? It is not unreasonable to suggest that it reflects a dramatic change in the willingness of the public and human services professionals to intervene and report sexual abuse. Thus, when the annual reported rates of child abuse are published each year and show yet another increase, it should be taken as an indication of progress in the fight to protect American children.

Recent increases in the rate of sexual abuse reported to the CPS have been much larger than increases in the rate of physical abuse because national consciousness and concern about physical abuse have been growing for many years whereas the concern with sexual abuse is more recent and hence has a more dramatic impact on the statistics. In neither case, however, can the increase in the reported rate be taken as evidence that the underlying incidence of physical or sexual abuse has been increasing.

The CPS reported rate is nonetheless an important indicator of efforts to deal with child abuse. Consequently, it has an equally important place in the research program outlined in this chapter.

National Data on the Incidence of Physical Abuse. In 1975 Straus, Gelles, and Steinmetz conducted a survey of a nationally representative sample of 2,143 American families to measure the incidence of physical abuse of children by parents and of spouses by each other.[5] In 1985 Gelles and Straus replicated the study on a sample of 6,002 families.[6] Comparison of the 1985 rate with the rate a decade earlier found a large and statistically significant *decrease.*

153

After examining many alternative explanations for the findings, Straus and Gelles conclude that the decrease was brought about by a combination of fewer serious assaults on children and fewer parents willing to tell an interviewer that they had been that violent toward one of their children. How much of the change was due to a change in behavior and how much to a change in willingness to report is not known. Straus and Gelles argue, however, that even if all the decrease from 1975 to 1985 was the result of greater reluctance to report because of the wide publicity given to child abuse during the decade, that is still an important change because it reflects a change in attitudes and awareness that is part of the process of changing behavior.

How can we explain the difference between the year-by-year increase in the CPS rate of physical abuse and the equally strong decrease in the rate found by Gelles and Straus? Straus and Gelles suggest that, rather than the rates being inconsistent, one is a function of the other.[7] They argue that the incidence declined (as measured in their two surveys) partly because of the vast increase in the extent to which intervention has occurred in cases of child abuse (as measured by the CPS rate).

The Straus-Gelles theory that the huge increase in the child abuse cases reported is an indicator of an increase in public and professional efforts to reduce child abuse and should therefore result in a lowered incidence, though plausible, has not been investigated. This chapter outlines how such research can be done. In the meantime we used what data were already available to conduct a preliminary analysis. We tested the hypothesis that states with the highest rate of reported child abuse tend to have the lowest incidence of abuse. The reporting data are for 1985 because 1985 was the most recent year with data for all fifty states.[8] The data on the incidence of child abuse are from the 1985 National Family Violence Resurvey (the measure is described in the next section).[9]

As hypothesized, we found a low negative correlation between reported rates and incidence ($-.30$, $p<.05$). A plot of the data showed two problems. First, two of the nine states in the low reported rate group (7–20) had such extremely high abuse rates that they might account for the observed correlation. We therefore reset the values of these two outliers from 20 to 10 (9.1 was the next highest value). This reduced the correlation to .26, just below the .27 needed to be statistically significant. Second, the plot suggested a decelerating rate of decrease, which is plausible if we assume that reported rates will come closer to the actual rates as reporting becomes more and more widespread. We therefore computed a polynomial regression (using the outlier adjusted data) and found a significant nonlinear relationship, as shown in figure 11–1.

Although the findings in the figure support the Straus-Gelles theory, other methodological and theoretical problems call for great caution. One methodological problem is that the theory refers to changes over time, whereas the figure shows differences among states. Second, the abuse rate for some states in the National Family Violence Survey is based on a precariously low number of households with children: an average of only 59 and a range of 3 to 285. Still another ground for caution is that the same analysis using 1984 and

FIGURE 11–1
PHYSICAL ABUSE RATE BY REPORTED ABUSE RATE,
FIFTY STATES AND THE DISTRICT OF COLUMBIA, 1985

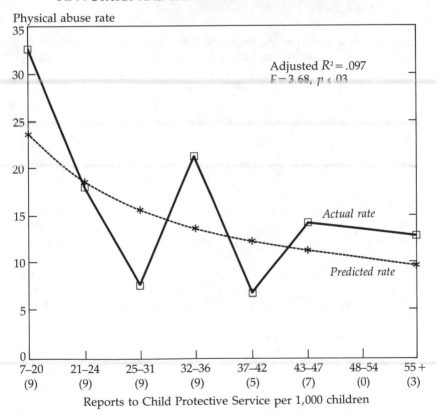

NOTE: In ½ S.D. (standard deviation) groups (mean = 31.1). Number of states in parentheses.

SOURCE: American Association for Protecting Children, *Highlights of Official Child Neglect and Abuse Reporting* (Denver: AAPC, 1985).

1983 reported data produced linear correlations that are lower and nonsignifiant (− .22 and − .25), though in the same direction.

Some theoretical issues are also not resolved by these data. Even if the results shown in the figure are correct, the findings by no means prove the Straus-Gelles theory. The theory asserts that the child abuse rate decreases as a result of beneficial intervention by CPS. The correlations, however, could be real but spurious. For example, they might reflect a concern with and sensitivity to child maltreatment in the cultural climate of certain states that leads people in those states both to a low level of child abuse and to a high level of reporting of those incidents that do occur. It is extremely important to resolve the theoretical and methodological questions we have raised about the results in the figure, and we hope that the research outlined in the rest of this paper can contribute to that goal.

State-by-State Data on the Incidence of Child Abuse. Although national surveys such as the Gelles and Straus study are an advantage for some purposes, they do not provide information on specific states. Consequently we suggest that surveys using the same methods to measure child abuse as were used in the National Family Violence Survey be carried out in a number of states.

The Conflict Tactics Scales (CTS). The technique used to measure physical child abuse in the National Family Violence Survey is known as the Conflict Tactics Scales (CTS). The CTS is a brief instrument designed to measure three aspects of parent-to-child behavior: reasoning, psychological aggression, and physical aggression.[10] The psychological aggression and physical aggression indexes are intended to measure the incidence and the severity of emotional and physical maltreatment of a child.

The CTS begins with the statement: "Parents and children use many different ways of trying to settle differences between them. I'm going to read a list of some things that you and (name of child) might have done *when you had a problem with this child.* I would like you to tell me how often you did it with (him/her) in the last year."

The list begins with the items from the reasoning scale, such as "discussed an issue calmly"; goes on to the items in the psychological aggression or emotional abuse scale, such as "insulted or swore at him/her"; and ends with the physical aggression or violence items, such as "slapped or spanked him/her" or "kicked, bit, or hit with fist." The acts of physical aggression that go beyond ordinary physical punishment and risk causing an injury that requires medical attention are used to form the measure of physical abuse.

Since the development of the CTS in the early 1970s, it has been used in two national surveys and in more than forty studies of spouse abuse by other investigators.[11] It has also been used by others to measure child abuse.[12] Studies using the CTS have made important contributions to knowledge of child abuse, including unique information on the incidence of physical abuse, on risk factors associated with abuse, on the effects of physical abuse on the child, and on changes in the incidence of physical abuse.[13]

There is not sufficient space in this paper to describe the CTS adequately, but a paper is available that provides detailed information on the use of the CTS to measure physical and psychological abuse of children, along with information on validity and reliability and norms.[14] We do not suggest that the CTS is a fully satisfactory instrument. It was originally developed to measure abuse between spouses. It was then modified for use in measuring child abuse, but additional refinement is needed, some of which is in process.[15]

Child Abuse Programs and Funding. Several of the research questions mentioned above, especially the questions of most direct policy relevance, require state-by-state data on kinds of programs, personnel, and funding of child abuse work. None of these data seem to be currently available. Consequently, a major part of the program of state research will need to be on developing a system for obtaining these data from each of the states. The following kinds of data need to be collected:

- number of staff assigned to CPS work
- training required for employment in CPS work and training provided to staff
- organization of CPS work, such as whether the staff are employees of the state or of local government
- program characteristics, such as whether there is a toll-free reporting line and whether child abuse cases must be reported to the criminal justice system
- number and size of voluntary groups, such as a state child abuse prevention committee or Parents Anonymous chapters
- presence or absence of prevention programs
- level of funding of CPS work and prevention work

This list is only illustrative and will need to be refined and expanded in conjunction with persons involved in state child abuse programs.

Sociocultural Characteristics of the States. All the sociocultural variables mentioned in this paper are available in the State and Regional Indicators Archive (SRIA) at the University of New Hampshire. The

SRIA contains a vast amount of other information on each of the states (approximately 15,000 variables), and the staff is experienced in obtaining such data and putting it into usable form.

The utility of the SRIA for work of this kind is illustrated by the fact that SRIA data have been the basis for a number of important studies, including *Social Stress in the United States* and *Four Theories of Rape in the United States*, as well as numerous journal articles on medical resources and their correlates, alcoholism, and homicide.[16]

Research Design

The ideal research design would include all fifty states. This is not a practical objective in the immediate future, however, and thus the research outlined in this chapter involves only eight states. If this research turns out to be as productive as we hope, the cost of including all fifty states can be weighed against the potential benefits. For now we suggest gathering the data on program effort for all fifty states and doing surveys to establish the incidence of child abuse in just eight states. Each of the surveys would interview a random sample of parents using the methods described below to estimate the incidence of physical and psychological abuse of children in those eight states.

The New Hampshire Pilot Study. The feasibility of the kind of survey we propose has been demonstrated by a pilot study conducted in April 1987.[17] This survey, carried out in collaboration with the New Hampshire Task Force on Child Abuse (a private voluntary group), interviewed 958 parents. The data used to compute the incidence of physical abuse were obtained using a modification of the Conflict Tactics Scales.

Objectives and findings. The immediate purpose of the New Hampshire survey was to provide data on the number and rate of children who were physically abused in 1986–1987 and to serve as a benchmark for similar studies in subsequent years for purposes of measuring progress in reducing child abuse.

The survey provided valuable data on how the rate of child abuse in New Hampshire compares with the rate for the rest of the United States, as measured in a recent national survey.[18] We found that the rate for New Hampshire is about one quarter of the U.S. rate. Our interpretation of this finding is that it reflects the low rate of other kinds of violence in New Hampshire. The New Hampshire homicide rate, for example, is about one quarter of the median state homicide rate.[19] The survey also provided information on the characteristics of families and parents where physical abuse occurred and documented and supported the view of the New Hampshire task force and the state CPS that there are many more cases than come to the attention of CPS.

Another purpose of the New Hampshire survey was to test certain revisions of the Conflict Tactics Scales and to conduct methodological analyses of the effects of question order on the response rate.[20] These analyses are being used to develop and refine the CTS further as a measure of child abuse.

Finally, the New Hampshire study was intended to bring child abuse to public attention. Surveys have a way of doing that, especially when they are locally relevant. This objective was highly successful. Each of the three television stations carried the story on the evening news. Public television did an entire large segment of its weekly magazine on the survey. Probably every newspaper in the state carried stories; some did a feature story in addition to the news story. The *Boston Globe* also covered the survey. In short, aside from the scientific contribution of the survey, it served to bring child abuse to public awareness.

Alternative Sources of Incidence Data. Several federal agencies conduct periodic epidemiological surveys. It might be possible to arrange to supplement one of these surveys to measure the incidence of child abuse. One example is the National Health Interview Survey. Another is the Behavioral Risk Factors Survey carried out each year by the Centers for Disease Control in cooperation with about thirty states. The Behavioral Risk Factors Survey has provided extremely valuable data on the progress being made (or not made) in primary prevention of heart disease, automobile injury, lung cancer, and alcoholism. Child abuse questions (modified from the Conflict Tactics Scales) could be added to that survey.

Because the thirty states participating in the Behavioral Risk Factors Survey include New Hampshire (under contract to the University of New Hampshire poll, David W. Moore, principal investigator), our estimate of the feasibility of adding data on child abuse is based on direct experience. It may be impossible, however, to develop a cooperative arrangement with either of the two surveys mentioned, and the delay would be a minimum of two years.

Sample of States. For the surveys on child abuse, we suggest using a three-factor, two-by-two-by-two design to select eight states, each of which would include a sample of 1,000 parents. Although eight states is not a large number, the total number of families in the surveys

TABLE 11–1

CLASSIFICATION OF STATES BY THREE DICHOTOMIZED FACTORS

Factor	Classification Scheme						
Program and funding level	High				Low		
Urbanization	High		Low		High		Low	
Legitimate violence	High	Low	High	Low	High	Low	High	Low
State type number	1	2	3	4	5	6	7	8

would be about 8,000. In addition, the two-by-two-by-two design means that comparisons among states on any of the three factors will always involve four states that are low on that factor and four states that are high.

Selection factor 1: program and funding level. The intensity of state services and prevention programs for child abuse can be used to select four states that rank high in relation to other states and four that rank low. This will permit us to determine whether the four states with more intensive programs have a lower rate of child abuse and whether they show a greater decrease in child abuse than the four states with a less intensive program effort.

Selection factor 2: urbanization. Four states with a high proportion of the population living in standard metropolitan statistical areas and four states with a low proportion of the population living in such areas should be selected. Urbanization is an important basis for choice because previous research shows that the rate of physical abuse is much higher in large urban centers and because the degree of urbanization is an indirect measure of many other important characteristics of the states.

Selection factor 3: other violence. Four states with a high score on a measure of "legitimate violence" should be selected to compare with four states having low scores.[21] Scores on the legitimate violence index are suggested as a basis for selection because both theory and empirical evidence suggest that the use of violence for socially permissible purposes tends to encourage its use for criminal and other illegitimate purposes.[22] Alternatively, a combination of scores on the legitimate violence index and rates of assault and homicide can be used as the basis for selecting states that are low and high in propensity to violence.

Factorial design. This selection of states will lead to the eight categories of states shown in table 11–1.

The Need for Longitudinal Surveys. Earlier we discussed the need to investigate the changes in the incidence of child abuse in the states and to relate those changes to changes in program effort and to sociocultural characteristics of the states. To accomplish these goals, epidemiological surveys must be conducted in the states at two or more times. For the initial research effort we propose that the epidemiological surveys be conducted in the first year of the project and again in the fourth year, allowing a three-year period for measuring change.

Summary and Conclusions

This chapter outlines policy-relevant research based on studying child abuse on a comparative, state-by-state basis. The only child abuse data now available on that basis are the officially reported numbers of cases. They provide an excellent measure of the degree to which the public and state agencies have intervened in cases of child abuse. This chapter argues for the importance of also collecting state data on the incidence of child abuse and on the programs and funding directed toward child abuse.

Fundamental to the approach outlined in this chapter is the assumption that the incidence of child abuse varies substantially among the states and that some states have responded with more vigor than others to the problem. Information on the varying rates of abuse, the sociocultural characteristics associated with high rates, and various levels of response to the problem can identify state characteristics that correlate most highly with child abuse and can suggest how states with the higher rates may lower them. The combination of data on specific families and data on the characteristics of the states in which the families live can be used to discover how individual factors associated with child abuse are either exacerbated or muted by the sociocultural environments within the various states.

The research requires two major data collection efforts: data on the incidence of child abuse and data on state sociocultural and political characteristics. Each of the two data collection efforts will

161

need to be replicated three years after the first data are collected to permit a cross-lagged panel analysis or other kinds of longitudinal analysis.

Incidence of child abuse. The data on the incidence of child abuse would be obtained by epidemiological surveys of parents in eight states. The first survey would be conducted in year 1 of the project, the second in year 4. In each survey approximately 1,000 parents from each of the eight states would be interviewed, and the incidence of child abuse would be measured with the Conflict Tactics Scales. The purpose of the two surveys is to measure the change in both the incidence of child abuse within each state and the relationship between the incidence and the sociocultural factors associated with it.

The eight states would be chosen according to three criteria:

• the extent of state programs and funding to deal with the problem of child abuse
• the degree of urbanization
• the degree of nonfamily violence, including both "legitimate" violence, such as corporal punishment in schools and the death penalty for certain crimes, and criminal violence

From each of the eight types of states, we would select one state for inclusion in the survey. Although it would be ideal to survey 1,000 parents in all fifty states, an effort of that magnitude seems too ambitious at this time. Instead, by carefully selecting the states according to the scheme outlined, it would be possible to control for three of the most likely influences on the incidence of child abuse. We would also be able to analyze the relationship between the incidence of abuse and other sociocultural factors. Our theoretical model suggests that these relationships will differ greatly among the eight categories of states.

Characteristics of states. In addition to the epidemiological surveys, data need to be collected from all fifty states on the amount of funding for child abuse programs. These data are, of course, essential to the identification of the eight state categories, but they can also be analyzed to determine their relationship to sociocultural and political characteristics of the states. The sociocultural data are already available in the State and Regional Indicators Archive. This information can be used to develop and test a model that explains why some states are more likely than others to respond to the problem of child abuse.[23]

Awareness of the problem of child abuse has grown dramatically in the past two decades, but we still have no reliable longitudinal measures of the problem within states—the entities that are primarily responsible for dealing with it. States need incidence data, not just reporting (that is, intervention) data. In the long run many states in addition to the eight in the proposed research may want to develop data collection efforts to provide continuous monitoring of the incidence of child abuse among their citizens.

The research described in this chapter would be expensive but far from prohibitively so. It would be a first and very substantial effort to examine the problem of child abuse from the perspective of the governmental units that have primary responsibility for dealing with it. This approach is a crucial next step in formulating policies that will contribute more effectively to the prevention and treatment of child abuse.

12

Is Violence Preventable?

Carol Petrie and Joel Garner

The United States is a violent place. The number of homicides reported to the police has almost tripled from 7,258 in 1962 to 19,257 in 1986. The murder rate, at 8.6 per 100,000, is higher than that of any other Western industrialized nation. Homicide is the eleventh leading cause of death. It is the greatest cause of death to young black men, their death from homicide being five times the national rate.

These rather grim facts have long been known and lamented and cannot be presented here as innovative research findings. Perhaps equally grim is the perceived inability of the society to do anything effective to prevent violence. This perception is particularly widespread among law enforcement and criminal justice officials, who presume that their primary job is to respond after a crime has been committed. This belief is nowhere more evident than in the annual statistical report of homicides in the United States, where the chief federal law enforcement agency in the country declares, "Supporting the philosophy that murder is primarily a societal problem over which law enforcement has little or no control is the fact that nearly 3 of every 5 murder victims were related to (16 percent) or acquainted with (42 percent) their assailants."[1]

This statement or one virtually identical with it has appeared in every issue of the uniform crime reports since 1962, when the Federal Bureau of Investigation first began reporting homicides by the circumstance and nature of the victim-offender relationship.[2] In 1962 the FBI used four categories to report the relationship of murderers to their victims. In 1966 a new reporting format appeared and was used consistently until 1976, when the current format totally separating relationship and circumstance was initiated. These changes in reporting format make it very difficult to assess the precise changes in homicide types since 1962.[3] Table 12–1, using the 1962 format, reports the data for that year and for 1986. What is clear is that homicides between strangers account for no more than 15 percent of all homicides. It is this finding over twenty-five years that appears to be the basis for the FBI's unwavering conviction that law enforcement can do little or nothing about homicide.

The data are so stark and consistent that they compel agreement with the FBI's observation—most homicides occur between people who have some sort of prior relationship. The victim and the offender may simply live in the same neighborhood, or they may be acquaintances or even friends. And homicides occur between those with the most intimate and long-lasting relationships, family members.

Relationship

The best information to date on the victim-offender relationship in homicides comes from *The Nature and Patterns of American Homicide*, by Marc Reidel, Margaret Zahn, and Lois Mock.[4] This study demonstrates the benefits of having access to and analyzing the raw data, rather than having to rely solely on published statistics. The investigators examined the supplemental homicide reports (SHR) submitted to the FBI by state and local police agencies for the years 1976, 1977, and 1978. This period was chosen because in 1976 the Uniform Crime Reports changed to an incident-based system that allowed the same information that had traditionally been collected on victims to be collected on offenders as well. Thus, for the first time, the victim-offender relationship could be determined.

For their published report, the authors divided homicide into

TABLE 12–1

HOMICIDES BY RELATIONSHIP, 1962 AND 1986

1962 FBI Relationship Category	1962		1986	
	Number	Percent	Number	Percent
Family situations	2,105	29	3,023	16
Altercations outside the family (acquaintance)	3,194	44	8,030	42
Felony type (stranger)	944	13	2,465	13
Unknown/not stated	1,016	14	5,739	30
Total	7,259	100	19,257	100

SOURCE: Federal Bureau of Investigation, *Crime in the United States* (Washington, D.C.: U.S. Department of Justice, 1963 and 1987).

three kinds of relationships: (1) family homicide, defined as homicide between husband and wife, parent and child, stepparent and stepchild, or those in "other" family relationships; (2) acquaintance homicide, defined as homicide in which victim and offender were known to each other but were not family; and (3) stranger homicide, defined as homicide in which victim and offender had no known previous connection. The proportions of murder by category for 1978 were similar to those reported for 1986 (see figure 12–1). Of 18,693 murders in 1978, homicide by an acquaintance was the most frequent type (38 percent), followed by family homicide (19 percent) and homicide by a stranger (13 percent) (30 percent were unclassified). Surprisingly, males were more often victimized than females, not just in the stranger and acquaintance categories, where the ratio was approximately five to one, but in the family category as well. There, the males constituted 57 percent of all homicide victims (see table 12–2).

An examination of raw data on homicide in 1978 bears out the findings in the family violence literature that more husbands murder their wives than the reverse. When we computed the 1986 numbers from the published statistics and compared them with the 1978 figures, we found a decrease in homicide behavior for both wives and husbands, but this change in behavior was somewhat more dramatic for the wives.

Contact

Knowledge of a prior relationship between offenders and victims of homicide does not by itself provide sufficient information to design violence prevention programs. Additional evidence for patterns in homicide, however, argues for preventability. This information does not provide direct guidance on how to prevent homicide or other violence; it merely establishes that prevention is possible. The first bit of evidence is this: the police and child protection agencies come in contact with a substantial proportion of homicide victims at least once before the homicide. Research findings from both Kansas City and Detroit for 1974 revealed that in 85 percent of the domestic homicides the police had been dispatched to that location at least once in the past two years.[5] In 50 percent of these cases the police had been dispatched five or more times. In addition, child protection agencies have contact with 25 percent to 38 percent of all fatalities where child abuse or neglect is suspected.[6]

Although some of these data are limited in scope and more than a decade old, the findings lend credence to the notion that the police and other social service agencies have sufficient opportunities to do

FIGURE 12–1
Homicides by Relationship, 1978 and 1986
(thousands)

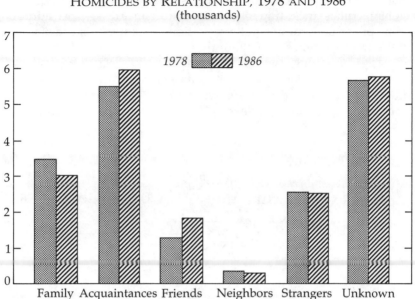

SOURCES: Marc Reidel, Margaret Zahn, and Lois Mock, *The Nature and Patterns of American Homicide* (Washington, D.C: U.S. Department of Justice, National Institute of Justice, 1985), and Federal Bureau of Investigation, *Crime in the United States* (Washington, D.C: U.S. Department of Justice, 1987).

something about homicide. Had the findings of this research been that the official agencies rarely had contact with homicide victims before their death, the prospects for prevention would be severely limited. With this information, however, we can build upon the roles of prior relationship and contact to study further what interventions ought to be implemented by which agencies in what kinds of situations.

Location

In addition to these two characteristics—the prior relationship between the offender and the victim and the existence of contact by official agencies before homicides—another salient characteristic about violence is the repetitiveness of calls for service. Recent research in Boston and Minneapolis has investigated the locations to which the police are dispatched.[7] Both studies have reported that small percentages of locations—residences, intersections, con-

167

venience stores—account for large percentages of the dispatches and that this geographic concentration exists for a variety of property and violent crimes including domestic disturbance cases. In addition, crime does not occur in equal proportions at all hours of the day, days of the week, or times of the month.

These findings, though still tentative, suggest that patterns of violence are spatial as well as relational. Findings from the Zahn and other research also confirm that violence between nonstrangers very frequently occurs in a residence. The police, of course, patrol spaces,

TABLE 12–2
Relationship and Gender of Victim, U.S. Homicides, 1978

Relationship	Total	Females		Males	
		Number	Percent	Number	Percent
Family	3,492	1,510	43.2	1,982	56.8
Acquaintances	7,043	1,366	19.4	5,677	80.6
Stranger	2,529	388	18.3	2,141	84.7
Unknown	5,629	1,177	20.9	4,452	79.1
Total	18,693	4,441	23.8	14,252	76.2

SOURCE: Marc Reidel, Margaret Zahn, and Lois Mock, *The Nature and Patterns of American Homicide* (Washington, D.C.: U.S. Department of Justice, National Institute of Justice, 1985).

not relationships, and do not enter residences without cause. If these findings hold up under further scrutiny, however, information about these locations can be used to concentrate prevention resources. If these findings do not hold up, if we cannot improve our prediction of violence through knowledge of where it has occurred, then our ability to prevent violence will be diminished. Some research efforts on the predictability of where crime occurs and how that information can be used to prevent future violence is under way.[8]

These three characteristics—the existence of prior relationships between victims and offenders, the extent of prior official contact with victims, and the concentration of crime in time and space—form the basis of our contention that violence is patterned, predictable, and maybe even preventable. These characteristics make the argument for prevention plausible; they do not in themselves make that argument true. These characteristics of violence lead to another, more than plausible conclusion. Since the bulk of homicide (and we suspect other forms of violence) is between people with a prior relationship, the prospects for violence prevention lie heavily with the prevention of family violence. In fact, a violence prevention program that does not focus on family violence or violence between nonstrangers cannot succeed.

We do not claim to know how to reduce violence. For a program of violence reduction to succeed, much more must be known about the patterns of violence, not only relational patterns but the full gamut of social, physiological, and psychological influences on violence. In the rest of this essay, we draw upon some published statistics and some raw data to compare family and other violence. The family violence literature defines family violence as a crime and recommends that it be treated as a crime by the criminal justice system.[9] We agree. We would add that many of the controversies regarding the nature and extent of violent crime within the family would benefit from direct comparisons between family and nonfamily violence and that these comparisons can best be studied within a criminological framework.

In this chapter we attempt to do just that—study family violence as crime is studied. The study of family violence within a common framework will broaden and advance knowledge accumulated from individual studies. No one study, no matter how well designed or implemented, can tell us very much. A body of research, bound together by a rigorous analytical structure, will in the long run be the best guide to understanding and preventing violence. We maintain that such a general criminological framework is emerging and can be applied to family violence research with salutary effects both for our understanding of family violence and for the emerging paradigm of criminal careers.

Criminal Career Paradigm

Emerging within criminology is a new framework for analysis. This paradigm is not a substantive theory like differential association or labeling theory but a structure for identifying and understanding various dimensions of a criminal career.[10] Though still innovative and not without controversy the criminal career framework offers the study of family violence a powerful tool of analysis and comparison.[11]

Distinguishing Prevalence and Incidence. The basic contribution of the criminal career framework is that the aggregate crime rate is made up of two components, the proportion of the population that are active criminals, that is, the prevalence rate, and the frequency with which those criminals commit crimes, the incidence rate.[12] For any particular period the number of crimes (C) is the product of the participation rate (d) and the individual offending frequency (L). Table 12–3 sets out the basic definitions and relationships between the central concepts in the criminal career framework.[13] To distinguish the crime rate from the prevalence rate from the incidence rate, three items of information are needed: the number of offenses, the number of offenders, and the size of the sample studied. In the next section we compute these rates for some of the most prominent studies in family violence research and in criminology, but before we do that it is valuable to explore further the potential of the criminal career framework.

The criminal career approach is concerned primarily with crime control. It seeks to reduce the number of *crimes* committed. This may mean reducing the number of persons who participate in illegal behavior or reducing the frequency with which current offenders commit crimes. By separating the dimensions of participation and frequency, this approach seeks to determine what policies will reduce the most crimes at the least cost to society. For example, the existence of 1,000 crimes (however measured or defined) may mean that (1) there are 1,000 offenders each committing one crime or (2) there is one offender committing 1,000 crimes. These extremes are unlikely, but the aggregate crime rate is composed of some combination of participation rates and frequency rates.[14]

This not very complicated distinction has serious implications for the design of any violence prevention program. To the extent that the participation rate in violence is high, violence prevention needs to focus on the general population. This might involve public education or broadly based interventions for the entire society. To the extent that the total number of violent incidents is driven by the high frequency of a relatively small number of offenders, different violence prevention strategies, such as the rehabilitation or the incapacitation of offenders, may be more appropriate.

The separation of prevalence and incidence derives in no small part from the recognition that in certain kinds of crime a small number of offenders account for a substantial portion of the known criminal activity. Perhaps the best known study in criminology, the Philadelphia birth cohort, found that 6 percent of all juveniles in the study (18 percent of all offenders) accounted for 52 percent of all police contacts.[15] Similar distributions have been found in numerous studies. This finding has led many criminologists to hypothesize that the factors relevant to the initiation of criminal behavior may differ from those relevant to the frequency with which crimes are committed by those criminally active.[16]

Drugs and alcohol are a good example. The evidence is strong that active criminals increase their rate of offending when they increase their drug use. Most offenders, however, initiate their careers years before they begin to abuse drugs. Whatever the exact causal mechanism between drugs and alcohol and crime, the distinctions generated by the criminal career framework lead to the tentative conclusion that drug abuse does not play a major role in the decision

TABLE 12-3
CRIMINAL CAREER CONCEPTS AND DEFINITIONS

Concept	Symbol	Measures
Offense-based Measures		
Aggregate crime rate per capita per year	C	Crimes per capita per year
Individual frequency per active offender	L	Crimes per year per active offender
Current participation rate	d	Percentage of a population commiting a crime within a year
Cumulative participation rate	D	Percentage of a population ever committing a crime
Arrest-based Measures		
Aggregate crime rate per capita per year	A	Arrests per capita per year
Individual frequency per active offender	m	Arrests per year per active offender
Current participation rate	b	Percentage of a population arrested for a crime within a year
Cumulative participation rate	B	Percentage of a population ever arrested

SOURCE: Alfred Blumstein, Jacqueline Cohen, Jeffrey Roth, and Christy Visher, *Criminal Careers and Career Criminals* (Washington, D.C.: National Academy Press, 1986).

to initiate criminal behavior but is probably a major influence on the amount of crime committed by active offenders.

Comparisons among Samples and Crime Types

The criminal career framework is designed for use with differing populations, differing definitions of offending, and different ways to measure criminal activity. Nothing in the criminal career framework imposes a definition of offending or limits the severity or definition of what constitutes a crime. The framework permits comparisons of shoplifting, assault, homicide, or any other crime. Different measures of the same crime are also accommodated so that the implications of different measures can be more easily appreciated.

As set out in table 12–3, the framework includes but takes pains to distinguish between measures of offending (self-reports, victimizations) and measures of official response to offending (arrests, convictions). The criminal career approach incorporates distinctions between measuring offenders' behavior on the one hand and behavior by criminal justice officials on the other. We rarely know (without direct observation) whether an individual is an active criminal or, if active, what his rate of offending is. What we can often examine are official records of arrests or convictions, but these reflect the activity and record-keeping ability of the police and the courts as well as the illegal behavior of the offender. Thus definitions have been established for the most common kind of criminal record data available for research, arrest rates. Caution in using official records to describe offending is always warranted; the criminal career paradigm has sought to ensure clarity by establishing firm definitions and distinctions between offending behavior and official records of that behavior.

This aspect of criminal careers is particularly valuable for research on family violence. Much of what we know about child abuse stems from reports of official agencies. The dramatic increases in the number of founded and unfounded cases in the past decade may reflect new reporting expectations and not a change in child abuse.

Finally, the criminal career framework is designed to incorporate research on nationally representative samples as well as samples of known offenders or victims. Clear definition of the sample is required, however, if the appropriate comparisons are to be made within this framework. In family violence research, as in criminology in general, representative samples are rare, and defining the exact nature of the study sample is as important to understanding the research findings as the kinds of criminality involved.

Correlates of Criminal Career Dimensions

The criminal career framework can be vitally important in exploring variations in crime rate and in discovering correlates and determinants of criminality. The Panel on Research on Criminal Careers of the National Academy of Sciences concluded that the most striking observation about participation is the high rate at which males ever become involved in crime. The academy's review of past research found that 50 to 60 percent of all males will be arrested at least once for a nontraffic offense; 23 to 36 percent will be arrested for an index offense.[17] Female participation was estimated at one-third to one-fifth that of males. Participation by blacks appears not to differ from that by whites for less serious robbery offenses, but for nontraffic offenses the ratio of participation rates is nearly two to one and for index offenses more than three to one. According to the academy report, virtually no one initiates a career before the age of eight but over half the persons ever arrested are first arrested by age eighteen. Initiation as recorded by self-reports starts many years earlier than records of first arrest.

The criminal career perspective seeks to focus on policy issues. There is little that can be done, for instance, to change someone's age, race, or sex. The academy focused, however, on some potentially influential considerations that might be susceptible to change through public policy. The panel's assessment of these issues was not that they were proven causes or correlates of criminality but that there was sufficient evidence to warrant further research on them.

A number of family influences were examined, including parental supervision and communication, criminality among parents, family disruption, and family size and structure. Early antisocial behavior has regularly been found to be related to subsequent delinquency. The link between social class and offending and arrest rates has been found to be complex but points consistently to an increase in participation by members of lower social and economic classes. For youth and adults the availability of legitimate means of obtaining resources may reduce the influence of illegal activities. The academy's assessment is that employment appears to reduce participation by adults but may increase it for youths, especially those under eighteen. A more important determinant of participation in criminal behavior may be with whom one works or plays. Peer group influences are an essential element in differential association, a major theory of juvenile criminal participation, and the academy's review considered not only negative influences but also the mediating role of parental supervision and involvement in conventional activities as factors influencing the decision to participate in criminal acts.

Family Violence

The academy's review of the correlates of prevalence and incidence rates is striking for its emphasis on property as opposed to violent offenses and its stark omission of any reference to family violence. Still, the framework is applicable to the phenomenon studied by family violence research, and the differentiation of frequency from participation is so central to family violence as to be almost definitional. Family violence is violence among people who have a continuing, intimate relationship. The prospects for repeated violence in these circumstances appear to be high. In the criminal career lexicon, these family violence offenders have a high rate of repeat offending. Battering is variously defined in the family violence literature as repeated acts of violence by a family member or the frequency rate for any violent act by a family member.

Participation and Frequency for Assault and Homicide

Can the criminal career framework be applied to family violence research? Table 12–4 is an initial effort at describing several major studies that permit the computation of participation and frequency rates for assault and homicide. Eight studies are included. We included two studies from the Bureau of Justice Statistics National Crime Survey and the National Youth Survey sponsored by the National Institute of Mental Health.[18] Family violence researchers will be familiar with the 1975 and 1985 surveys of Murray Straus and Richard Gelles.[19] For contrast, we included the Rand survey of incarcerated felons in California.[20] Our last two studies are the U.S. homicide data referenced in the first section.[21] This sample of studies is intended to be illustrative, not comprehensive.

The range of samples in the list of studies is quite broad. The National Crime Survey, the National Youth Survey, and the Gelles and Straus research are all nationally representative samples. The Gelles and Straus survey is designed to include households with certain characteristics (intact couples with children aged three to seventeen, and so on). The crime survey is representative of all households.[22] The National Youth Survey is a representative sample of youth aged eleven to seventeen. The Rand survey is an opportunity sample of inmates in California prisons and jails and represents nothing but that.

These surveys vary sharply among themselves on whether they are self-reports of offending or victimization reports. The Gelles and Straus data are both. The uniform crime reports supplemental homicide reports for the nation for 1978 are official records of victimizations, as are the eight city homicide data from Reidel, Zahn, and Mock. Except for the homicide studies, we purposely limited our reporting to items roughly comparable to assault. Our use of "assault" to describe a great variety of behavior (within and between studies) is not as precise as the definitions given in the original studies.

We selected these studies because of their importance and because they were readily available, either in published form or as raw data or both. We wanted to display participation and frequency rates among studies, some of which included crimes of family violence. We discovered how difficult that is to do, especially for frequency rates.

Participation and Frequency Rates

The Bureau of Justice Statistics normally publishes aggregate victimization rates and the numbers of victimizations weighted to reflect the U.S. population. In 1985, however, they published victim prevalence rates for a wide variety of crimes reported.[23] This research reported an individual's risk of being a victim of certain crimes. That risk is simply the number of *victims*, not the normally published number of *victimizations*. The bureau reported that 31.5 per thousand, that is, 3.15 percent, of the U.S. population over twelve years of age were victimized at least once during 1982. This prevalence rate varied by crime type: 2.46 percent of the population were assaulted, 0.89 percent were the victims of aggravated assault, and 1.69 percent were the victims of simple assault. There are no new findings here. More people are the victims of simple assault than of aggravated assault, and the percentage of the population victimized in any one year is small.

The bureau also reported the participation rates by sex. Thus, 4.07 percent of males and 2.31 percent of females were victims of violent crime. Because the bureau separately reported the number of victimizations by sex for 1982, we were able to compute a frequency rate for these crime types.[24] The last three columns of table 12–4 report the results of this computation. The frequency rates for violent crimes as reported in the National Crime Survey do not vary much. The highest is 1.11 for any violent act against females. The lowest is 1.00 for simple assault against males. Not only are these frequency rates consistent between the sexes, they are consistently low compared with results of other studies. Thus the victimizations reported

TABLE 12-4
ANNUAL PREVALENCE AND INCIDENCE RATES FOR VIOLENCE, EIGHT STUDIES, 1975–1986

Study	Sample	Source	Crime Type	Total		Male		Female	
				Prevalence Rate	Incidence Rate	Prevalence Rate	Incidence Rate	Prevalence Rate	Incidence Rate
National Crime Survey, 1982[a]	128,000 individuals	Victimizations	Any violence	3.15	1.09	4.07	1.07	2.31	1.11
			Assault	2.46	1.07	3.22	1.06	1.77	1.08
			Aggrevated assault	0.89	1.05	1.30	1.05	1.05	1.04
			Simple assault	1.69	1.03	2.09	1.00	1.32	1.05
National Crime Survey, 1978–1982[a]	640,000 interviews	Victimizations	Robbery, rape, and assault	n.r.		n.r.		0.42	1.62
National Youth Survey[b]	National probability ages 11–17	Self-reported crimes	Assault	6.1	3.9	8.7	4.4	3.1	2.6
	ages 15–21		Assault	4.6	3.9	6.4	4.4	2.5	2.5
Gelles and Straus, 1975[c]	3,520 households	Self-reports and victimizations	Spouse assault	n.r.		3.8	n.r.	4.6	n.r.

176

Study	Sample	Method	Crime					
	1,146 households with children	Self-reports and victimizations	Child assault	3.6	n.r.	n.r.	n.r.	n.r.
Gelles and Straus, 1985[d]	1,428 households with children	Self-reports and victimizations	Spouse assault		n.r.	3.0	n.r.	4.4	n.r.
		Self-reports and victimizations	Child assault	1.9	n.r.	n.r.	n.r.	n.r.
Peterson and Braikere	643 California inmates	Self-reports	Assault	59.0	2.40	n.r.	n.r.	n.r.
Uniform crime reports 1986[f]	U.S. population	Official reports	Homicide	.01	n.a.			
Reidel and Zahn, 1978[g]	8 U.S. cities	Official reports	Homicide	.02				

(Table continues)

TABLE 12–4 (Continued)

NOTES:

    n.r.—not reported

    n.a.—not available

SOURCES:

a. Patrick Langan and Christopher Innes, *The Risk of Violent Crime*, Bureau of Justice Statistics Special Report (Washington, D.C.: U.S. Department of Justice, 1985).

b. Delbert Elliott, S. Ageton, D. Huizinga, B. Knowles, and R. Kanter, *The Prevalence and Incidence of Delinquent Behavior: 1976–1980*, National Youth Survey Report no. 26, 1983.

c. Murray A. Straus, Richard J. Gelles, and Suzanne K. Steinmetz, *Behind Closed Doors: Violence in the American Family* (Garden City, N.Y.: Anchor Press, 1980).

d. Murray A. Straus and Richard J. Gelles, "Societal Change and Change in Family Violence from 1975 to 1985 as Revealed by Two National Surveys," vol. 48 (1986), pp. 465–79.

e. M.A. Peterson and H. B. Braiker, *Doing Crime: A Survey of California Prison Inmates*, Report R-2200-DOJ (Santa Monica, Calif.: Rand Corporation, 1980).

f. Federal Bureau of Investigation, *Crime in the United States* (Washington, D.C.: U.S. Department of Justice, 1987).

g. Marc Reidel, Margaret Zahn, and Lois Mock, *The Nature and Patterns of American Homicide* (Washington, D.C.: U.S. Department of Justice, National Institute of Justice, 1985).

to the National Crime Survey for violent crimes for males and females are primarily driven by the number of victims and not by the number of victimizations per victim.

Just the opposite is true for the National Crime Survey data on the violent victimization of women by family members.[25] Over the five years 1978 to 1982 an average of 420,000 women a year reported being raped, robbed, or assaulted by family members. The average annual number of victimizations for these victims was 680,000. These numbers provide an estimate of prevalence rates for women of 0.42 percent.[26] The average number of victimizations per victim is 1.62, that is, the number of victimizations increased by 62 percent because some of the victims were assaulted more than once. This rate should be compared with the 1.09 average frequency rate for the 1982 National Crime Survey, where the number of victimizations was only 9 percent higher than the number of victims. Unfortunately, from these data we can compute only the *average* number of victimizations per victim. We cannot tell from the published statistics how many victims were attacked twice, three times, or more.

The contrast between the two studies highlights the importance of separating prevalence and incidence rates, but it does not put family violence rates in the context of violence rates generally. Table 12–4 reports the rates for other studies, including some familiar data on family violence from Gelles and Straus. They report offense prevalence rates of "child assault" of 3.6 percent for 1975 and 1.9 percent for 1985.[27] They also report offense prevalence rates for "spouse assault" of 3.8 percent in 1975 and 3.0 percent in 1985 by males and 4.6 percent for 1975 and 4.4 percent for 1985 by females. Although these are household (not individual) rates and are generated from a combination of victimizations and self-reports of offending, the levels appear to be comparable to the participation rates reported by the 1982 National Crime Survey. Since Gelles and Straus do not report the number of offenses or victimizations, it is not possible from the published data to compute an average frequency rate for their data.[28]

The computations in table 12–4 require more development, but they are a first cut at comparing the prevalence and incidence of different kinds of violence among studies. Too much could be made of the precision suggested by the two decimal points. We are more interested in the comparative approach and the larger picture. We have included several studies of violent offending for which prevalence and incidence rates have already been computed. The National Youth Survey reports an annual participation rate of 6.1 percent: 8.7 percent for males and 3.1 percent for females. The youth of this sample is more typical of criminological studies since much offending behavior occurs among teenagers. In fact, the criminal career framework explicitly incorporates notions of career termination because such a large percentage of offenders active in their teens drop out in their early twenties.[29]

While we have been focusing on one correlate of offending, sex, the inclusion of the National Youth Survey findings is intended to illustrate another well-grounded correlate of offending, age. Family violence research does not explicitly control for the fact that family violence offenders, though not necessarily their victims, are likely to be older than the populations normally studied by criminologists. The data permit the computation of annualized frequency rates for these youths.[30] The frequency rates for both males and females in the National Youth Survey are higher than the rates computed from the National Crime Survey for family violence. We have not yet determined whether the National Youth Survey data can be disaggregated by the victim-offender relationship so that family violence rates can be computed for this sample.

We also included the most prominent study of frequency rates, the Rand survey of inmates in California prisons and jails. Asked about their offending during the last year they were not incarcerated, 59 percent of these inmates reported at least one assault. The number of reported assaults per offender, however, was less than that reported by the National Youth Survey for both males and females.

Our last two studies in table 12–4 are the two homicide data sets from *The Nature and Patterns of American Homicide* by Reidel, Zahn, and Mock. Our intent here is to contrast assault participation rates with homicide participation rates for males and females. The contrast is instructive. Homicide is a severe and well-documented crime. It is always of concern to the public and frequently studied by criminologists. It is a rare event and only a minuscule proportion of all the violence that occurs in our society. Yet it is the crime most investigated by the police and most frequently cleared by arrest. Nevertheless, as discussed earlier, homicide traditionally has been seen as an unpreventable crime.

Reidel, Zahn, and Mock's examination of national homicide patterns was discussed earlier. In an effort to compare urban patterns of murder with national patterns, however, the authors also analyzed homicide records from police departments and medical examiners in eight cities for 1978.[31] The test year was chosen because it was recent enough to reflect the current patterns of homicide and distant enough to allow for court processing of most cases. Here the findings presented a somewhat different picture. In the eight cities males were far more often victimized than were females in all three homicide categories, family, acquaintance, and stranger. In two of the cities, Philadelphia and St. Louis, the ratio was close to three to one.

We were so surprised by this published finding that we examined the raw data from the eight cities.[32] The authors included a variable on the victim-offender relationship with thirty codes. Table 12–5 reports the distribution of those categories by the sex of the victim. In every category except former-spouses, male victims outnumbered female victims. In the former-spouses category the distribution was virtually equal.

This raised the question of who was doing the offending in these cities. Was this similar to homicide by acquaintances and strangers, that is, males killing other males in the family? In the aggregate this appears to be the case, particularly when the "other family" category is included. Still intrigued, we looked at the victim-offender relationship by the sex of the offender.

Table 12–6 illustrates the participation of women as offenders in family homicide, at 40 percent of the total. In the more intimate relationships where the offenders are adults—spouses, parent and child, former spouses, and lovers—the result is even more dramatic; women offenders numbered 110 and men offenders 112 (see table 12–7). In cases of parents murdering their children, the split between male and female offenders was nearly equal.[33] Indeed, in their published report, Reidel, Zahn, and Mock note that while nationally women constituted a minority of arrests in every homicide category, in several cities women made up as many as half the family homicide arrests (Oakland, Newark, and Chicago).[34]

When we examine these data in the context of table 12–4, it becomes clear that family violence involves complex behavior on the part of the offenders and that the patterned interactions between offender and victim may also play a role in the kind of family violence that leads to homicide. Further, these complex interactions may have implications for the design of criminal justice interventions in family violence and for the design of general violence prevention programs.

Conclusions

Homicide and perhaps other kinds of violence are distinguished by three characteristics salient to prediction. These are prior relationship between the victim and the offender, prior contact between victims and official agencies, and concentration of offenses in time and by

TABLE 12–5
Relationship and Gender of Homicide Victim, Eight U.S. Cities, 1978

Relationship		All Homicides	Female Victim		Male Victim	
Victim	Offender		Number	Percent	Number	Percent
Family						
Husband	Wife	65	0	0	65	100
Wife	Husband	48	48	100	0	0
Ex-husband	Ex-wife	4	0	0	4	100
Ex-wife	Ex-husband	5	5	100	0	0
Parent	Child	17	3	18	14	82
Child	Parent	32	11	34	21	66
Stepparent	Stepchild	6	0	0	6	100
Stepchild	Stepparent	10	4	40	6	60
Other		60	9	15	51	85
Total		247	80	32	167	68
Acquaintances						
Male lover	Female lover	38	0	0	38	100
Female lover	Male lover	42	42	100	0	0
Male lover	Male lover	14	0	0	14	100
Employer	Employee	5	1	20	4	80
Employee	Employer	3	1	33	2	67
Friends		206	26	13	180	87
Acquaintances		280	23	8	257	92
Neighbors		38	9	24	29	76
Accomplices		11	0	0	11	100
Other known		99	14	14	85	86
Total		736	117	16	619	84
Strangers						
Police	Felon	1	0	0	1	100
Felon	Police	70	3	4	67	96
Guard	Citizen	1	0	0	1	100
Citizen	Guard	5	0	0	5	100
Client	Clerk	9	0	0	9	100
Clerk	Client	13	1	8	12	92
Hostage		1	0	0	1	100
Kidnapped person		1	1	100	0	0
Strangers		264	25	9	239	91
Other		62	7	11	55	89
Total		427	37	9	390	91
Unknown relationship		262	44	17	218	83
Total homicides		1,672	278	17	1,394	83

NOTE: Cases excluded where victim's gender is not known.
SOURCE: Marc Reidel, Margaret Zahn, and Lois Mock, *The Nature and Patterns of American Homicide* (Washington, D.C.: U.S. Department of Justice, National Institute of Justice, 1985).

TABLE 12–6
Relationship and Gender of Homicide Offender, Eight U.S. Cities, 1978

| Relationship | | All | Female Offender | | Male Offender | |
Victim	Offender	Homicides	Number	Percent	Number	Percent
Family						
Husband	Wife	65	63	100	0	0
Wife	Husband	48	0	0	48	100
Ex-husband	Ex-wife	4	4	100	0	0
Ex-wife	Ex-husband	5	0	0	5	100
Parent	Child	17	4	24	13	76
Child	Parent	31	14	45	17	55
Stepparent	Stepchild	6	2	33	4	67
Stepchild	Stepparent	10	0	0	10	100
Other		58	10	17	48	83
Total		242	97	40	145	60
Acquaintances						
Male lover	Female lover	37	37	100	0	0
Female lover	Male lover	42	0	0	42	100
Male lover	Male lover	12	0	0	12	100
Employer	Employee	5	1	20	4	80
Employee	Employer	3	1	33	2	67
Friends		200	16	8	184	92
Acquaintances		269	17	6	252	94
Neighbors		38	9	24	29	76
Accomplices		10	0	0	10	100
Other known		93	6	6	87	94
Total		709	86	12	623	88
Strangers						
Police	Felon	1	0	0	1	100
Felon	Police	59	2	3	57	97
Guard	Citizen	1	0	0	1	100
Citizen	Guard	5	0	0	5	100
Client	Clerk	8	1	13	7	87
Clerk	Client	11	0	0	11	100
Hostage		1	0	0	1	100
Kidnapped person		1	0	0	1	100
Strangers		222	10	5	212	95
Other		56	5	9	51	91
Total		365	18	5	347	95
Unknown relationship		63	1	2	62	98
Total homicides		1,379	202	15	1,177	85

Note: Cases excluded where offender's gender is not known.
Source: Same as source for table 12–5.

TABLE 12–7

RELATIONSHIP AND GENDER OF HOMICIDE OFFENDER, INTIMATE
CASES, EIGHT U.S. CITIES, 1978

Relationship		All	Female Offender		Male Offender	
Victim	Offender	Homicides	Number	Percent	Number	Percent
Husband	Wife	65	63	100	0	0
Wife	Husband	48	0	0	48	100
Ex-husband	Ex-wife	4	4	100	0	0
Ex-wife	Ex-husband	5	0	0	5	100
Parent	Child	17	4	24	13	76
Stepparent	Stepchild	6	2	33	4	67
Male lover	Female lover	37	37	100	0	0
Female lover	Male lover	42	0	0	42	100
Total		224	110	49	112	50

SOURCE: Same as source for table 12–5.

location. Contrary to conventional wisdom, these characteristics lead us to believe that at least some forms of serious violence can be predicted and prevented.

In this chapter we have sought to illuminate several issues about violent offending. In particular, we believe a strong case can be made for focusing both violence research and prevention programs on family violence. This focus on family violence research should be undertaken within the context of criminal careers, and research on criminal careers should include family violence. By comparing existing research on assault and homicide, we have illustrated the value of comparing participation and frequency rates within the family and not within the family. The data analysis we report here suggests the importance of studying female offending as well as male offending for purposes of prediction, early intervention, and prevention.

13

How Research
Makes a Difference
to Policy and Practice

Russell P. Dobash and R. Emerson Dobash

Research results and the ideas and concepts associated with them constitute only one element in the broader process of public discourse and policy formation. The optimistic days of the 1970s when policy makers and researchers appeared to be forging a new synthesis that would inform the social and political strategies of that era are over. The social and behavioral sciences are experiencing a period of regression; research and the academics who conduct it are not as important as they once were, or thought they were, in the process of policy formation and implementation. In societies where expert knowledge is associated with the number of times one appears on television or the rating of one's books on lists of nonfiction or even fiction best sellers, all forms of systematic knowledge are debased. Furthermore, conservative political agendas, with an emphasis on fiscal stringency and individual responsibility, have dramatically reduced the importance of social research. In some instances the media and those who control them seem to count more in public policy formation than research does. This interpretation is overpessimistic and certainly not one we would wish to embrace in considering how research should inform policy. To contemplate a nihilistic view of our role is too painful, but we do not wish to dismiss this view and will return to this thorny question in our conclusion.

Examining how research strategies shape results and how these approaches and results may shape policy requires us to consider a number of complex issues and the links between them.

We must consider the range of methodologies and methods employed in the investigation of violence in the family, giving special

---

Portions of this chapter appear in R. Emerson Dobash and Russell P. Dobash, *Violence, Women and Social Change* (London: Routledge, forthcoming).

attention to teasing out their underlying assumptions and to assessing how they shape research questions and procedures. We must examine how diverse epistemologies and research strategies may affect the conclusions and inferences researchers draw about the subject under investigation. We must look at alternative formulations of how research enters public discourse and policy. We must locate the role of researchers in this complex mosaic of social, cultural, and political enterprise.

A number of research methodologies have been employed to study violence in the family arena, but three predominate: empiricist, instrumental positivist, and interpretive-contextual. Each has its adherents and defenders, who view their method as the best or most valid approach to studying violence and the issues related to it. A range of positions on the nature of the relations between research and policy can be described as rationalist social engineering, enlightenment, and critical.[1] The role of researcher can be roughly specified as that of the detached scholar, the state counselor, the partisan, or what might tentatively be called the critical sympathizer.

The chapter begins by considering the recent analysis of the relationship between research and policy formation. The implications drawn from this work guide the evaluations of research work on violence in the family. An analysis of the major research traditions includes a consideration of the way methodological assumptions shape research results and examples of the way they have shaped public discourse and policy.

Policy and Research

Positivism, Empiricism, and Rational Decision Making. The orthodox conception of policy formulation gives preeminence to the role of research. In this rational decision-making model, policy makers recognize a need for information on a particular problem and identify a gap, and the researchers' role is to fill it. As Carol Weiss says, "A problem exists and a decision has to be made, information or understanding is lacking either to generate a solution to the problem or to select among alternative solutions; research provides the missing knowledge. With the gap filled a decision is reached."[2]

The strong variant of this approach stresses an orderly sequential process: a consensus in the formation of goals, a formal, rational consideration of possible alternatives, an explicit calculation of the costs and benefits of various options, and the ultimate selection of an optimal choice.[3] Such a conception has several underlying assumptions about policy formation, research, and the public's role in the process. This approach is most closely associated with the researcher as the detached scholar or state counselor.[4]

The rational deductive model has its roots in the Enlightenment of the late eighteenth century, when philosophers and the predecessors of modern social science first began to think that research could solve social and political problems. Ideals such as these have been prominent in the postwar era. The British welfare state and the U.S. War on Poverty envisaged a society based on planned social change guided, at least partially, by the results of social research. In this meritocratic and, one might argue, elitist vision, researchers would be the princes and princesses of social change. Detached scholars, usually with humanistic leanings, would gather valid knowledge uncontaminated by the wider world. Using this knowledge, politicians and policy makers would create just programs to implement the implications drawn from research.

State counselors would play a more active role, providing valid knowledge that would point to specific and direct interventions in the social world. Working closely with the state, they would help formulate new policies inferred from research results. Researchers and their findings would play a crucial role in solving problems in an incremental and linear fashion. Together researchers and policy makers would build a better society using an expanded base of knowledge derived from increasingly sophisticated research.

In this social engineering model, the results of research constitute hard facts, objectified, universally valid information that can be translated into logically consistent policies and practices. Dissemination of hard facts is viewed as straightforward and unproblematic in a world where all agree on the goals of a just society. As the scholar or state counselor, the researcher produces "unequivocal," certain knowledge about social and cultural issues from which decisive pronouncements are made. In this role the researcher remains above the babble and confusion of political and social processes, uncontaminated by government concerns and the demands of political pressure groups. Because of the presumed superior and unassailable position of science and often the authority of academia, the researcher assumes a privileged position. The community and even policy makers are the passive recipients of objectified knowledge. The heroic individualism of this position allows no dialogue, exchange, or adjustments in the position of researchers, who conduct research, present findings, and advise governments "as one sees fit."[5]

The rational decision-making model is allied to and has much in common with empiricist and logical positivist approaches to social research.[6] In this tradition the researcher is viewed as standing aloof from the wider world, operating as an objective, detached observer who, in the early empiricist tradition, merely gathered and collated facts. Logical positivism and more recent variants of this tradition emphasize the importance of theory testing, rigorous concept formation, and statistical analysis in the study of society; the collection of facts is not enough. The emphasis is on theory, from which hypotheses are deduced to be tested against "reality." Once data are gathered, statistical analysis allows the generalization of results and eventually the creation of general laws about how society operates. Procedures such as these are seen as commensurate with rational policy formation.

Research on Policy Making. The assumptions of rational policy formation, empiricism, and logical positivism have been subjected to increasing scrutiny, leading to considerable skepticism about their claims. Research on decision making reveals a process that bears little resemblance to the logical progression portrayed in much of the prescriptive literature.[7] Systematic knowledge about the process of policy making reveals a complex, multilayered enterprise proceeding in an aimless and diffuse manner. National policy formation is especially complex, influenced by the mass media, pressure group activity, and informal networks of communication and influence. Policy making is not a linear process proceeding along an even, upward-sloping trajectory; it ebbs and flows, meanders, and sometimes gets lost before returning to its main course.

In the final outcome, the sidetracks and meanderings may be far more important than the apparent main course. Instead of talking about a logic of policy making, we need to consider policy incidents involving improvised responses. According to Weiss, the adaptations that lead to policy adjustments and developments include reliance on custom and implicit rules, "impromptu accommodation," mutual adjustment of competing interests, accretion, negotiation, use of the tried and accepted regardless of the problem, and a muddling through by ad hoc actions that may be formalized into legislation.[8] What role is there for research in this nonlinear process that is clearly not bounded by the often rigid constraints of time associated with the usual research project?

We might answer that research plays no part. Yet both research and experience demonstrate that, at least in the United States, government officials value research. The skeptical might question this apparent enthusiasm. It may be that policy makers value research because it buys time until public enthusiasms for a particular issue have waned, because it can be used as a control and monitoring device in local communities, or because, if conducted in a particular manner, it can provide support and vindication for traditional practices or divert public attention away from certain aspects of an issue to other, less critical ones.

Is this too pessimistic? Perhaps. Viewed more positively, even these functions might be seen as constructive. Diversion to other issues may open new perspectives on a problem, and the evaluation of programs for control may result in greater financial support for valuable innovations. Social science may also help clarify assumptions, discover strategic points of intervention, and delineate different definitions of a problem.[9] These and other contributions are important; yet the most significant and enduring role of research is to offer new formulations of problems and to encourage new ways of perceiving and conceptualizing issues. Weiss calls this the enlightenment function of research, and she suggests, "The ideas derived from research provide organizing perspectives that help people make sense of experience."[10] Thus conceptual and theoretical work is crucial.

The evidence suggests that research plays a diffuse, often secondary role in the meandering route to the creation of new policies. Government officials rarely digest research results directly. Results gradually seep in through a process of reading, discussions about the problem, and lateral thinking about other issues. Research may be only a bit player in this process, and it certainly has no privileged position. As Weiss concludes, "Social science has no monopoly on knowledge and insight";[11] other forms of knowledge are just as important. Policy formation may not even involve policy makers. In the United States much policy is created outside government through the pronouncements and dictates of the courts. Within government, policy makers use information gained from their own experience in past policy events and new knowledge gained through interactions with colleagues and pressure groups. Ideas and concepts associated with or emerging from research may help shape assumptions that guide policy formulation.

Unfortunately, not all research is adequately conceptualized and rigorously conducted. Serious methodological flaws, sloppy conceptualization, and unwarranted or exaggerated inferences from results can all enter into policy work. There is no guarantee that policy makers will read or digest high-quality results; they may choose research that confirms or reinforces their own views of problems regardless of its quality. Of course, this leaves aside the thorny question of what counts as adequate and good research.

Challenges to Positivism and Empiricism. This new, rather less heroic, conception of the role of research and the researcher includes an alternative imagery of the nature of the research enterprise. It could be argued that although everyone knows about the complex political chicanery associated with policy formation, the purely logical nature of research enshrined in the positivist tradition remains intact. Not a bit of it. Researchers do not operate in some scholarly attic or vacuum unaffected by the social and political world in which they operate. Historical and philosophical investigations have revealed the significance of social, personal, and political factors in the production of science.[12] They have shown that research in all spheres of social and physical sciences, not just in policy research, is deeply affected by the context in which it is conducted. Problem identification, concept formation, theoretical imagery, research methods, statistical analysis, the interpretation of results—that is, the entire research process—are affected, if not determined, by the particular outlook of investigators and the context in which they work. Intuition, bold conjectures, and hunches play just as much a part in science as logic and analysis. Findings such as these have grave implications for those who would offer us positivist-based blueprints as sure routes to knowledge.

Additional challenges to positivistic approaches have been made from alternative epistemological positions. Phenomenological and ethnographic approaches that rely on qualitative and interpretive methods have undercut the philosophical foundations of positivistic efforts.[13] Proponents of this position propose that the externality of knowledge as posited by positivists is an illusion. Knowledge is produced only through a social process of interpretation and social production; it is not something out there but is a socially produced product that is always provisional. Thus certain knowledge is impossible.

Those who adhere to this view of knowledge object on philosophical and sometimes ethical grounds to positivists' objectification of people and the social world in which they live. For them the social world is composed of interacting and knowing subjects engaged in the creation of an ever-developing reality. This does not mean that no patterns recur in social life. Interpretive social scientists argue that social life cannot be understood and explained without careful attention to its unfolding and interactive qualities. What we need, they argue, are more detailed analyses, case studies, participant observation, and in-depth interviews that embed the phenomena under investigation in the wider context of the daily lives of the subjects involved in research. Others have argued that we must also go beyond the immediate and everyday context to consider how wider institutional, cultural, and historically based contexts influence human behavior.

Positivist and empiricist approaches have also been criticized from other theoretical positions. Critical Marxists and feminists propose other epistemological approaches to knowledge and policy formation. Critical realists object to what they see as the superficiality of explanation associated with positivism.[14] Positivists treat explanation as a demonstration of a connection or co-occurrence between independent and dependent variables. Although they usually argue that correlation is not causation, they often act as if it were and rarely go beyond their empirical generalizations. Realists see this as inadequate, merely a starting point. Realist explanations demonstrate how these observed features of reality are connected, how they operate to produce the effect. They look for the underlying nature of phenomena, seeking to go beyond immediate appearances. Correlations are merely the surface appearance. On their own they do not provide an explanation. Feminists, though not yet offering a unified epistemology, often echo the criticisms of interpretive and critical observers. Feminists emphasize gender and power relationships as important for all forms of analysis. Following the interpretive tradition, many feminist writers also stress the subjective aspects of social analysis.[15]

Starting with certain variants of the interpretive approach, these generally critical traditions have proposed new roles for the researcher. In the 1960s Howard Becker and Alvin Gouldner exposed the value-free stance of positivism as an illusion, and Becker proposed a partisan role for the social scientist.[16] It was never clear quite what Becker meant by this, but one might infer that he proposed a more active part for researchers in defending or protecting the underdog. Presumably, partisans should work in and for the community, engaged in action research and providing support for the community. Action research made it legitimate to be involved with voluntary groups. Just as one could work as state counselor, one could work as a community research counselor. The problem with this proposal, as with the earlier model of state counselor, is that its proponents never specified or analyzed this role. They failed to recognize the contradictions associated with such an activity. They also failed to specify what kind of research partisans might do since it seems probable that empiricist, positivist, and interpretive research could all aid the community. Nonetheless, they pointed to new possibilities. We think their prescriptive advice was extremely naive, however. In our subsequent discussion of the contextual approach we sketch a fourth way of working, what we provisionally call the critical sympathizer.

191

All of this may seem rather basic, a familiar aspect of the new orthodoxy of social science. We may all know of these criticisms and the approaches available, but we often act either as if they do not exist or as if the interpretive and contextual approaches are inferior rustic cousins. In the research conducted in the United States on violence in the family, the reliance on positivistic methods is nearly monolithic. While we readily acknowledge the importance of this kind of work, the neglect of other approaches has had serious consequences for our knowledge and understanding of family violence. An overreliance on empiricist and positivist procedures has led to the relative neglect of meaningful conceptualization, explanation, and understanding.[17] Limitations such as these have significant consequences for policy formation since ideas and concepts, not particular findings, affect policy. Poorly formulated ideas and concepts developed ad hoc or post hoc provide unfortunate, sometimes dangerous, direction for policy. A fuller, more measured analytical approach would be more fruitful. We would endorse Weiss's prescriptions:

> To serve the longer-term policy needs of officials, research should be grounded in relevant theory and existing knowledge; it should look at issues comprehensively in all their . . . complexity; it should be done with the greatest methodological skill that advances in research and analytic techniques have made possible. . . . The critical ingredients will be independence of thought, conceptual sophistication and methodological rigour.[18]

Only contextual forms of analysis using the best and most sophisticated qualitative and quantitative methods can lead to valid interpretations of social reality that may inform policy deliberations. This is not a call for a retreat to methods. As Weiss states, researchers also need to be informed about the "shape and contour of policy issues if their work is to be relevant to current debates."[19] Researchers should also be attuned to the concerns, demands, and interpretations of the community and of women working on violence against women. This wider context shapes research questions and the results we produce. To be aware of it enriches and enhances our research and theoretical interpretations.

In the remainder of the chapter we consider how empiricist and positivist approaches often fail to provide interpretive knowledge of the social world and examine some of the wider consequences of these methods for the role of the researcher and for policy formation. We finish by considering the contributions of the interpretive and contextual methodologies.

Positivist and Empiricist Approaches

What follows is not a rejection of quantitative approaches. The purpose of this discussion is to point out the limitations of these efforts and to offer directions for other forms of research. Examples of positivistic approaches are numerous in the area of domestic violence, but one of the most sophisticated is the work of Richard Berk and his colleagues at the University of California. These researchers have pursued a rigorous program of methodologically and statistically sophisticated research primarily aimed at elucidating the operation of the criminal justice system.[20] Using highly developed statistical causal models and quasi-experimental designs, they attempt to demonstrate how various institutional and individually based variables contribute to police action or decision making. The strength of this agenda is in its clear, carefully delimited research designs and complex statistical analysis. The agenda illustrates an unswerving commitment to a positivist method, which is often contrasted to what is apparently seen as inferior interpretive work.

This research has made important contributions, but its commitment to measurement and statistical analysis may have important analytical limitations. The topics chosen for study and especially the manner in which phenomena are conceptualized often appear to be at least partially, if not wholly, determined by how amenable they are to measurement. Problems are not chosen for theoretical reasons or because of wider community or policy concerns; the methods call the tune. This instrumental positivism can lead to contrived specification of variables that have more to do with whether they can be subjected to certain forms of statistical analysis than to the theoretical, or even the empirical, nature of the concepts and phenomena under investigation.

A recent example is an interesting study of women's use of shelters.[21] A shelter stay is evaluated in terms of the relationship between a woman's "genuine exploration" of alternatives, such as a shelter, and the effect of a stay on subsequent violence. This is an interesting and important issue, and through statistical analysis of a multitude of status and demographic variables the researchers conclude that "a shelter stay can dramatically reduce the likelihood of new violence."[22]

As positivists rather than empiricists, these researchers discuss the implications of their results in the context of wider knowledge about shelters. They fail, however, to investigate women's perceptions and experiences of using a shelter. Rather than asking a woman about issues associated with the use of a shelter—how useful it might

193

be; whether a shelter stay is seen as a viable alternative; what else is seen as an alternative; what are some of the problems associated with leaving her home and a violent man; and other issues of perception, evaluation, and judgment—they employ external status variables to determine the significance of a stay in a shelter. In addition, concentrating on one outcome, an increase or decrease in violence, fails to take account of a host of other potential benefits of the shelter and ignores other factors that may affect subsequent violent attacks. This limitation arises not because of the researchers' lack of awareness of other possibilities but because of a need to concentrate on variables that can be measured in a certain way. The consequence of such an approach may be a narrowing of the policy conception of the nature of the problem confronting women who attempt to leave their violent partners.

Quasi-experimental work, though equally sophisticated in its methods, presents additional problems. First, as in all research of this nature, there is great difficulty in controlling relevant variables. The arrest study by Sherman and Berk, for example, shows an elegant clarity of purpose but nonetheless suffers from several inherent problems of controlling relevant variables by conflating arrest and detention into the category called arrest.[23] The results showing that arrest appears to deter men from beating their partners do not point unequivocally to the significance of arrest. Even if arrest and detention are disentangled and one or both are shown to have a deterrent effect on violence, we are still left with the main question, Why does it work? The researchers readily admit that their research does not answer this question; yet it is crucial if we wish to develop policy and concrete actions based on the results.

We need to investigate how arrest makes a difference, to provide the inferential links. To do so, we need more qualitative information about men's reactions to arrest, perceptions of it, and motives for stopping their violence. Such information would allow us to make more informed judgments about the effects of arrest as a form of intervention and might help to avoid such unforeseen consequences as the use of arrest laws to discriminate against men of color. Such is the political nature of the research process that we should be reminded that the apparent enthusiasm for the implications of this research may have more to do with the demands of a law-and-order society and the recent history of successful class actions and lawsuits against the police than with the results of research. Clearly, the wider political and cultural context has had a significant effect on the acceptance of this research. If such results had been achieved in the early

1970s when crisis intervention was in vogue, they would have most probably been ignored.

Empiricism is another approach in the positivist tradition. The contemporary variant of empiricism is often called abstracted empiricism since its adherents generally seek to explain the social world by isolating phenomena and separating them from the context in which they occur.[24] Individuals and social issues are analyzed with little concern for locating them in the social world in which they exist. For the empiricist, improved measurement and statistical manipulation constitute the sole or major avenue to valid knowledge. Theoretical discourse beyond statistical generalizations is not permitted. Explanations, if proffered, are usually post hoc observations about specific results. Empiricist research is primarily a technical exercise, and improved technology is seen as the best route to explanation. Such assumptions have guided much research within the United States, especially by those who use the social survey.

We do not doubt the utility of social surveys based on probability samples of the population. They are powerful instruments for social investigation. Sociologists employ surveys as a means of investigating significant variables that are not amenable to experimental methods— that is, most social phenomena.[25] Using carefully stratified and clustered samples, researchers can control certain variables while manipulating those considered crucial in the production of the phenomena under investigation. If we think class is a significant variable in the generation of violence, we can use sampling or statistical manipulation to estimate the effects of class differences on violence in the chosen sample. If certain criteria are met, these findings may be extrapolated to the population from which the sample was drawn. This method, when used properly, is an important technique for gathering information about social issues. When used to study the problem of violence in the family, however, the methods associated with the sample survey have had unfortunate consequences for social science and for public perceptions of the problem and policy formulation.

A national survey using a well-constructed data collection instrument can help estimate the extent of family violence within a population, and the results might inform policy makers. Unfortunately, the national survey, rather than elucidating the extent of the problem of violence in the family, has contributed to considerable confusion and misrepresentation of the significant features of violence in the American family.[26] This has occurred because of a failure to recognize the limitations of the social survey, faulty conceptualization, and adherence to an empiricist method as the only route to valid knowledge. Criticisms of this national survey research and its major conclusions have been widespread and persistent and have included the inappropriateness of survey methods for studying a sensitive and unshareable problem such as severe violence, the use of abstract scales, the narrow focus on individuals rather than families, poor rates of response, generalizing from small, inadequate samples of violent individuals, exaggeration of small statistical differences, faulty theoretical generalizations, and ignoring or dismissing alternative counterfactual evidence.[27]

The most unfortunate, now widely publicized and criticized aspect of this empiricist research agenda is the "finding" that "1.8 million wives are physically abused by their husbands each year (3.8 percent) while nearly two million husbands are physically abused by their wives (4.6 percent)."[28] Researchers using this approach claim to have identified both a battered husband and a battered wife syndrome; they speak of near "equality between the sexes" in the use of violence and even of more battered husbands than battered wives.

These claims and the debate surrounding them seem ludicrous to a British or European audience. Public and government thinking in Britain never doubted this was a serious problem and defined it as serious violence against women in the home. Yet violence in the family may be manifestly different in the United States, or we may be mistaken about the nature of violence in the countries in which we live. It is possible, however, that the research may need to be scrutinized as a possible source of a differing reality. Many other researchers and most of those working in the community in the United States and Britain, in women's groups, social services, and criminal justice, come up with very different evidence and conclusions that support the position that violence between adults in families is predominantly violence against women.[29] The difference in findings and conclusions emerges from a rigid adherence to a particular method and, in the face of criticism, defensiveness and retrenchment.

It is no use pretending that we are innocent bystanders in all this. We stand with others as antagonists in the public and academic debates raging on this very significant issue. The fires of this debate have recently been inflamed by the publication of an especially disingenuous paper.[30] To unravel this research and its claims, we must traverse the methodological terrain that led to such conclusions. This critique includes criticisms from within the tradition of logical positivism as well as those derived from an alternative interpretive or contextual position.

The basic method employed in these surveys is the use of abstracted scales meant to measure the extent and presumably the nature of violent acts between family members. These measures are incorporated into a wider scale aimed at assessing conflict within the family, the conflict tactics scale.[31] Although we have reservations about scales, they can be useful; if carefully constructed, they can assist us in determining the nature of a problem or the psychological state of individuals.[32] Unfortunately, the construction, use, and interpretation of the conflict tactics scale have led to serious misrepresentation of the problem of violence in the home.

Positivists propose that research involve a careful theoretical explication of concepts from which one can deduce appropriate measuring devices. It is often assumed that this process of operationalizing concepts is a straightforward logical task. All of us who have tried it know that it is not and that it takes careful working and reworking to get a good approximate fit. "Approximate fit" is, of course, the appropriate phrase since this can never be an exact procedure. If we do not begin with carefully developed concepts, if we exclude important elements of the concepts in measurement procedures, or if we rely on statistical operations to give meaning to our concepts, we are in danger of producing work with a poor fit between ideas and research procedures.

We do not know how the concepts of conflict and violence were developed and operationalized in this survey research, but it is clear that a number of important features of violence were omitted. The direction of the violence, its impact, and, most important, its intention and motivation were omitted from the scale, despite the researchers' own statement that any definition of violence must include intentions. Thus we appear to have a poor fit between definition and measurement. The most profound problems occur, however, through the use of post hoc assumptions and statistical manipulations in the analysis of results.

Without studying intentions, initiation, motivations, the nature of injury, and the process of violent events, the researchers can only rely on post hoc judgments to give meaning to the observed results. To consider severity of violence, they speculate that certain violent acts should lead to various levels of serious injury. They assume, for example, that "hit" and "*attempt* to hit with something" (our emphasis) are acts that will have serious physical consequences and include these in a scale of severe violence acts. They assume that pushing and shoving will not result in injury. Those of us who are unfortunate enough to have experienced violence or who have studied it more closely know that such assumptions are not warranted. Being shoved over a stairway banister or into a sharp object such as the edge of a

table can have serious consequences, whereas attempting to hit someone with something results in an injury only if the attempt ends in a
landed blow causing an injury. In addition, hitting or trying to hit
with something could mean with a pillow, a flying cookie, or a
marshmallow. The point is, an outcome cannot be assumed; therefore
scale construction is not valid. One cannot, without additional evidence, assume that certain acts are more serious than others.

This error is amplified by using the results from the scale in an
additive, summary manner to produce "violence indexes" for individuals. Discrete acts of aggression or violent events occurring over an
extended period of time are combined to give an overall picture of
violence, potentially misrepresenting levels of violence in relationships.

These methodological problems are further compounded by using words such as "battered" and "beaten" to describe outcomes of the
behaviors measured on the conflict tactics scale. No one would quib-
ble with findings that women sometimes use violence, but a post hoc
assessment of these acts as resulting in battered or beaten husbands or
the existence of a battered husband syndrome is not warranted on the
basis of such research. Such claims demonstrate lack of care in concept formation, mostly arising from post hoc empiricism. A glance at
the Oxford English Dictionary or Webster's would have revealed the
inadequacy of this formulation; there the words "beat" and "batter"
refer to "heavy bruising blows," "strike violently," "blow after blow,"
"to punish by striking repeatedly and hard." From the results actually
obtained in this research, terms such as "battered" and "beaten" are
totally inappropriate.

Criticisms from another methodological tradition highlight additional inadequacies. Interpretive social scientists and some in the
positivist tradition have emphasized the significance of context in
understanding human behavior. Motives, intentions, the immediate
circumstances associated with an event, and the interactions preceding violence have all been seen as crucial for an understanding of this
phenomenon.[33] Those following an interpretive tradition would argue that it is either misleading or useless to explore complex human
behavior, such as violent events, through social surveys and abstract
scales. They would argue that to understand human behavior we
must employ more intensive methods. Without a consideration of
context we can say little about the initiation and direction of the
violence and its effects.

Another important aspect of interpreting results is a consideration of the wider academic and social contexts to which our results
pertain. If these results had initially been considered in the context of

existing evidence demonstrating that when women use violence they usually do so in self-defense, in a protective manner, or as a response after years of abuse, it would have been difficult if not impossible to find "battered husbands." Indeed, other conclusions might have been reached if the knowledge of the battered women's movement and of social, legal, and medical agencies had been considered. This knowledge and other equally valid research demonstrate that the significant social problem is persistent violence directed at women. Certainly, other violence sometimes occurs, but to treat all violence as if it is of national significance and to ignore the usual direction and consequences of violence is a grave misjudgment with serious consequences for public discourse and policy deliberations on violence in the family. One can only guess at the motives of researchers who rush into print and gain media attention with such misleading and potentially damaging results. If these researchers had relied less on the methods and logic of abstracted empiricism and engaged in dialogue with community groups and other researchers, they might have made more meaningful contributions to our understanding of violence in the family.

Recent responses to these criticisms have acknowledged many of the methodological inadequacies associated with the use of the conflict tactics scale and suggested the need for qualitative research and further improvements of the scale; yet this response shows a continued failure to consider context and simply offers more empiricist solutions.[34] The solution for assessing severity of violence, for example, is to use a weighting system of the conflict tactics scale scores based on the "height and weight of each spouse," an obvious empiricist strategy. Presumably the heavier the spouse, the more serious the slap or punch. In both its initial and its revised forms, this research tells us very little about the nature and consequences of violent events. To know who threw the first cookie and how much he or she weighed does not tell us much about the antecedents of violence and tells us nothing about how and why it happened. More research of this nature can only continue to lead to confusing and misleading results.

Context and Interpretation

Contextual interpretive methods are usually characterized as more intensive than positivist and empiricist approaches. Although some observers think subjectivist and quantitative methods are incompatible, we think they can often be complementary. In our own work we have used both quantitative and subjectivist methods to provide an empirical base for a comparative contextual interpretive analysis of the problem of violence against wives. To assess the extent of the problem of violence against women, we analyzed police and court records, conducted in-depth interviews with battered women, and analyzed historical evidence about the problem.[35] Over 34,000 police and court records—all the cases for a one-year period in two Scottish cities—were analyzed. These official data were used to describe police responses and to estimate the extent of reported violence and were compared and contrasted with interpretive findings. In this way quantitative work can provide us with structural and aggregate knowledge of a particular phenomenon while the intensive, contextual approaches can provide the understanding, explanation, and meaning missing from the skeletal knowledge derived from the positivist approach.

These approaches, however, are often attempting to answer different questions. Empiricists use quantitative methods to establish the distribution of a problem and, in a reductionist manner, to establish the individual characteristics of those involved. Some interpretive analysts also use quantitative results to estimate the extent of a problem, but they would never employ such methods to characterize individuals or to give meaning to their analysis. Interpretive approaches focus on processes, activities, relations, and episodes or events in the lives of individuals to provide explanations and understanding. Instead of describing the characteristics of the persons involved, interpretive approaches are employed to explain their experiences and perceptions. For example, rather than measure discrete facets of a violent act, the analyst would be concerned about describing the entire violent event, the processes leading to it, and the wider contexts in which it occurs.

Intensive and comprehensive studies of a given phenomenon will provide meaningful concepts, explanations, and understanding, but they are time consuming and cannot be done through sample surveys. This presents us with the often cited disadvantage of intensive methods: lack of representativeness. This problem is not easily overcome. Attempting to study events and processes makes it difficult, usually impossible, to specify a known universe before conducting research, a prerequisite of sampling. This means not that such research cannot be generalized but that such generalizations cannot be made on statistical grounds. The generalizability of intensive interpretive research is achieved through corroboration leading to a preponderance of supportive evidence. This is a bit like the process of triangulation. The difference is that instead of comparing the findings of a few very narrow statistically based studies to establish the authority of a finding, comparisons are made of much larger bases of knowledge. In our own research this meant using supporting evidence from sources as diverse as historical documents, contemporary records, in-depth interviews, and the findings from other research on violence against women.

In the remainder of this chapter, we illustrate this methodology by our own work on violence against women. For the purposes of this illustration we concentrate only on selected aspects of the research, particularly the violent event, the violent relationship, and the method of locating these within a wider social and institutional context.[36] A core feature of the methodology we employed is an analysis of the actual violence experienced by women in the family.[37] We were not merely concerned, as interpretive researchers are, to identify and understand the meanings women and men attach to these events. We were also interested in the concreteness of the violence: when it happens, how it happens, its essential features, how men and women respond to it, what circumstances precede violence, what consequences it has for the relationship, and how it changes over time. These are merely a few of the issues of concern, and not all of them were apparent when we began the research.

After a year of preliminary work, we concluded that the best means of investigating violence was to concentrate on violent events, violent relationships, and the wider responses to them. We assumed violent events would have a great significance for women, a salience that would maximize recall. Consequently, in the intensive and lengthy interviews we conducted with women who experienced violence, we asked them about the first, worst (as they defined it), and last episodes of violence they had experienced. We also asked them to describe a typical, or usual, violent event. In this way we studied violent events not through statistical manipulation but through the full accounts of the women. This provided a comprehensive picture of the men's violence, the women's responses, their feelings and emotional reactions, approaches to agencies, and responses from them. A lengthy interview schedule employed structured and semistructured questions and open and closed response categories. The approach enabled us to come to a fuller understanding of the immediate and wider contexts of the violence.

We also considered it crucial to understand the violence in the context of the history of the relationship. Through this method we sought to establish how the daily lives of men and especially women are altered as they become husbands and wives in our society and how this process relates to violence. What became apparent through interviews with battered women, police accounts of such cases, and historical evidence was that violence and women's reactions to it occur within the context of male demands and expectations. This was especially apparent when the violent relationship was examined over time. Women revealed that an increasing sense of expectation and domination accompanied marriage or the creation of a permanent relationship, and this figured strongly in the occurrence of violence.

Obtaining information about specific violent events is a significant aspect of interpretive work associated with variants of phenomenology, but this approach usually stops at an investigation of the immediate and fails to locate events and individual interpretations in a wider context.[38] Much like empiricists, subjectivist researchers do not go beyond the immediate interactional contexts of violence. We decided we needed to go further, to place the violence and the relationships in which it occurred in the context of institutional and historical evidence and analysis. This combination of information held the key to going beyond a description of the violence and the interpretations of individuals to work on a more holistic explanation.

In this way we moved beyond the interview into the realms of historical and institutional analysis.[39] Some of the questions we sought to answer were how to explain these observed patterns of violence, demands, and domination and what the sources of such patterns are. Answers to these questions were not apparent in the interview materials, and mere post hoc assessments seemed inadequate. This wider form of analysis enabled us to interpret the violence and violent relationships and to establish the links between the ideological and cultural supports of male domination and violence against women in the family.[40] It helped us, for instance, to understand the context of negotiation that immediately precedes the violence and to understand why women feel guilty and find it difficult to leave their partners. These patterns could not be understood without being grounded in women's historically structured subordination within the family, which requires them to engage in continual negotiations with their husbands. Guilt and an inability to leave must be located in the context of a moral order that makes the family the responsibility of women and an economic order that makes it extremely difficult for women to leave violent men and live on their own with children.

Such relationships and patterns cannot be demonstrated by focusing on the characteristics of individuals or by statistical manipulations. They must be developed within a wider explanatory net that includes quantitative, historical, institutional, and qualitative evidence. In this way, we can establish connections between observed patterns and explanations. This can only be achieved through an interpenetration of evidence and arguments, what Dreyfus and Rabinow have termed "interpretive analytics."[41]

Researchers and Community Groups. Throughout this research we were closely engaged with the battered women's movement. Often such work was mutually supportive, although occasionally we disagreed over concepts, interpretations, and political strategies. Community groups have significant and important information gained through years of experience of assisting battered women. This is valid knowledge that should be incorporated in academic research. This engagement and dialogue enriched our work, gave us insights and new ways of looking at issues, informed our formation of concepts, and forced us to consider how our results and explanations would enter into wider public and policy debates. We hope that these exchanges and the results and interpretations presented in our work aided those in the movement and the case of battered women.

Attempting to work with community groups in a nonhierarchical manner is not an easy task. It has taught us many things about research, community action, and the naiveté of most prescriptive proposals. A. Touraine has proposed that researchers play the role of supportive critic of community groups, investigating the operation of the group, clarifying goals, and keeping the group on course.[42] While we reject the more elitist aspects of Touraine's work, especially his view that researchers should provide theoretical interpretations and corrections of group activities, we endorse his position that researchers should relate to community groups as critical sympathizers. We must be sensitive to the concerns and demands of community groups, just as some of us are responsive to the demands of policy makers because they provide research funds. We should be more concerned about assessing the effects of institutional reforms and forms of intervention than about concentrating on causal analysis based on the assumption of individual differences. We support Barbara Hart's assertion that researchers should be more attuned to the investigation of the potential for social change associated with community action.[43] Such concerns are best investigated through the use of the contextual, interpretive, and holistic methodology outlined in this chapter.

Working with community groups does not mean researchers are captured by the ideals of community groups or rejecting state agencies. Researchers should advance their evidence and theoretical positions in diverse forums, and we have been involved in work with housing officials, social workers, the police, and members of the medical profession. We must also present our ideas and evidence in a form that is accessible to members of the battered women's movement and professional groups. The important point here is that academic posturing, obtuse descriptions of methods, and abstruse language do not enhance presentation, although they may impress colleagues. We need to write in a style that is intelligible to a wide audience, though never losing sophistication and rigor. In short, researchers need to be responsible for and about their evidence and present it with care in diverse forums.

It is crucial to ask whether improved methods and explanations based on a contextual approach will make a difference to policy making. We do not equate contextual, interpretive methodology solely with qualitative methods. They do, however, play a crucial role. This method and the wider methodology associated with it lead to more meaningful conceptualization, understanding, and informed policy analysis. The approach is not inferior to positivistic methods, nor is it a mere adjunct. It is an equally powerful scientific approach and in many respects superior to the alternative. Clearly, empiricism and positivism will continue to play a dominant role in research on family violence. We think that these approaches, though useful, are only partial. Positivistic researchers should be more temperate in their claims, recognize the limits of this kind of research, and be more receptive to evidence and interpretations derived from other methodologies. Such concerns may go unheeded in the context of the rampant empiricism associated with research and policy making in the United States. Policy makers, it seems, feel secure with numbers. They may not want interpretations and may see research as merely providing numbers that they can manipulate and interpret for the benefit of political masters or agendas associated with the agencies in which they work.

Methods and methodologies aside, the theoretical substance of explanations may be the major determinant of their incorporation in policy formulation. The explanations offered by feminist and critical approaches threaten preexisting perceptions and practices. Whether critical and feminist perspectives will be incorporated in policy work will probably have more to do with the politics of policy formulation than with the methods, methodologies, and evidence employed to support these positions. In the final reckoning politics may be all important.

14

The Effects of Research on Legal Policy in the Minneapolis Domestic Violence Experiment

Lawrence W. Sherman
and Ellen G. Cohn

When should research *not* be used to influence policy? Until recently few social scientists had the luxury of asking this question, since so much research was ignored by policy makers. But social science is having an increasingly demonstrable effect on legal policy.[1] And in several recent cases published social research reports have been attacked by other researchers as too flawed or limited to serve as a reliable guide to legal decision making.

The research by Robert Martinson and by Douglas Lipton and others on the ineffectiveness of rehabilitation, for example, was widely cited by policy-making opponents of rehabilitative programs yet attacked by correctional researchers for concluding too much from too little evidence.[2] The Peter Greenwood scale of predictive factors for selective incapacitation was apparently quite influential among criminal sentencing decision makers but was criticized by researchers as too often inaccurate.[3] The Kansas City preventive patrol experiment has been widely discussed in decisions about police staffing levels but criticized by researchers as too weak a test of the deterrent value of patrol.[4] All three studies received substantial press attention when they were released.

In all the criticism of these studies, however, we can find no suggestion that the studies should not have been publicized or that

Opinions expressed in this essay are solely those of the authors and do not reflect the official position of the National Institute of Justice. We wish to thank Charles Wellford for his support of this research, Edwin E. Hamilton for gathering the data for the first panel survey, Albert J. Reiss, Jr., for his comments about the Minneapolis experiment, and Joel Garner for providing valuable comments on an earlier draft, which was presented to the Australian Institute of Criminology's National Conference on Domestic Violence, Canberra, November 1985.

their conclusions were prematurely released to policy makers who would misuse them. Yet Richard Lempert has suggested just that about another highly publicized study, the Minneapolis domestic violence experiment.[5] The experiment, a randomized test of police actions for misdemeanor domestic assault, found that arresting produced a lower prevalence of repeat violence than two alternatives.

Lempert describes the Minneapolis study as "arguably the best field experiment on a criminal justice policy problem done to date."[6] But he also suggests that the results have been "prematurely and unduly publicized, and that police departments that have changed their arrest practices in response to this research may have adopted an innovation that does more harm than good."[7]

Lempert's principal argument against publicizing the Minneapolis experiment and other policy-relevant studies is that publicity should await replication. He suggests that legal research should follow medical practice, which he says "painstakingly tests new drugs for safety and effectiveness before putting them into general distribution."[8] Lempert's specific claim about the Minneapolis experiment is that "if an anti-cancer drug had been tested instead of an anti-crime drug, substantial additional testing would have been required before the drug were made available for general distribution."[9] He also suggests a need for more systematic study of how research is publicized and influences policy, a general issue made all the more important by the apparently growing influence of research on legal behavior.[10]

The first part of this chapter provides some systematic evidence on how the Minneapolis experiment was publicized and its apparent effects on urban police policy, drawing on interviews with the principal investigators and a three-wave panel survey of urban police departments. The second part examines Lempert's claims that the publicity and influence were premature, given the limitations of the Minneapolis research, the evidentiary basis for the police practices that preceded that experiment, and actual practices in medical research. The article concludes that research on legal effectiveness should be reported when it is completed; any regulation of its use should be directed to legal officials, not to researchers.

Publicity and Influence on Policy

Publicizing the Research. Lempert claims that the Minneapolis experiment was *unduly* publicized, which suggests that somewhat less publicity might have been acceptable. This claim implies that researchers—or anyone—can control the amount of coverage a story receives. That premise is largely falsified by the available social research on news organizations.[11] While it may be possible to prevent a story from becoming news—as President Richard Nixon tried to do with his "plumbers" to stop leaks—it is very hard for news makers to obtain less (or more) coverage for a story once it is released. A finite amount of newspaper space and broadcasting time is available, and the competition for it is intense. News makers are therefore largely at the mercy of editors.

The Minneapolis experiment was announced in Washington, a city in which over 500 members of Congress, all federal agency heads, and thousands of special-interest organizations compete for national and local news coverage. In this context it is quite difficult for any news of scientific developments to attract press attention. Federal agencies supporting research routinely put out press releases summarizing the results, but many of them are never reported. At best they may receive a few paragraphs buried deep in the main news section of the *New York Times* or wire service coverage that editors in cities around the country may or may not decide to include.

As Leon Sigal points out, the target audience for press maneuvers is not the general public but attentive decision-making elites.[12] The purpose of doing policy research is to influence those elites, which can be done much more easily if press coverage is successfully obtained. Press coverage also helps justify continued or increased funding for research programs, as the American Sociological Association suggests in its efforts to obtain more publicity for sociological research.[13] The Washington culture of social science policy research takes news seeking for granted and news getting as very good luck.

The interesting question about the extensive coverage the Minneapolis experiment received is therefore not, as Lempert suggests, why the researchers and the sponsoring organizations sought it out. The interesting question is why there was *so much* news coverage. Several factors may account for it, both intrinsic and extrinsic to the substance of the research.

Intrinsic factors. The substance of the research touched two eternal topics of human interest: sex and violence. But it also addressed the major changes in domestic power relationships produced over the preceding two decades by the feminist movement. The very idea of using police to redress the imbalance of physical power between men and women in love relationships was, in Herbert Gans's terms, a highly "suitable" story for editors.[14] The suitability extended to several editorial domains: national news, local police news, science news, and women's news. It satisfied a major suitability criterion of impact on large numbers of people.[15] And as Lempert suggests, the results were part of a larger story about the increasing punitiveness of American criminal justice.[16]

Extrinsic factors. The researchers, one of whom has described himself as a "publicity hound," also carefully orchestrated the release of the experimental results in an attempt to receive maximum press coverage.[17] Such attempts do not usually succeed, but the intrinsic factors made the decisions about how to manage the story more important. Those decisions included their persuading the Minneapolis area public television station to film a documentary on the research during the field phase of the experiment, which provided action film footage for several national television news shows covering the announcement of the experimental results many months later—by which time there would have been no experiment to film.

More important was their decision to release the story in two waves: the preliminary results in April 1983 and the final results in May 1984. This decision entailed the risk of violating the press's "repetition taboo," which can apply for twelve to twenty-four months.[18] But the preliminary results were released through an exclusive story in the *New York Times* Tuesday science section, not through a press release. The *Times* story, which the reporter agreed to write only if the research was legitimated by comments of three distinguished senior scholars who had read the preliminary report, was picked up by 107 newspapers nationally.[19] But it was not picked up by the Associated Press or United Press International wire services.

When additional data had been analyzed, the research had been published in the *American Sociological Review,* and a simplified version of the report had been mailed to some 3,000 policy makers, the project director decided to seek additional publicity through a Police Foundation press release. This decision was made in the context of an internal battle over the succession to the presidency of the foundation, in which the project director was one of the potential candidates. Rather than bowing to institutional pressures for excessive publicity, as Lempert suggests, the project director was refused permission to put out a Police Foundation press release.[20] He then recommended that the National Institute of Justice staff put out a press release. The manager of the research program funding the experiment (who was later picked to manage its replications) agreed, but he had to overcome opposition by superiors who thought the story was old news.

A third key decision was to release the final results on the Sunday of Memorial Day weekend. This timing increased the chances that the story would face less competition on a "slow news day," even slower than Sundays without a three-day weekend.[21] Over 300 newspapers carried the story, largely because the Associated Press and other wire services did run it this time. In the ensuing nine months the Police Foundation received over 2,500 requests for the report from around the country, many of them from citizens' groups, battered women's shelters, and the like, compared with only some 500 requests in the year after the release of the preliminary findings.

The researchers' goals for publicizing this research were not to convey the technical contents of the report but to get the attention of the key audiences of persons affecting police department policies. The researchers say they were not proarrest but rather proresearch, with a commitment to see research have an influence on policy. Their specific objectives were to have the key audiences at least recognize the message out of the masses of information with which they are inundated every day. They also wanted to have the audiences recall the information with accuracy and then use it in thinking about the relevant policy issues. At the most ambitious level they wanted the audiences to be influenced by the recommendations of the research. The data presented below provide some indication of the effects of that publicity strategy on the key audiences' recognition and accuracy of recall of the findings and the findings' influence on police policy.

The Effects of the Publicity. A national telephone survey of police departments serving cities of over 100,000 people was completed just before the second wave of the Minneapolis results was released. It would have been better, of course, to have completed the first wave of the survey of police practices before the preliminary report was released in 1983, but that was not done. The survey was repeated in June 1985 and in June 1986.

Methods. Both the 1984 and the 1985 telephone surveys used the same universe of cities as the sampling frame, with the minor exception that the 1984 survey identified 173 cities of 100,000 and the 1985 survey identified three more cities inadvertently omitted in 1984. The 1984 survey obtained 146 responses, for a response rate of 84 percent. The 1985 survey obtained 173 responses, for a response rate of 98 percent. The 1985 survey also obtained 143 responses from among the 146 cities that responded in 1984, for a 98 percent response rate in that panel. The 1986 survey reached all 176 cities.

The same interview schedule was used in all three surveys, with some additions in 1986. The schedule began with an introduction that made no mention of the Minneapolis experiment but did mention the

209

organizational affiliation of the interviewer. The first question was the department's current policy for dealing with minor domestic violence. Subsequent questions asked whether domestic violence arrests were increasing and tested respondents' recognition of the research and accuracy of recall of the principal findings. Other items explored the effects of the study on department policy and closed with the department's willingness to replicate the experiment.

In both surveys the interviewer was instructed to ask for the head of the planning and research department. But since not all cities of over 100,000 have a planning and research unit, the interviewers often had to accept responses from other spokespersons. Moreover, in some 52 percent of the cases, the 1985 respondents did not clearly identify the unit where they worked. Of those we could identify, 9 percent of the 1985 respondents were planning directors, 24 percent were members of the planning staff, 2 percent were members of the training division staff, 2 percent were operations division staff members, and 10 percent were staff members of the chief's office or other affiliated units. The 1986 responses were clearer: 22 percent planning directors, 24 percent planning division staff members, 19 percent staff members of the chief's office, 12 percent staff members of the operations (patrol) division, 12 percent staff of the criminal investigation (detective) division, and 11 percent other.

The 1985 and 1986 surveys attempted to reach the same respondents as the 1984 survey in those 146 agencies, but transfers and attrition often meant that other people responded. As a result, some inconsistencies appear. For example, in 1984 the Houston respondent said that the department's policy had been influenced by the Minneapolis experiment. In 1985 the Houston respondent said the opposite. This kind of discrepancy is symptomatic of the larger problem of attempting to determine the policies and practices of police departments through telephone survey methods. As many police chiefs can attest, it is no easy matter even for them to find out just what their officers are doing, let alone for a telephone interviewer who can only elicit the views of whomever the department assigns to answer the call.

The value of this method probably lies more in its reliability as an indicator of patterns of change than in its validity as a precise measure of police policy and practice. Even among cities claiming to have a policy of arresting suspects in minor spouse assault cases, for example, the policy may not be understood or widely followed in the field. The field research Kathy Ferraro reports in one department that adopted such a policy illustrates the inherent problems in communication from police headquarters to police officers on patrol.[22] This

telephone survey method is intended to measure not the actual behavior of police officers but rather the prevailing values and attitudes
of top executives about what field personnel ought to be doing.

Results. The findings of all three waves suggest a steady increase
in the influence of the Minneapolis experiment on police policy.
Recognition of the study and accuracy of recall were high in all three
waves, at least by the standards of general public knowledge of news
events. The influence of the study on policy making was small but not
negligible in the first wave and increasingly substantial in the second
and third waves. To produce reliable estimates of the change, only
panel results are displayed (see table 14–1).

Recognition. The recognition of the Minneapolis experiment was
relatively high from the preliminary findings alone. A year after the
initial press release, one-third of the respondents were sure they had

TABLE 14–1

RECOGNITION OF MINNEAPOLIS EXPERIMENT, DOMESTIC VIOLENCE
POLICIES, AND ARREST TRENDS IN 146 POLICE DEPARTMENTS, CITIES
OVER 100,000, 1984–1986

	1984		*1985a*		*1986*	
	Percent	Number	Percent	Number	Percent	Number
Recognition						
Yes	32	47	69	98	67	98
Maybe	9	13	1	1	2	3
No	59	86	31	44	31	45
Current policies						
Arrest	10	15	31	45	46	67
Mediation	38	56	17	24	16	24
Sending suspect						
away	3	5	6	8	3	5
Officer's						
discretion	48	70	46	66	34	50
Domestic arrest						
trends						
More	24	35	35	50	47	69
Same	28	41	25	36	25	37
Less	10	14	6	8	2	3
Don't know	38	56	34	49	25	37

a. N = 143.
SOURCE: Author.

TABLE 14–2

ACCURACY OF RECALL, INFLUENCE OF RESEARCH, AND WILLINGNESS TO
REPLICATE AMONG PANEL POLICE RESPONDENTS RECOGNIZING
MINNEAPOLIS EXPERIMENT, 1984–1986

	1984[a]		1985[b]		1986[b]	
	Percent	Number	Percent	Number	Percent	Number
Accuracy						
Arrest	43	26	73	72	80	79
Mediation	7	4	4	4	4	4
Separation	3	2	5	5	5	5
Don't know	47	28	18	18	11	11
Research influenced policy						
Yes	7	4	31	31	44	44
No	88	53	61	60	47	47
Don't know	5	3	8	8	8	8
Willingness to replicate[c]						
Yes	15	22	28	28	n.a.	n.a.
No	12	17	25	25	n.a.	n.a.
Maybe	47	69	44	44	n.a.	n.a.
Don't know	26	38	2	2	n.a.	n.a.

n.a. = not available.
a. N = 60.
b. N = 99.
c. 1984, N = 146.
SOURCE: Author.

heard of the experiment. The second round of publicity apparently helped double the recognition of the report. A year after the final report was publicized, two-thirds of the respondents were sure they had heard of it, just as they were two years later.

Accuracy. As table 14–2 shows, not all those claiming to have heard of the experiment were bluffing. In 1984 almost half of those respondents correctly identified the results of the experiment; most of the others admitted that they could not recall. The second round of publicity improved the accuracy of their memories by over 50 percent, with 73 percent of those claiming to have heard of it correctly recalling which police treatment the experiment found most effective in cases of minor domestic violence. By 1986 accuracy had risen to 80 percent.

Influence. Among those who said they had heard of the experiment, a majority of respondents in the first two waves of the panel said that the experiment had not influenced policy in their departments. But by the third wave that was no longer the case, and 44 percent of the respondents who knew about the experiment said it had influenced their policy. This constituted 30 percent of the full panel sample.

The "influence" of the research was not always a change to an arrest policy. Only twenty-four of the thirty-six departments in the full 1985 sample of 173 that reported some influence also reported a policy of encouraging arrest. The changes they referred to included "a greater emphasis on arrest when mediation fails," rather than the previous policy of viewing arrest as a last resort. Others referred to new training, and a few said the experiment got the department to pay greater attention to the problem of domestic violence.

Policies. The best test of influence may be to look at the policies themselves. The leading policy for minor domestic violence, as reported in the first two surveys, was no policy: complete officer's discretion, with arrest in third place. But by the third wave arrest was the leading policy. Arrest policies increased 360 percent between the first and third waves of the survey, rising from 10 percent of panel respondents to 46 percent (table 14–1). The explanation for this rapid increase cannot lie entirely with the Minneapolis experiment, since several other relevant events occurred within the same period: the recommendations concerning arrest made by the Attorney General's Task Force on Family Violence, the showing of the television movie "The Burning Bed," and a general growth in the anti-family-violence movement.[23] But researchers say police told them the experiment was often cited by local lobbying groups meeting with police officials to request that more arrests be made.

Lawsuits. Another reason that arrest policies may have increased is the fear of lawsuits for failure to make arrests. A 1985 verdict for $2.6 million (later settled for $1.9 million) against a Connecticut police department (*Thurman* v. *Torrington*) was widely publicized and may have prompted some departments to change their policies. Surprisingly, the 1986 survey showed more problems with litigation for making arrests than for failing to make them. Of all 176 departments, only 5 percent reported being sued for failure to make arrests; 15 percent had been sued for false arrests for domestic violence.

Arrest trends. Whatever their policies may be, the majority of respondents in all three waves reported that the actual number of arrests for domestic violence had either increased or stayed about the same over the preceding year. The percentage reporting increased arrests over the prior year rose from one-fourth in 1984 to one-third in 1985 and to almost half in 1986 (table 14–1).

Willingness to replicate. Given Lempert's argument that replication should precede publicity, it is interesting to note the effect of publicity on the feasibility of replication. The willingness to replicate almost doubled from 1984 to 1985 among those respondents who claimed to have heard of the study, from 15 percent to 28 percent (table 14–2).

It seems, then, that more publicity (or the passage of time, or both) helps to make replication possible. Without any publicity it might not have been possible to replicate the experiment in more than one or two cities. But when the National Institute of Justice solicited proposals for replication in early 1986, nineteen police departments participated in or filed their own replication proposals (six replications were funded). It is not surprising that publicity should have this effect for this kind of research design; when a research procedure is potentially controversial, publicity about its use in another city documents a precedent that provides a measure of protection for decision makers bold enough to replicate.

Summary. This case study of the effect of the Minneapolis experiment is quite limited. It has completely omitted the question of the experiment's influence on several state laws imposing mandatory arrest on local police (thereby making replication impossible in those states, contrary to the recommendation of Lawrence Sherman and Richard Berk), local mandatory arrest laws, and other laws increasing police powers to arrest.[24] It has also omitted any close analysis of how much change the policies produce or the failures of implementation after police departments adopt arrest policies.[25] Most important, the longitudinal design of the case study cannot control for the influence of factors other than the Minneapolis research on police policy. Just as law and social science have developed a broad literature on the effects of U.S. Supreme Court decisions on police behavior, further research can address the empirical issues in the effects of research on police practice.

Nonetheless, this case study supports Lempert's basic premise. The publicity about the Minneapolis experiment reached a large number of police departments and apparently had a substantial influence on police policy. Thus it is important to ask whether the publicity and influence were premature.

Was the Publicity Premature?

Lempert's claim that the publicity was premature until the experiment had been replicated raises major issues about the relationship of research to policy.[76] Addressing those issues requires this case study to answer three questions about the Minneapolis experiment:

• How severe were the threats to the internal and external validity of the experiment as published in 1984?
• How does the quality of scientific evidence in the Minneapolis experiment compare with the evidence supporting police practices before the publicity over the experiment?
• What is the practice in medical research with respect to the approval of drugs or treatments, which Lempert argues should be the standard for social research on legal processes?

Answering these questions provides a context for discussing when research should be publicized and when policy makers should be influenced by it.

The Limitations of the Minneapolis Experiment. The Minneapolis misdemeanor (simple) assault experiment found that the measured percentage of offenders who repeated an act of domestic violence against their victims over a six-month follow-up period after a police intervention was half as great for offenders randomly assigned to arrest (and those arrested when other alternatives failed) as for offenders randomly assigned to nonarrest alternatives.[27] The experiment also found that offenders randomly assigned to arrest were significantly less likely to reoffend than others not randomly assigned to arrest—including some who were actually arrested in preapproved exceptions to the randomization protocol.[28] That is, both the designed and the delivered treatment distributions showed that arrest worked best. The measurement of recidivism included both official records of 100 percent of the sample and at least one interview (and up to twelve interviews) with 65 percent of the victims. Analytic techniques included linear and logistic regression and proportional hazard rate time-to-failure models.

As in any field experiment involving human beings, a number of factors could not be controlled. A review of the internal and external validity issues is appropriate so that the reader can evaluate the policy implications the researchers drew from the findings and the policy effects they attempted to achieve.

Internal Validity. *Randomization.* Despite substantial evidence that the officers in the Minneapolis experiment did not compromise the randomization in any serious way, it is at least possible that they decided to exclude certain nonarrest cases from the study after arriving at the scene.[29] (Any unrandomized arrests were detected by independent monitoring by Police Foundation researchers.) Since the agreement with the Minneapolis police did not allow the experimental officers to receive all domestic calls, it was very difficult for observers to ride with those officers and witness the rare case in which violence had occurred and the offender was still present.[30]

Differential reporting by victims. One rival hypothesis for the lower rate of repeat violence among those arrested is that they "intimidated" their victims into neither calling the police in cases of future violence nor telling the Police Foundation interviewers about it in their biweekly interviews. Sherman and Berk concluded that the intimidation hypothesis was unlikely, for two reasons.[31] First, in 55 percent of all cases in the experiment, someone other than the victim called the police. It is possible that the offender managed to intimidate all the others who might call the police as well, but that seems unlikely. Second, the victims' response rates to the interviewers did not vary according to the police action against the offenders. This seems to make *differential* intimidation unlikely, since it is more plausible that an intimidated woman would not show up for an interview than that she would show up and lie. That is, intimidators would probably try to discourage the contact entirely rather than to shape its contents. Nonetheless, we cannot rule intimidation out entirely as a rival hypothesis.

Sample size. The sample size and base rate of repeat violence were both large enough to detect main effects of the alternative treatments. Neither the sample size nor the distributions of subpopulations were adequate, however, for thorough testing for interaction effects. Arrest may work best in general, but we do not know whether it works best, for example, for black males with two years of college education earning $20,000 to $25,000 per year who have been married ten years or more. It is entirely possible that arrest may backfire for some kinds of offenders, increasing their propensity to violence against the same or other potential victims. Advances in personal computers would make it easy for police to process this kind of detailed information in determining what action to take. But large sample sizes are needed to produce reliable predictions on which such software would be based.

Analysis. The Sherman and Berk analysis was limited to two basic methods: analysis of the prevalence (or percentage) of offenders who had at least one repeat incident and analysis of the time to "failure"— the length of time between police intervention and the first repeat incident.[32] This analysis omits two other policy-relevant questions: What was the difference among treatments in the frequency of offending, or the average number of repeat offenses per offender over the follow-up period?[33] What was the difference in the seriousness of repeat offending, measured by injury and hospitalization? If the total number of incidents or the average seriousness was lower for any of the nonarrest treatments than for the arrest group, that would have complicated the policy implications seriously. But the Sherman and Berk analysis did not address those issues.[34]

Follow-up period. Although there is no evidence that a longer follow-up period would alter the results, it is possible that the longer-term results are different. Anne Witte and her colleagues, in a re-analysis of the data, have found that most of the deterrent effect disappears by the end of the six-month follow-up period.[35] If the trend continues, arrest could actually increase overall violence beyond six months.

Displacement. As Albert Reiss has pointed out, it is possible that arrest of an offender merely displaces the offender's violence onto another victim, so that no net reduction in domestic violence is achieved.[36] Alternatively, victims may enter into new relationships where they become abused. Although the Minneapolis data showed no difference among treatment groups in the *rate* at which relationships broke up, the timing was not clear; moreover, the response rate was too low to rule out the Reiss hypothesis. Testing it would require tracking both victims and offenders separately, not just their relationship, with both official records and interviews.

External Validity. More troubling than the possible threats to internal validity were the clearly established threats to external validity. These were also the principal concerns of Lempert and others who ask whether policy decisions in other cities should be made on the basis of the Minneapolis results.[37]

Jail time. As Sherman and Berk point out, Minneapolis may be unusual in jailing suspects arrested for domestic assault for at least one night.[38] Thus the treatment tested in Minneapolis was arrest plus immediate but brief jail time, rather than arrest and immediate release. The effects of arrest in cities practicing immediate release might be very different, including the offender's possible return to the

217

victim while he is still in a drunken rage, whereupon he might inflict even more serious damage.[39]

Mediation quality. It has been argued that Minneapolis was not a fair test of the effects of mediation, since the participating police officers did not have special training in family crisis intervention.[40] All of them had the standard patrol officer's training in those skills, which was very little. The skills of a highly trained special police unit devoting most of its time to domestic violence might be much more effective, however, perhaps producing better results than arrest. The Minneapolis findings may not generalize well to cities where such units are in operation, but they should generalize to the larger number of cities without such units.

Interaction of interviews and arrest. All the arrests, as well as the other treatments, were accompanied by an intensive effort of Police Foundation interviewers to get in touch with the victims. These efforts included up to twenty phone calls and visits and lasted up to six months. They cannot account for any differences among treatments, since they were apparently equal for all the treatments, as were the response rates.[41] But they do raise questions about how effective arrest would be in the absence of this form of "surveillance," which may have had some deterrent effect on the offenders. As Sherman and Berk concede, it is an open question whether the same effects would be found without the interviews.[42]

Absence of theory. As Lempert suggests and Berk and Phyllis Newton emphasize, the theoretical basis for the observed deterrent effects of arrest is poorly understood.[43] In the language of Thomas Cook and Donald Campbell, Sherman and Berk report only on the "molar" relationships but not their "micro-mediation": the links in the causal chain between police action and the likelihood of further violence.[44] Documenting such links would probably require interviews with offenders, guided by some model of causation to focus the questions.

City context. The setting, of course, is a major external validity issue. Minneapolis is not America, nor is any city truly "comparable" to any other. Variations in weather, ethnic composition, age structure, prevailing crime rates, and general sanctioning levels might all affect the responses of offenders to alternative police actions for domestic violence.[45] Minneapolis is an extreme case on many of these dimensions. For at least six months a year its weather prevents men ordered out of the house from spending the night out of doors. It has one of the smallest minority populations of any major city, the largest Native American population, and probably the largest proportion of white Protestants. Both its homicide rate and its imprisonment rate are among the lowest in the country. Whether arrest would work as well in Miami, San Diego, or Pittsburgh is an open question. But the only way to answer that question is to replicate the experiment in as many cities as possible, cities that represent different points on these many contextual dimensions—just as Lempert recommends.

Alternative procedures. The Minneapolis conclusion that arrest works "best" clearly has no external validity in comparisons with other procedures not included in the research design. Different findings might result, for example, from extending the design to include offenders who had already left the scene (by randomly picking some to be tracked down). Or victim "empowerment" officers could be randomly assigned within each treatment, with officers paying either great attention or little attention to the victims. Or the aftermath of the intervention could be randomly assigned, with police follow-up visits to some offenders and not others or some arrested offenders diverted to mandatory counseling but not others. All these complexities are possible and commonplace in many cities and could fruitfully be examined in future replications. Moreover, the external validity of the arrest-works-best conclusion is limited to the two comparison treatments only.

Summary. The list of possible threats to the internal and external validity of the "arrest works best" finding is clearly quite extensive. But that can probably be said for any single piece of research. As Lempert points out, it is not the conduct of the experiment that is at issue but rather the fact that it was a single experiment. In comparison with most other policy studies and even with other randomized experiments, the Minneapolis experiment actually suffered quite minor threats to validity.[46] The question Lempert raises is really, *How much evidence is enough to change policy or practice?*

Perhaps it is best to answer that question neither in relation to the validity of research in general nor in relation to the potential strength of evidence derived from multiple replications. Either of those methods creates a bias in favor of the status quo for its own sake. A better test is to compare the evidentiary strength of any recommendations derived from new research with the strength of the evidence in support of the status quo. In the case of police policy on domestic violence, that test is not difficult.

The Existing Knowledge Base for Practice. At the time the Minneapolis experiment's findings were published, the existing knowledge base for police practice was virtually nonexistent. Most police officers were guided by their experience in handling such cases, which gave them an intuitive judgment about what works best. But this kind of experience suffers from highly selective feedback. Unlike craftsmen who can see the results of their finished products, big city police may never see the "product" of their work—defined as the subsequent rates of crime after the police officer's intervention. If there is a recurrence while the officer is on the same shift and the same beat, feedback may occur. But otherwise it is possible in many cities for police officers responding to a domestic call to remain unaware that the problem culminated in a murder the next day. Such lack of feedback is probably more common for less extreme outcomes.

This point is important because of the hyperscientistic tendency to criticize any and all experiential learning as a basis for policy decisions.[47] We do not dismiss all experience as a knowledge base for police decision making. But given the flawed and erratic system of feedback to officers on their handling of minor domestic violence, that particular kind of experiential learning must be discounted as a reliable knowledge base for making policy decisions.

The published research literature, in 1983, was even less help as a guide to practice. For all the ink expended in describing, explaining, or criticizing police practices in minor domestic violence, only one study that we could find claimed to provide any systematic empirical evidence evaluating the effectiveness of any of the policy alternatives in reducing subsequent domestic violence.[48] And that study was arguably interpreted incorrectly.[49]

The study exposed eighteen specially selected volunteer police officers to 160 hours of training at the City College of New York and to weekly consultation with graduate students in clinical psychology over a two-year period. The officers were assigned to a Harlem precinct where they worked as "generalist-specialists," handling routine police calls when available but receiving all the precinct's calls for domestic disputes. They were encouraged to negotiate the dispute at the scene in some depth, taking as much time as they needed. They were also encouraged to refer disputants to social service agencies. The evaluation report on the project by Morton Bard claimed its success at, among other things, reducing the occurrence of family assaults, family homicides, and assaults on police officers.[50]

Donald Liebman and Jeffery Schwartz's examination of the New York City study's findings, however, found that many of Bard's conclusions were unsubstantiated by the data and some conclusions were actually contradicted.[51] The demonstration precinct had a significantly higher percentage of repeat disturbance calls than the comparison precinct. It also had more homicides and more family homicides than the comparison precinct. The demonstration precinct suffered an increase in homicide while the comparison precinct enjoyed a decline. The same was true of assaults and family assaults. The finding that injuries to officers were reduced was based on no injuries to officers in the experimental precinct and one injury in the comparison precinct.

Even without these problems, the N-2, after-only comparison design suffered enormous threats to internal and external validity.[52] Nonetheless, the program was acclaimed as a success and widely imitated under the Law Enforcement Assistance Administration sponsorship of family crisis training.

When the Minneapolis experiment was undertaken, then, the existing level of knowledge about the consequences of alternative police actions was not only low but misunderstood. There were not even any prospective nonrandomized follow-ups of offenders or households treated with different methods. Virtually no one had reported any data on what happened after police left, regardless of the method police employed.[53] The research literature had focused on the police themselves as the object of explanation and prediction, rather than on the problem of violence.

Consequently, there was no reliable basis for choosing any policy, let alone an established basis for practice that should not be changed on the basis of "merely" a one-site randomized field test. Compared with the existing state of knowledge, the Minneapolis experiment, with all its limitations, constituted a substantial advance over what had been known before. Had similar evidence become available about a medical treatment, it would not have been subjected to further testing before approval, as Lempert suggests.[54] Rather, any doctor who failed to use a treatment proved effective with this level of evidence could have been sued for malpractice.

The Medical Model of Research and Practice. Lempert's comparison of arrest policies for domestic violence with a new cancer drug breaks down on several points.[55] One is that, contrary to his assertion, there is no requirement or standard practice of replicating randomized clinical trials. A second point is that arrest was not a new "drug" in the sense of no prior general use; police had been making some arrests for domestic violence for centuries, since legislatures "approved" such treatments in passing laws against assault. A third point is that the theoretical rigor in medicine is often no higher than it is in the sociology of law. Fourth, Lempert's premise that delayed implementation of research is more cautious may apply to construction projects but not to life and death human problems that cannot be delayed pending further research.

Replications in medicine. The relationship of research to medical practice is different and far more regulated for new drugs than it is for other kinds of treatments. But the regulation is a relatively recent development. Before World War II drugs could be marketed freely without testing.[56] Even after the war, tests were largely limited to toxicity levels. In the wake of the thalidomide and DES disasters, the Food and Drug Administration (FDA) raised the level of evidence required to prove the safety and effectiveness of new drugs, but it was not until 1969 that the FDA required evidence from randomized clinical trials before granting marketing approval for new drugs.[57]

The Bureau of Drugs Clinical Guidelines established four phases of human drug testing, following positive results among animals.[58] Phase I uses healthy volunteers to measure the toxicity, or unhealthy side effects, of the drug. Phase II trials test the drug's effectiveness on a small number of patients, who are monitored very closely. Phase III is a randomized controlled trial on a large number of patients. If this *single* trial is successful, the drug can be approved. Phase IV is postmarketing surveillance, including long-term, large-scale follow-up of morbidity and mortality (such as the heart attack rate associated with the birth control pill).

In theory, additional trials could be conducted after approval is obtained, but this seems to be rare. On the contrary, many doctors would find it unethical to withhold a treatment already found effective in one randomized controlled trial. As a medical journalist points out, "In principle, randomized trials are performed only when there is no clear evidence as to which therapy is best."[59] It is not at all clear, despite the limitations of the Minneapolis experiment discussed below, that physicians would find it ethical even to proceed with replications, let alone to withhold treatment until the replications are completed. In the early stages of the Minneapolis replications, several of them were opposed by victim's rights groups for precisely that reason.

The standard medical research goal seems to be one large randomized trial that is intended to "settle" a question, or at least a narrowly defined segment of it. Problems may develop that may limit the trial's conclusiveness, but the ideal is *not* to have to replicate. Consider, for example, the trial of the vaccine for hepatitis B, described as the "finest clinical trial in the history of medicine."[60] The fifteen-year time span between the discovery of an agent and the licensing of the vaccine was reportedly the shortest ever. The controlled trial was preceded by tests on chimpanzees and on 200 human volunteers from the Merck Company (which developed and manufactured the vaccine), none of whom developed any adverse effects. The investigators recruited 1,083 high-risk volunteers from the gay community in Greenwich Village, 96 percent of whom returned for the second injection (of either vaccine or a placebo drug) and 85 percent of whom stayed in touch with the study over the follow-up period. On the basis of its finding that the vaccine was 81 percent effective in preventing infection, the FDA apparently licensed the vaccine for general use.

More recently the controversy over the clinical trial of the experimental drug AZT for treating acquired immune deficiency syndrome (AIDS) demonstrates the enormous pressure on medicine to rush treatments into practice without ideally thorough testing. Doctors treating AIDS patients lobbied the Congress to force the National Institutes of Health (NIH) to abandon the 282-patient randomized controlled trial before it was completed, since an uncontrolled phase II study of fifteen patients had found some life-prolonging effects. They argued that the FDA should approve the drug for more general use on the basis of the initial research. The *Wall Street Journal* even attacked the alliance of regulators and researchers for playing God in withholding the treatment from general use. Both the controversy and the experiment were cut short when nineteen placebo patients and one AZT patient had died by the twenty-fourth week of the study. The FDA released the drug for general use, and it is clear there will never be a replication of the trial.[61]

Nor will there be a replication of the aborted 1985 clinical trial of the heart attack victim's life-saving drug tissue plasminogen activator (TPA), which the National Heart, Blood, and Lung Institute of NIH stopped for ethical reasons. "Investigators felt that TPA was so superior to an alternative drug, streptokinase, that they could not ethically withhold TPA from patients in the trial who were not receiving it."[62] This conclusion was reached despite an initial finding that the drug caused severe brain damage in 2 percent of the cases, a problem that led the FDA to withhold approval of the drug until late 1987, when further phase II studies showed the brain damage rate to be 0.4 percent.

Theoretical rigor in medicine. Lempert might approve of such adopting of medical treatments with limited controlled experimentation because the theoretical basis for predicting the effectiveness of a treatment is presumably stronger than comparable theoretical developments in social science. As Lempert puts it, "We should remember that the key to generalizing in science is theory. . . . If we simply assume that what has occurred in one setting will occur in another, our generalizations will rest on shaky ground whenever the settings differ in important particulars. Making policy on the basis of a single study is always dangerous in part because one study is almost never sufficient to develop a reliable theory."[63]

Precisely the same point is debated in medical research. Dr. Emil Freirich, a professor of medicine who claims that randomized controlled trials are widely overused in medical research, argues that the biological heterogeneity of human populations is "enormous," so that it may well be inappropriate to generalize to populations beyond those selected for any medical study.[64] Despite social scientists' assumptions that human bodies are less variable in their biochemistry than cities are in their criminology, one could easily argue that a vaccine that "works" on a gay population in New York might not work in other settings where diet, water content, sanitation, the epidemiology of the disease, and other factors are different. Yet the hepatitis B vaccine was approved for national use after a single trial on that "unique" population.

Testing new versus existing treatments. Moreover, randomized controlled trials are hardly used to test all new or existing treatments in medicine.[65] The total annual cost of treatments not so tested that may be ineffective has been estimated by the editor of the *New England Journal of Medicine*, Arnold Relman, at $10 to $15 billion.[66] The impact on the patients may be incalculable. Some doctors believe that randomized trials should be the standard of care for both surgical and other treatments, but many treatments grow "like Topsy" and are only later (if ever) subjected to tests to settle debates—much like criminal justice treatments and sanctions.

A good case in point is the medical response to breast cancer detected early, when the tumor is still confined to the breast—encompassing some 60 percent of all breast cancer patients. In the early 1960s, when many such patients refused to suffer the disfigurement of a full mastectomy, Harvard physicians developed the now famous lumpectomy, cutting out the tumor but leaving the breast intact, and following the surgery with radiation. Follow-up of 357 women treated from 1968 to 1978 showed only eighteen cases of recurrence. This evidence (and even less evidence at earlier stages) was sufficient for many physicians to recommend that their patients undergo lumpectomies, while other physicians remained adamantly opposed to anything less than radical mastectomy. Ultimately, randomized controlled trial found no difference in five-year survival and recurrence rates for such patients.[67]

The lumpectomy/mastectomy trial also illustrates the division in medicine over the "when to publicize" issue that Lempert raises. The results were originally submitted for publication almost a year before they finally appeared in the *New England Journal of Medicine*. Although the reason for the delay was not made public, it was widely speculated that on peer reviewer recommendations the journal decided to ask for more time to elapse in the follow-up period to increase the statistical power of the data analysis. The delay upset many physicians who wanted the formal guidance of published results to help them to decide what course of treatment to recommend. The delay was all the more upsetting because of widespread rumors that oral presentations of the findings at medical conferences had reported no difference in treatment outcomes. Their concern illustrates the complexity of the timing issue Lempert raises.

Delaying the announcement of test results until the evidence is stronger is not necessarily a more cautious approach. The physicians who had to act on over 100,000 breast cancer patients during the year's delay in publication may, as it turns out, have unnecessarily disfigured many of those patients. If they had prematurely recommended lumpectomies, however, and later evidence had shown higher rates of breast cancer recurrence, they would have increased the risk of death. These problems of type I and type II error have no obvious solution but require the kind of judgment that will always be debatable.

The costs of delay. The important point is that there are costs and controversies entailed in publication delay, as well as in potentially premature publicity. Medical practices, like crime control practices, deal with continuing human problems. Decisions about such problems cannot be postponed like a decision to build a dam or a highway, for example, until a careful study of environmental impact and other issues has been completed. The cost of delay for such construction projects is usually just the delay of a new benefit, rather than the positive imposition of harm or ineffectiveness at saving lives. In attacking the FDA's two-year delay in approving the heart attack drug TPA, for example, the *Wall Street Journal* accused the FDA of having "sacrificed thousands of American lives on the altar of pedantry."[68]

Moreover, in both medical and crime control practice, policies can be changed much more quickly than a dam or highway can be torn down. Medical research publication practices assume that practitioners will continue to follow new research, that science is constantly evolving, and that practice should continue to change with new knowledge. The question in medicine is never "What is the final and ultimate truth?" but rather, "What is the best available knowledge at this time?"

Consensus from conflicting results. Medical research is often plagued with conflicting evidence from research, just like social science. One solution medicine has adopted may be applicable to social science as well. Since 1977 the NIH have sponsored a Consensus Development Program.[69] The program convenes a distinguished group of experts without conflicts of interest to review the evidence on controversial questions of medical practice and produce recommendations for doctors. Over sixty topics have been considered, including breast cancer screening, caesarean childbirth, and liver transplantation. At least four other countries have adopted similar programs.

Perhaps legal practices could benefit from similar consensus development panels, especially where legislatures have allowed officials to exercise discretion. But even considering such an approach opens the broader questions of regulation of legal research and practice that Lempert raises.

Conclusion: Research and Regulation

This article has considered whether the Minneapolis domestic violence experiment was "unduly and prematurely publicized," how much influence on policy the experiment had, and whether that influence was inappropriate. The evidence suggests that the researchers tried quite hard to publicize it and that their efforts produced some effects on policy. The evidence also suggests that the policy influence was not premature or inappropriate, at least not by medical standards. Legal researchers seem fully justified in releasing and publicizing research results as soon as they have been favorably reviewed.

Legal practice and medical practice can both benefit from research on two kinds of questions: new technologies never used before (such as the Greenwood scale or electronic monitors for house arrest) and technologies long in use but never tested before (such as preventive patrol or arrests for domestic violence). Such practices can be more or less effective, and research on them can be more or less reliable. The question Lempert raises is where, if anywhere, the process of decisions to change policies should be regulated.

By criticizing the publicity about and the influence of the Minneapolis experiment, Lempert may imply that *researchers* either should be regulated or should regulate themselves to prevent policy from being changed on insufficient research grounds. This clearly has no basis in the medical model, since there is no restraint (other than normal peer review) on either publication or publicity for medical research. Rather, strict application of the medical model would imply some regulation of practitioners, based on some standard of research.

Civil litigation, especially against police, has increasingly employed research to regulate legal practice, just as it regulates medical malpractice. But there is no FDA for new or existing legal practices. Nor is there an NIH consensus program. Perhaps such structural changes are warranted. But they seem most likely to happen, as they did in medicine, after sufficient development and funding for the research enterprise make the need for them obvious.

In late 1987 the Minneapolis domestic violence experiment was being replicated in six cities under funds from the National Institute of Justice. This is one of the largest programs of replication ever launched in legal research. Neither the federal funds for the experiments nor the willingness of those police departments to randomize arrest would have been as likely to occur if there had not been so much publicity about the original experiment.[70]

For those who would use research to improve legal effectiveness—which is hardly a universal goal among social scientists of law—this case study of the Minneapolis experiment has a broader lesson.[71] Rather than changing practice prematurely, publicity about new research can speed up the process by which practice can be more reliably tested. Since no study is final, publicity about each new study can focus attention and funding on further research. If further studies reach different conclusions, publicity about them can influence policies to change yet again. If legal policies are to be based on science, they must be able to change along with the constant evolution of scientific knowledge. Anything that can speed up that evolution, including publicity, should probably not be discouraged.

15

The View from the
National Institute of Justice

James K. Stewart

I want to start with a story. Coming back from the Gulf of Iran is a captain on board a battleship. He has a number of distinguished battle ribbons, and he is feeling pretty good: he is a graduate of Annapolis, and he has this tremendous ship with 7,000 people on board. As he is approaching the United States, he sees a series of lights on the horizon. It is dark, and they are trying to maintain radio silence.

The person on the bridge says, "There is a ship approaching us on a collision course." The captain says, "Tell them to move off. But don't break radio silence, just blink to them." So they send a message with a series of lights that says, "We are on a collision course with you; move two degrees to the south." A light flashes back, "We acknowledge, but this is a dangerous tack that you are on. Move two degrees to the north." He says, "Signal back, and tell them who I am." So they signal, "This is Captain Jones, graduate of Annapolis, leader of the U.S. Navy; we command you to move two degrees to the south." A blink back a minute later says, "We acknowledge; this is Chief Petty Officer Smith, and I am from the U.S. Coast Guard; please move two degrees north." He flashes back, "We are a battleship. Move two degrees to the south." That will settle the argument. The light blinks back, "We acknowledge that you are a battleship; we are a lighthouse, and we suggest you move two degrees to the north."

I feel a little like the chief petty officer, when I am helping with the research area and try to communicate some ideas to the mighty captains of policy who are going to make decisions. The captain feels much better when he has the information that he should move off. Sometimes policy makers feel the same way, because in the political arena there is always a debate, and what we ought to do is to inform it with some empirical evidence.

We may get to the point where we can categorically say that this is truth, but we need to be able to perform quality research, research that is of use, informs the public, and leads the field as opposed to research that is either superficial or too specific.

That is one of the things I tried to do when I moved to the National Institute of Justice. I have a national plan on this, and I am trying to give very large credibility to the kind of work that you are doing.

There is a wealth of knowledge that will provide policy makers not with the answer but with a range of options. We have to come up with serious, responsible options, because the choices are going to be made, and we ought to have a chance to inform those choices.

The area of domestic violence is very tough to handle, on the one hand, and very trivial on the other. Why is it trivial? Why do people have such a difficult time dealing with it?

First, it is an issue that involves sovereignty. Essentially, a family is like a nation of two or three or four. Subliminally, other people in government feel that way about it. What right do we have to invade this sovereign nation?

The second thing is that the criminal justice system does not do well with crimes between persons that have an established relationship. We do well with crimes by strangers. But here is somebody that has a continuing relationship. What is the proper intervention to make?

If we can get people to look at it differently, not as a trivial matter between people that have a continuing relationship but as something different and more important, then we change the debate. That is what we have to do. And that debate has been changed.

All of you have dedicated yourselves to this. We are not in a position to say it is a good thing to do because you are talking about the children or because you are talking about the wives. People do not understand it in those terms. But judges do care about the murder rate in the United States. We try to explain to them that most murder occurs among friends, lovers, and business associates. If we are going to make a difference in the murder rate in America, we ought to do something about spouse abuse, because we can make a difference by a different kind of treatment. Then we move a long way toward changing the debate, moving away from the idea that it is a trivial pursuit or a negotiation between people involved in a sovereignty. When we bring up murder, it sounds more important than if we bring up personal relations; so we have to recast it.

We have to be careful that we cast it in such a way that the state does not make an unjustified intrusion. The family is the substantive unit of virtually all our societies, and we do a poor job with families. There is so much stress on them already that we may not survive as a civilization.

We can change ideas very effectively. The Crime Control Institute has found that over two-thirds of the nation's largest police departments have changed their policy regarding arrest as the preferred action in spouse abuse. That will give you an idea of the power behind properly managed research that gets out in the area.

It is a waste of money to come out with contradictory or inconsistent results. When I go up to get the budget, they say, "You guys can't ever find out anything. We are going to cut your budget to save some money."

Why do we put the money into this? Because we finally have a policy that we can say works, and we ought to try to see how generalizable it is, what we can learn about its limits, and what we can learn about its potential. That is vitally important. Besides that, we are looking for a range of options, what works under different circumstances in controlling future violence—not eliminating future violence but controlling and influencing. That is a powerful argument, and that is why we are doing it.

If we do studies in four or five locations, we often get a design drift. So we have created a panel of experts that has the power to terminate experiments. They are going to make site visits, watch how projects develop, and have regular consultations with each project. I think this will eliminate the sort of inconsistencies that occur. It will give you, as researchers, a better chance to get consistent data and to influence policy much better.

The other responsibilities that we are involved in that are related are drug abuse and crime, the sentencing effects on crime, and criminal careers. We have created the Drug Use Forecasting Program. We have used expert judgments to determine what kinds of drugs are being used and how drug use relates to crime. In the DUF program we get urine specimens from volunteers who have been arrested to get a snapshot of what kinds of drugs they seem to be using.

This gives us new information about how to tailor a treatment program, an education program, an enforcement program. It gives us knowledge that we never had before, much better than the self-reports and survey information, and it may help us in spouse abuse. One thing that we found was that drug use among those arrested is uniformly and surprisingly high; it exceeded all the expert judgments of police researchers and medical people. The drug used varies dramatically from region to region, so that we need different kinds of treatment programs, because we have different kinds of markets. That is an important breakthrough, and this is a rich data source for researchers in the future.

We have limited resources, and we have to use those strategically as best we can. That is one of the reasons that I insist on quality research, better information systems, better data bases, and better access to things like the DUF program.

When I came on, President Reagan wanted us to watch and see how we could better manage this. One of the things, and it was the most expensive part of doing research, was collecting data and only a few people could get into it, because that was all the money we had. We could only fund a few programs, and we found that the data collected were kept by the researchers so that they could write articles, and nobody did any secondary analysis. We tried to change that. We have been able to get data tapes cleaned up, so that you and other researchers can do secondary analysis on existing data sets. We can get lots of looks at the same kind of data, which I think will give us an ability to do research in the criminal justice and social science fields that we did not have before. We have set aside $10,000 stipends to reanalyze the data tapes.

There is not enough money around to do research. We are severely constrained. The National Institute of Dental Research gets $144 million a year to do dental research, and very few people have died because of bad teeth. Yet we spend $18 million a year on criminal justice research. How do we try to make the kind of investment that makes a difference?

We pay about $38 per person in America to do medical research. We have licked smallpox and polio, and people with leukemia are living longer. We have to think the same way about crime—we may not eliminate crime, but we may be able to ameliorate it and work marginally on it, and that is what our strategy ought to be.

We are spending eight cents per capita on criminal justice research. You may be getting what you pay for from medical science, but you are not getting what you pay for from your investment in criminal justice research. We now have more people getting killed than ever before, we have much more violence on our streets than ever before, and your chance of being a victim of a violent crime over your lifetime is about 90 percent, where it was only about 10 percent two generations ago. The sense of crime is on all of our minds, destroys our economy, changes our life style, ruins our education.

I am not encouraging you to say that the government ought to weigh in as the exclusive people here. We ought to form partnerships. We ought to pool our resources, for it is one of the most important investments we could possibly make in the future of our civilization.

I have changed the way the National Institute of Justice operates. First, we no longer are institutionally oriented. We used to give the police $3 million a year, the courts $1 million, and corrections $2 million to do research. That was the way we politically cut up the pie.

If you give the courts money, they spend it on figuring out how to manage their calendar better. If you give the police money, they figure better ways to assign their police cars and to study for promotional examinations. They are looking at special problems, and that is what we ought to be looking at when we do criminal justice research. I have created a problem-oriented series of programs that overarches our system. I have divided research into two areas. One is crime prevention and public safety, and the other is apprehension and prosecution. Those are two separate kinds of tasks.

We are looking at career criminals, how the courts deal with career criminals, how corrections deal with them, how the police deal with them. If you want to try to solve that problem, how does the institution that you are going to study contribute to the solution? That is what we must do—rethink how we approach crime in our justice institutions in the United States. That is what I am trying to do.

I have moved very hard to bring researchers and practitioners together. Every time I have a meeting I have practitioners and researchers. Every time I have researchers together I invite a couple of practitioners as well, so they can get an idea that this is a bigger community. For the researchers we have had the tremendous benefit of increasing the market for the utility of what they are doing. For the practitioners the incentive is that we give them more options and inform their judgments and help them when they are doing litigation.

The research field has matured dramatically. We have a much better field in the past eight years than we had before.

The Burden Foundation is helping us with violence prevention education, the Department of Health and Human Services is supporting our spouse abuse replications with $150,000, and the Office of Juvenile Justice Delinquency Prevention is giving us $200,000 to fight crime in the schools. The National Institute of Justice is the broadest and the most creative justice research agency in America, and it is headed by a presidential appointee. That is very important. We have been able to establish and maintain independence, and we have also been able to bring prestige to the kind of work that you do, because a presidential appointee has access to a number of policy meetings.

We are going to do a longitudinal study, over at least five years, in six cities, in partnership with the MacArthur Foundation. We will put in $1.4 million a year, MacArthur will put in $1.4 million a year, and we hope that other foundations will come in for $1 million a year, for this five-year period. Very important information will be gained from a longitudinal survey of not just pathological but also healthy people—what are the kinds of things that encourage violence, criminal careers, narcotics? Domestic violence ought to be one of the things we look at. This will give us a very rich data base, and we may be able to answer some questions with much more confidence.

This is not going to be done by a single institution. I have insisted that it be broad-based. It is much too important to be done by just one person or just one institution. It is long-term, it is costly, but it will help us get better information about what is going on.

I have insisted, as a professional and as a scientist, that we maintain peer review. I have used researchers and practitioners together on peer review committees; there are always at least two researchers and one practitioner. The practitioner says whether it is important and the researchers say whether methodologically it can work. People in Washington think that they could make all the decisions themselves. That is bad for research, and that is why I have insisted that we make it broader. That is why I have insisted that researchers make the judgments.

My idea is to try to open it up and make progress, but I am trying to shoot toward bigger things, the bigger things that really influence policy. It is the bigger things that make a difference in having fewer violent activities, fewer people in drug clinics, less crime on our streets.

That is exactly what the president has wanted. He wanted us to reach out and to make sure that the whole country is involved. The wealth of our country is our brain power, our ability to think. That is what we ought to be investing in.

The Department of Justice's budget has gone from $2.5 billion when I was Attorney General William French Smith's special assistant to $7 billion. The National Institute of Justice's budget went from $25 million when I took over down to $16 million and now has moved up to $18 million. Originally, much of the quality of the research that was going on was inferior and did essentially a disservice. That is why I went to peer review, and that is why I held up most of the grants. I said it must be better.

When we give money, it has to be for policy-relevant research. We still do basic research, but the most important thing is that research be policy-relevant. Think about what policies we ought to form to reduce the amount of domestic violence and what the state ought to do.

You ought to inform policy, rather than inform a debate among scholars. A debate among scholars is important, but we are all in this boat together, and our country works so well because we all have some input into it.

233

Afterword

The Harry Frank Guggenheim Foundation sponsors a program of research and study designed to advance the understanding of social problems related to dominance, aggression, and violence. Grants are made for projects, in any discipline, that promise to further the foundation's intellectual and practical objectives. We have complemented the grant-making program with spotlighting areas that would benefit from close attention and encouragement, building interdisciplinary understanding through conferences and workshops, introducing academic researchers to those responsible for public policy decisions, and underwriting publications, such as this one, aimed at bringing relevant findings to a wider audience.

Douglas Besharov and I met at an American Enterprise Institute seminar on welfare and the family, where conclusions derived from social science were subjected to rigorous examination in the light of policy successes and failures, and academics were held accountable for the results of their advice in relation to the economics of poverty and social support (reported in AEI's *The New Consensus on Family and Welfare*). We agreed on the timeliness of examining the assumptions and attitudes that influence the design and interpretation of research in family violence and encouraging a critique of the methods and skills that characterize research in the field and its use in policy making. We agreed to hold a conference for foundation grantees and others doing excellent research into family conflict and dysfunction. The conference would explore new ideas about research and analyze the methodological weaknesses of earlier research. This volume is the result of that conference.

Since 1972, when the foundation began to make research grants, we have supported much first-class research on violence in the family. During that time, the field has moved from the margins of research interest and has become an important academic focus. We have found it necessary, however, to reject a high percentage of proposed projects, because compared with studies of aggression from other disciplines, many seemed weak in theory and methodology. It is disturbing to a grant maker when funds are not sufficient to support all worthy comers, but it is equally perturbing when a particular area of study does not produce a sufficient number of deserving proposals for the available funds.

Some of the methodological problems in this field are shared with other research in social science—problems in collecting reliable long-term data and refining quantitative measures—compounded by the sensitivity of and sanctions against its subject matter. Other problems—such as the dilemma of singling out a control group among people in need of intervention and the tension between the requirements of scientific validity and the pressure for responsible action—are special to this young discipline. Problems of recruitment and personality; questions of denial and reliability in respondents; ethical issues involved in such research, such as long-term commitment to treatment and follow-up in the study group; the relationship of economic, educational, and welfare issues to family violence problems and policy; and the legal and ethical positions of social workers—these concerns were discussed at the March 1987 conference.

Researchers in family violence are a disparate group—some highly activist, others primarily concerned with survey and enumeration, and many in between. Increasingly, many are turning their attention toward the kind of self-examination suggested here. We hope that this publication encourages discussion of such areas as the influence on research design by expectations from the clinical and policy arenas; the relationship of the scientific researcher to victims and their advocates, and to perpetrators and the criminal justice system; the impact of research results on efforts to ameliorate the social problem (clinically on the level of the individual and more widely in terms of public policy); and the effect of all these considerations on the definition of family violence and the imperative to understand and interpret it.

The foundation's perspective, from its research program in which aggression is defined and approached from many directions, suggested that if family violence researchers would learn about research on aggression in other disciplines and focus some attention on the study of family interaction rather than on correlates of violent acts, they would broaden the intellectual base of their research and protect it from ideological imperatives. The field seems ready to progress beyond description and correlation toward generation and testing of hypotheses on the model of traditional social science, with an interest in ethnographic description and a self-sense of identity previously lacking.

An effort to consolidate disciplinary approaches would be particularly important, especially in the investigation of child abuse (typically from a perspective of social work and public policy) and of spouse abuse (from the more academic field of social psychology, with influence from feminist political perspectives). It would be important also to add the strengths of other, classic disciplines (statistical rigor, anthropological techniques for fieldwork, brain and endocrine physiology, and history's view of change and continuity in abuse and treatment) and technological advances (videotape as a research tool and biofeedback and stress management techniques) to the repertoire of the researcher interested in family violence.

By no means are these academic concerns meant to imply an ivory-tower preoccupation with methodology divorced from the urgency and subjectivity faced by those studying family violence. This volume addresses crucial questions which also concern the Harry Frank Guggenheim Foundation: What changes in research strategy are needed for a contribution toward solving the problems of domestic violence and conflict? What do policy makers need to know to act responsibly and effectively? The American Enterprise Institute's efforts to bring the insights of scientists to the attention of those responsible for social policies are building necessary bridges from academia to government. It is the foundation's concern that the information carried over those bridges be the best possible advice based on the most competent, independent, and creative investigation.

This book contains papers prepared for an American Enterprise Institute conference on family violence research held March 20 to 23, 1987. Augmenting these papers are brief statements from the key federal officials responsible for supporting research in family violence.

KAREN COLVARD
Program Officer
Harry Frank Guggenheim Foundation

Notes

Chapter 1: Qualitative Research on Spouse Abuse

1. I. S. Lincoln and E. G. Guba, *Naturalistic Inquiry* (Beverly Hills, Calif.: Sage, 1985).

2. A. Browne, "Assault and Homicide at Home: When Battered Women Kill," in L. Saxe and M. J. Saks, eds., *Advances in Applied Social Psychology* (Hillsdale, N. J.: Lawrence Erlbaum, 1986), vol. 3; B. E. Carlson, "Battered Women and Their Assailants," *Social Work*, vol. 2 (November 1977), pp. 455–60; L. V. Davis, "Battered Women: The Transformation of a Social Problem," *Social Work* (July–August 1987), pp. 306–11; K. J. Ferraro, "Rationalizing Violence. How Battered Women Stay," *Victimology*, vol. 8, nos. 3–4 (1983), pp. 203–12; J. Finn, "Men's Domestic Violence Treatment: The Court Referral Component," *Journal of Interpersonal Violence*, vol. 2, no. 2 (1987), pp. 154–65; D. A. Ford, "Wife Battery and Criminal Justice: A Study of Victim Decision-making," *Family Relations*, vol. 32 (October 1983), pp. 463–75; R. J. Gelles, "Abused Wives: Why Do They Stay?" *Journal of Marriage and the Family*, vol. 39 (November 1976), pp. 659–68; E. W. Gondolf, "Fighting for Control: A Clinical Assessment of Men Who Batter," *Social Casework*, vol. 66, no. 1 (1985), pp. 48–54; E. W. Gondolf and J. Hanneken, "The Gender Warrior: Reformed Batterers on Abuse, Treatment, and Change," *Journal of Family Violence*, vol. 2, no. 2 (1987), pp. 177–91; S. K. Hanks and P. Rosenbaum, "Battered Women: A Study of Women Who Live with Violent Alcohol-abusing Men," *American Journal of Orthopsychiatry*, vol. 47, no. 2 (1977), pp. 291–306; K. E. Koslof, "The Battered Women: A Developmental Perspective," *Smith College Studies in Social Work*, vol. 54, no. 3 (1984), pp. 181–203; T. Mills, "The Assault on the Self: Stages in Coping with Battering Husbands," *Qualitative Sociology*, vol. 8, no. 2 (1985), pp. 103–23; D. K. Snyder and L. A. Fruchtman, "Differential Patterns of Wife Abuse: A Data-based Typology, *Journal of Consulting and Clinical Psychology*, vol. 49, no. 6 (1981), pp. 878–85; M. J. Strube and L. S. Barbour, "The Decision to Leave an Abusive Relationship: Economic Dependence and Psychological Commitment, *Journal of Marriage and the Family*, vol. 46 (November 1983), pp. 785–93.

3. G. T. Hotaling and D. B. Sugarman, "An Analysis of Risk Markers in Husband to Wife Violence: The Current State of Knowledge," *Violence and Victims*, vol. 1, no. 2 (1986), pp. 101–24

4. A. Rosenbaum, and K. D. O'Leary, "Marital Violence: Characteristics of Abusive Couples," *Journal of Consulting and Clinical Psychology*, vol. 49, no. 1

(1981), pp. 63–71; T. A. Schwandt, "Some Consequences of the Value-free Claim for the Conduct of Inquiry," unpublished qualifying paper, inquiry methodology, School of Education, Indiana University, 1980.

5. G. B. Spanier and E. E. Filsinger, "The Diadic Adjustment Scale," in E. E. Filsinger, ed., *Marriage and Family Assessment* (Beverly Hills, Calif.: Sage, 1983).

6. H. Scwartz and J. Jacobs, *Qualitative Sociology: A Method to the Madness* (New York: Free Press, 1979).

7. G. Lakoff and M. Johnson, *Metaphors We Live By* (Chicago: University of Chicago Press, 1980), p. 4.

8. M. B. Scott and S. Lyman "Accounts," *American Sociological Review*, vol. 33, no. 1 (1968), pp. 46–62.

9. Ferraro, "Rationalizing Violence: How Battered Women Stay"; Ferraro and Johnson, "How Women Experience Battering: The Process of Victimization."

10. T. Mills, "The Assault on the Self: Stages in Coping with Battering Husbands," *Qualitative Sociology*, vol. 8, no. 2 (1985), pp. 103–23.

11. Zvi Eisikovits and J. L. Edleson, "Violence in the Family: A Study of Men Who Batter," a request of H. F. Guggenheim Foundation for a second year of research support (in preparation).

E. Webb, D. T. Campbell, R. D. Schwartz, and L. Sechrest, *Unobtrusive Measures in the Social Sciences* (Boston: Houghton Mifflin, 1966).

13. Lincoln and Guba, *Naturalistic Inquiry*.

14. N. K. Denzin, *On Understanding Emotion* (San Francisco: Jossey Bass, 1984); R. E. Dobash and R. P. Dobash, *Violence against Wives* (New York: Free Press, 1981); M. Elbow, "Theoretical Considerations of Violent Marriage," *Social Casework*, vol. 58, no. 16 (1977), pp. 515–26.

15. Denzin, *On Understanding Emotion*.

16. Lincoln and Guba, *Naturalistic Inquiry*.

17. U. Bronfenbrenner, "Toward an Experimental Ecology of Human Development," *American Psychologist*, vol. 32 (July 1977), pp. 513–31. N. K. Denzin, *The Research Act*, 2d ed. (New York: McGraw-Hill, 1978).

18. Eisikovits and Edleson, "Violence in the Family: A Study of Men Who Batter."

19. Lincoln and Guba, *Naturalistic Inquiry*.

20. M. Bograd, "Family Systems Approaches to Wife Battering: A Feminist Critique," *American Journal of Orthopsychiatry*, vol. 54, no. 4 (1984), pp. 558–68; L. Wardell, D. I. Gillespie, and A. Leffler, "Science and Violence against Wives," in D. Finkelhor et al., eds., *The Dark Side of Families: Current Family Violence Research*. (Beverley Hills, Calif.: Sage, 1983).

21. D. R. Loseke and S. E. Cahill, "The Social Construction of Deviance: Experts on Battered Women," *Social Problems*, vol. 31, no. 3 (1984), pp. 269–310.

22. Zvi Eisikovits and J. L. Edleson, "Treating the Violent Man: A Critical Review of the Evidence."

23. Lincoln and Guba, *Naturalistic Inquiry*.

CHAPTER 2: METHODOLOGICAL ISSUES AND NEW DIRECTIONS FOR RESEARCH ON VIOLENCE IN RELATIONSHIPS

1. Richard J. Gelles, "Violence in the Family: A Review of Research in the Seventies," *Journal of Marriage and the Family*, vol. 42 (1980), pp. 873–85.

2. Lenore E. Walker, *The Battered Woman Syndrome* (New York: Springer Publishing Company, 1984).

3. Lettie L. Lockhart, "A Reexamination of the Effects of Race and Social Class on the Incidence of Marital Violence: A Search for Reliable Differences," *Journal of Marriage and the Family*, vol. 49 (1987), pp. 603–10.

4. Suzanne K. Steinmetz, "Occupation and Physical Punishment: A Response to Straus," *Journal of Marriage and the Family*, vol. 33 (1971), pp. 664–66; Suzanne K. Steinmetz, *The Cycle of Violence: Assertive, Aggressive, and Abusive Family Interactions* (New York: Praeger Publishing Company, 1977). Murray A. Straus, "Some Social Antecedents of Physical Punishment: A Linkage Theory Interpretation," *Journal of Marriage and the Family*, vol. 33 (1971), pp. 658–63; Murray A. Straus, "Leveling, Civility, and Violence in the Family," *Journal of Marriage and the Family*, vol. 36 (1974), pp. 13–30.

5. Murray A. Straus, "Measuring Intrafamily Conflict and Violence: The Conflict Tactics (CT) Scales," *Journal of Marriage and the Family*, vol. 41, (1979), pp. 75–86.

6. Diane R. Follingstad, Ann Neckerman, and Julia Vormbrock, "Reactions to Victimization and Coping Strategies of Battered Women: The Ties That Bind," *Clinical Psychology Review*, vol. 8 (1988), pp. 373–90; Irene H. Frieze, "Power and Influence in Violent and Nonviolent Marriages" (Paper presented at the meeting of the Eastern Psychological Association, Philadelphia, Pa., April 1979); Alan Rosenbaum and K. Daniel O'Leary, "Marital Violence: Characteristics of Abusive Couples," *Journal of Consulting and Clinical Psychology*, vol. 49 (1981), pp. 63–71.

7. Straus, "Measuring Intrafamily Conflict and Violence: The Conflict Tactics (CT) Scales."

8. Eugene J. Webb, Donald T. Campbell, Richard D. Schwartz, Lee Sechrest, and John B. Grove, *Nonreactive Measures in the Social Sciences* (Boston: Houghton Mifflin, 1981).

9. Dennis A. Bagarozzi and C. Winter Giddings, "Conjugal Violence: A Critical Review of Current Research and Clinical Practices," *American Journal of Family Therapy*, vol. 11 (1983), pp. 3–14.

10. Richard A. Berk and Phyllis J. Newton, "Does Arrest Really Deter Wife Battery? An Effort to Replicate the Findings of the Minneapolis Spouse Abuse Experiment," *American Sociological Review*, vol. 50 (1985), pp. 253–62; Lawrence W. Sherman and Richard A. Berk, "The Specific Deterrent Effects of Arrest for Domestic Assault," *American Sociological Review*, vol. 49 (1984), pp. 261–72.

11. Douglas K. Snyder and Lisa A. Fruchtman, "Differential Patterns of Wife Abuse: A Data-based Typology," *Journal of Consulting and Clinical Psychology*, vol. 49 (1981), pp. 878–85.

CHAPTER 3: IMPLICATIONS OF BIASES IN SAMPLING TECHNIQUES FOR CHILD ABUSE RESEARCH AND POLICY

1. T. J. Reidy, "The Aggressive Characteristics of Abused and Neglected Children," *Journal of Clinical Psychology*, vol. 33 (1977), pp. 1140–45.

2. D. M. Bousha and C. T. Twentyman, "Mother-Child Interactional Style in Abuse, Neglect, and Control Groups: Naturalistic Observations in the Home," *Journal of Abnormal Psychology*, vol. 93 (1984), pp. 106–14.

3. M. Straus, R. Gelles, and S. K. Steinmetz, *Behind Closed Doors: Violence in the American Family* (Garden City, New York: Anchor Press, 1980).

4. C. M. Mouzakitis, "An Inquiry into the Problem of Child Abuse and Juvenile Delinquency," in R. J. Hunner and Y. E. Walker, eds., *Exploring the Relationship between Child Abuse and Delinquency* (Montclair, N.J.: Allanheld, Osmun, 1981), pp. 220–32.

5. L. Young, *Wednesday's Children: A Study of Child Neglect and Abuse* (New York: McGraw-Hill, 1964).

6. K. Burgdorf, *Recognition and Reporting of Child Maltreatment* (Rockville, Md.: Westat, 1980); D. Gil, *Violence against Children: Physical Child Abuse in the United States* (Cambridge, Mass.: Harvard University Press, 1973); R. J. Light, "Abused and Neglected Children in America: A Study of Alternative Policies," *Harvard Educational Review*, vol. 43 (1974), pp. 556–98; S. Zalba, "Battered Children," *Transaction*, vol. 8 (1971), pp. 58–61.

7. Straus, Gelles, and Steinmetz, *Behind Closed Doors: Violence in the American Family*.

8. Burgdorf, *Recognition and Reporting of Child Maltreatment*; Gil, *Violence against Children: Physical Child Abuse in the United States*.

9. Straus, Gelles and Steinmetz, *Behind Closed Doors: Violence in the American Family*.

10. G. J. McCall, and N. M. Shields, "Social and Structural Factors in Family Violence," in M. Lystad, ed., *Violence in the Home: Interdisciplinary Perspectives* (New York: Brunner/Mazel, 1986), pp. 98–123.

11. R. Stark and J. McEvoy, "Middle Class Violence," *Psychology Today*.

12. D. Gil, *Violence against Children: Physical Child Abuse in the United States*.

13. C. A. Rohrbeck, and C. T. Twentyman, "Multimodal Assessment of Impulsiveness in Abusing, Neglecting, and Nonmaltreating Mothers and Their Preschool Children," *Journal of Consulting and Clinical Psychology*, vol. 54, (1986), pp. 231–36; C. S. Widom, "Does Violence Beget Violence? A Critical Examination of the Literature," Manuscript under review, 1987.

14. *Boston Sunday Globe*, June 14, 1987.

15. C. S. Widom, "Family Violence and Infanticide" (Paper presented at conference on postpartum depression and criminal responsibility, Pennsylvania State University, State College, Pennsylvania, May 28–30, 1987).

16. C. Adams-Tucker, "Proximate Effects of Sexual Abuse in Childhood: A Report on 28 Children," *American Journal of Psychiatry*, vol. 139, (1982), pp. 1252–56.

17. M. A. Perry, L. D. Doran, and E. A. Wells, "Developmental and

Behavioral Characteristics of the Physically Abused Child," *Journal of Clinical Child Psychology,* vol. 12 (1983), pp. 320–24.

18. D. A. Wolfe, and M. D. Mosk, "Behavioral Comparisons of Children from Abusive and Distressed Families," *Journal of Consulting and Clinical Psychology,* vol. 51 (1983), pp. 702–8.

19. W. H. Friedrich and A. J. Einbender, "The Abused Child: A Psychological Review," *Journal of Clinical Child Psychology,* vol. 12 (1983), pp. 244–256.

20. H. P. Martin and P. Beezley, "Behavioral Observations of Abused Children," *Developmental Medicine and Child Neurology,* vol. 19 (1977), pp. 373–87.

21. C. W. Morse, O. J. Sahler, and S. B. Friedman, "A 3-Year Follow-up Study of Abused and Neglected Children," *American Journal of Diseases of Children,* vol. 120 (1970), pp. 439–46.

22. American Humane Association, *Highlights of the 1979 National Data* (Englewood, Colorado: 1981); Gil, *Violence against Children: Physical Child Abuse in the United States.*

23. According to the Census Bureau, in 1986 nearly a quarter of all American children live with just one parent, in contrast to the situation in 1960 when only one child in ten was living in a single-parent household.

24. Morse, Sahler, and Friedman, "A 3-Year Follow-up Study of Abused and Neglected Children.

25. R. M. Barahal, J. Waterman, and H. P. Martin, "The Social Cognitive Development of Abused Children," *Journal of Consulting and Clinical Psychology,* vol. 49 (1981), pp. 508–16.

26. Ibid.

27. L. P. Groeneveld and J. M. Giovannoni, "Disposition of Child Abuse and Neglect Cases," *Social Work Research and Abstracts,* vol. 13 (1977), pp. 24–30.

28. Straus, Gelles, and Steinmetz, *Behind Closed Doors: Violence in the American Family.*

29. American Humane Association, *Highlights of the 1979 National Data.*

30. Friedrich and Einbender, "The Abused Child: A Psychological Review."

31. Gil, *Violence against Children: Physical Child Abuse in the United States.*

32. Ibid.

33. E. H. Newberger et al., "Pediatric Social Illness: Toward an Etiological Classification," *Pediatrics,* vol. 50 (1977), pp. 178–85.

34. Straus, Gelles, and Giovannoni, *Behind Closed Doors: Violence in the American Family.*

35. Gil, *Violence against Children: Physical Child Abuse in the United States;* L. H. Pelton, "Child Abuse and Neglect: The Myth of Classlessness," *American Journal of Orthopsychiatry,* vol. 48 (1978), pp. 608–17.

36. R. J. Gelles, "Violence in the Family: A Review of Research in the Seventies," *Journal of Marriage and the Family,* (November 1980), pp. 873–885.

37. Groeneveld and Giovannoni, "Disposition of Child Abuse and Neglect Cases."

38. H. R. Blount and T. A. Chandler "Relationship between Childhood Abuse and Assaultive Behavior in Adolescent Male Psychiatric Patients," *Psychological Reports*, vol. 44 (1979), p. 1126; D. O. Lewis and S. S. Shanok, "Medical Histories of Delinquent and Nondelinquent Children," *American Journal of Psychiatry*, vol. 134 (1977), pp. 1020–25.

39. R. E. Tarter, A. M. Hegedus, N. E. Winsten, and A. I. Alterman, "Neuropsychological, Personality, and Familial Characteristics of Physically Abused Delinquents," *Journal of the American Academy of Child Psychiatry*, vol. 23 (1984), pp. 668–74.

40. E. Hartstone and K. V. Hansen, "The Violent Juvenile Offender: An Empirical Portrait," in R. A. Mathias, ed., *Violent Juvenile Offenders: An Anthology* (San Francisco: National Council on Crime and Delinquency), pp. 83–112; P. C. Kratcoski, "Youth Violence Directed toward Significant Others," *Journal of Adolescence*, vol. 8 (1985), pp. 145–57; S. C. Wick, "Child Abuse as Causation of Juvenile Delinquency in Central Texas," in R. J. Hunner, and Y. E. Walker, eds., *Exploring the Relationship between Child Abuse and Delinquency* (Montclair, NJ.: Allanheld, Osmun, 1981), pp. 233–39.

41. Kratcoski, "Youth Violence Directed toward Significant Others."

42. C. George and M. Main, "Social Interactions of Young Abused Children: Approach, Avoidance, and Aggression," *Child Development*, vol. 50 (1979), pp. 306–318.

43. Perry, Doran, and Wells, "Developmental and Behavioral Characteristics of the Physically Abused Child"; Wolfe and Mosk, "Behavioral Comparisons of Children from Abusive and Distressed Families."

44. G. A. Wasserman, A. Green, and R. Allen, "Going beyond Abuse: Maladoptive Patterns of Interaction in Abusive Mother-Infant Pairs," *Journal of the American Academy of Child Psychiatry*, vol. 22, no.3 (1983), pp. 245–52.

45. J. A. Aragona and S. M. Eyberg, "Neglected Children: Mothers' Report of Child Behavior Problems and Observed Verbal Behavior," *Child Development*, vol. 52 (1981), pp. 596–602.

46. Gelles, "Violence in the Family: A Review of Research in the Seventies."

47. A. H. Green, "Child Abuse: Dimension of Psychological Trauma in Abused Children," *Journal of the American Academy of Child Psychiatry*, vol. 22 (1983), pp. 231–237.

48. M. R. Yarrow, "Problems of Methods in Parent-Child Research," *Child Development*, vol. 34 (1963), pp. 215–26.

49. R. Gaines, A. Sandgrund, A. H. Green and E. Power, "Etiological Factors in Child Maltreatment: A Multivariate Study of Abusing, Neglecting, and Normal Mothers," *Journal of Abnormal Psychology*, vol. 87 (1978), pp. 531–540.

50. Ibid.

51. M. T. Orne, "On the Social Psychology of the Psychological Experiment: With Particular Reference to Demand Characteristics and their Implications," *American Psychologist*, vol. 17 (1962), pp. 776–83.

52. Straus, Gelles, and Steinmetz, *Behind Closed Doors: Violence in the American Family.*

53. Mouzakitis, "An Inquiry into the Problem of Child Abuse and Juvenile Delinquency."

54. R. L. Jenkins, "The Varieties of Children's Behavioral Problems and Family Dynamics," *American Journal of Psychiatry,* vol. 124 (1968), pp. 1440–45.

55. D. O. Lewis, E. Moy, L. D. Jackson, R. Aaronson, N. Restifo, S. Serra, and A. Simos, "Biopsychological Characteristics of Children Who Later Murder: A Prospective Study," *American Journal of Psychiatry,* vol. 142 (1985), pp. 1161–67; D. O. Lewis, S. S. Shanok, J. H. Pincus, and G. H. Glaser, "Violent Juvenile Delinquents: Psychiatric, Neurological, Psychological and Abuse Factors," *Journal of the American Academy of Child Psychiatry,* vol. 8 (1979), pp. 307–19.

56. Aragona and Eyberg, "Neglected Children: Mothers' Report of Child Behavior Problems and Observed Verbal Behavior"; Wolfe and Mosk, "Behavioral Comparisons of Children from Abusive and Distressed Families."

57. R. S. Lazarus and R. Launier, "Stress-related Transactions between Persons and Environment," in L. A. Pervin and M. Lewis, eds., *Perspectives in Interactional Psychology* (New York: Plenum, 1978).

58. V. DeLissovoy, "Toward the Definition of 'Abuse Provoking Child,'" *Child Abuse and Neglect,* vol. 3 (1979), pp. 341–50.

59. M. L. Kohn and E. E. Carroll, "Social Class and the Allocation of Parental Responsibilities," *Sociometry,* vol. 23 (1960), pp. 372–92.

60. M. J. Hindelang, T. Hirschi, and J. G. Weiss, "Correlates of Delinquency: The Illusion of Discrepancy between Self-Report and Official Measures," *American Sociological Review,* vol 44 (1979), pp. 995–1014.

61. J. M. Levanthal, "Risk Factors for Child Abuse: Methodologic Standards in Case-control Studies," *Pediatrics,* vol. 68 (1981), pp. 684–90.

62. F. Schulsinger, S. A. Mednick, and J. Knop, *Longitudinal Research: Methods and Uses in Behavioral Science* (Boston: Martinus Nijhoff, Publ., 1981).

63. R. Q. Bell and D. Pearl, "Psychosocial Change in Risk Groups: Implications for Early Identification," *Prevention in Human Services,* vol. 1, pp. 45–59.

CHAPTER 4: IMPROVED RESEARCH ON CHILD ABUSE AND NEGLECT THROUGH BETTER DEFINITIONS

1. M. Holmes, *Child Abuse Programs: Practice and Theory* (Washington, D.C.: U.S. National Institute on Mental Health, 1977), p. 113.

2. J. Giovannoni and R. Becerra, *Defining Child Abuse* (New York: Free Press, 1979), pp. 13–14.

3. A. Rivlin, *Systematic Thinking for Social Action* (Washington, D.C.: Brookings Institution, 1971); C. Weiss, *Using Social Science Policy Research in Public Policy Making* (Lexington, Mass.: Lexington Books, 1977).

4. J. Giovannoni, *What Is Harmful to Children? A Survey of Experts and a Literature Review* (Washington, D.C.: U.S. Community Services Administration, Department of Health, Education and Welfare, 1977), p. 4.

5. F. G. Bolton, R. H. Laner, and S. P. Kane, "Child Maltreatment Risk among Adolescent Mothers: A Study of Reported Cases," *American Journal of Orthopsychiatry,* vol. 50 (1980), p. 489; E. M. Kinnard and L. V. Klerman,

"Teenage Parenting and Child Abuse: Are They Related?" *American Journal of Orthopsychiatry,* vol. 50 (1980), pp. 481–88.

6. Giovannoni and Becerra, *Defining Child Abuse,* p. 15.

7. U.S. National Center on Child Abuse and Neglect, *Annual Analysis of Research* (Washington, D.C.: Government Printing Office, 1978).

8. Giovannoni and Becerra, *Defining Child Abuse,* p. 14.

9. U.S. National Center on Child Abuse and Neglect, *Annual Analysis of Research.*

10. Burt Associates, *Report and Plan on Recommended Approaches for Determination of National Incidence of Child Abuse and Neglect,* vol. 2 (Washington, D.C.: Burt Associates 1975), pp. 124–25.

11. K. Burgdorf and C. Eldred, *System of Operational Definitions* (Rockville, Md.: Westat, 1978).

12. M. Wald, "State Intervention on Behalf of 'Neglected' Children: A Search for Standards," *Stanford Law Review,* vol. 27 (1975), pp. 985–1040.

13. Utah Code Ann., section 78-3A-2(17) (1977).

14. Ill. Ann. Stat. Ch. 37, s702-04 (Smith-Hurd Supp. 1976).

15. C. H. Kempe, *Children in Peril* (Xerox Films, Media Concepts, 1972).

16. S. Katz, *When Parents Fail: The Law's Response to Family Breakdown* (Boston: Beacon Press, 1971).

17. In re Stilley, 6 Ill. Dec. 873, 363 N.E.2d. 820 (Ill. 1977).

18. In Interest of Nitz, 11 Ill. Dec. 503, 368 N.E.2d 111 (Ill. 1977).

19. Jacabelis v. Ohio, 378 U.S. 184 (1964). Steward, J., dissenting.

20. Wald, "State Intervention on Behalf of 'Neglected' Children.

21. Bolton, Laner, and Kane, "Child Maltreatment Risk among Adolescent Mothers," p. 489; Kinnard and Klerman, "Teenage Parenting and Child Abuse," pp. 481–88.

22. A. Cohn, "Effective Treatment of Child Abuse and Neglect," *Social Work,* vol. 513 (November 1979), pp. 516–17.

23. N. Polansky, C. De Saix, and S. Sharlin, *Child Neglect: Understanding and Reaching the Parent.* (New York: Child Welfare League of America, 1973).

24. Behavior Associates, *The Parents Anonymous Self-Help for Abusing Parents Project: Evaluation Study for 1974–1976.* Report submitted to U.S. Office on Child Development. (Washington, D.C.: [AUTHOR,] 1976).

25. E. Zigler, "Controlling Chld Abuse in America: An Effort Doomed to Failure," in R. Bourne and E. Newberger, eds., *Critical Perspectives in Child Abuse* (Lexington, Mass.: Lexington Books, 1979), pp. 171–213.

26. D. Gil, *Violence against Children: Physical Child Abuse in the U.S.* (Cambridge, Mass.: Harvard University Press, 1970); Polansky, De Saix, and Sharlin, *Child Neglect.*

27. Bolton, Laner, and Kane, "Child Maltreatment Risk Among Adolescent Mothers," p. 489; Kinnard and Klerman, "Teenage Parenting and Child Abuse," pp. 481–88.

28. R. Helfer and C. H. Kempe, *The Battered Child* (Chicago: University of Chicago Press, 1972).

29. Giovannoni and Becerra, *Defining Child Abuse,* p. 15.

30. J. I. Layzer and B. Goodson, "Impact Evaluation of Twenty Child

Abuse and Neglect Demonstration Treatment and Innovative Projects." Abt Associates, Cambridge, Mass., 1979. Working draft.

31. Giovannoni and Becerra, *Defining Child Abuse*, pp. 14–15.

32. Helfer and Kempe, *The Battered Child*.

33. V. J. Fontana and D. J. Besharov, *The Maltreated Child* (Springfield, Ill.: Charles C. Thomas, 1977)

34. Polansky, De Saix, and Sharlin, *Child Neglect*.

35. The Act provides that " 'child abuse and neglect' means the physical or mental injury, sexual abuse or exploitation, negligent treatment, or maltreatment of a child under the age of eighteen . . . under circumstances which indicate the child's health or welfare is harmed or threatened thereby. . ."

36. U.S. National Center on Child Abuse and Neglect, *Annual Analysis of Research*, p. 1.

37. U.S. National Center on Child Abuse and Neglect, *Annual Analysis of Research*.

38. U.S. National Center on Child Abuse and Neglect, *Child Abuse and Neglect: Grants Program FY 1978* (Washington, D.C.: Government Printing Office, 1978), p. 7.

39. R. Gelles, "Overview of Research into Child Abuse and Neglect." Hearings. Subcommittee on Domestic and International Scientific Planning, Analysis and Cooperation, House Committee on Science and Technology, 78th Cong., 2nd sess., 1978, H. Rept. 276, 278.

40. Ibid.

41. U.S. National Center on Child Abuse and Neglect, *Request for Proposal: National Study of the Incidence and Severity of Child Abuse and Neglect* (Washington, D.C.: Government Printing Office, 1975).

42. Burgdorf and Eldred, *System of Operational Definitions*.

43. Gil, *Violence against Children*.

44. E. Elmer, "Traumatized Children, Chronic Illness, and Poverty," in L. Pelton, Ed., *The Social Context of Child Abuse and Neglect* (New York: Human Services Press, 1981).

CHAPTER 5: CONTRIBUTIONS OF RESEARCH TO CRIMINAL JUSTICE POLICY ON WIFE ASSAULT

1. Neil Gilbert, *Capitalism and the Welfare State: Dilemmas of Social Benevolence* (New Haven, Conn.: Yale University Press, 1983).

2. Sandra Wexler, "Battered Women and Public Policy," in Ellen Boneparth, ed., *Women, Power, and Policy* (New York: Pergamon Press, 1982).

3. Laurie Wardell, Dair L. Gillespie, and Anne Leffler, "Science and Violence against Wives," in David Finkelhor et al., eds., *The Dark Side of Families* (Beverly Hills, Calif.: Sage Publications, 1983).

4. David Gil, *Violence against Children: Physical Child Abuse in the United States* (Cambridge, Mass.: Harvard University Press, 1970).

5. Murray A. Straus, Richard Gelles, and Suzanne Steinmetz, *Behind Closed Doors: Violence in the American Family* (New York: Doubleday and Company, 1980).

6. Richard J. Gelles, *The Violent Home* (Beverly Hills, Calif.: Sage Publica-

tions, 1974); W. K. Goode, "Force and Violence in the Family," in Suzanne K. Steinmetz and Murray A. Straus, eds., *Violence in the Family* (New York: Harper & Row, 1974); Del Martin, *Battered Wives* (San Francisco, Calif: Glide, 1976); J. E. O'Brien, "Violence in Divorce-prone Families," *Journal of Marriage and the Family,* vol. 33, no. 4 (1971), pp. 692–98; Mildred D. Pagelow, Testimony before the U.S. Commission on Civil Rights, January 1978; Maria Roy, *Battered Women: A Psychological Study of Domestic Violence* (New York: Van Nostrand Reinhold Company, 1977); J. Sprey, "On the Management of Conflict in Families," *Journal of Marriage and the Family,* vol. 33, no. 4 (1971), pp. 722–31.

7. Morton Bard and Joseph Zacker, "The Prevention of Family Violence: Dilemmas of Community Intervention," *Journal of Marriage and the Family,* vol. 33 (1971), pp. 627–82; Raymond I. Parnas, "The Police Response to the Domestic Disturbance," *Wisconsin Law Review,* vol. 31 (1967), pp. 914–60.

8. Both Dobash and Dobash and Stark and Flitcraft note that the "discovery" of family violence in the 1970s is hardly new. "Virtually every 20 years . . . the popular press has joined women's groups and charitable organizations to denounce wife beating, child abuse, and related forms of family violence in the strongest terms"; Evan Stark and Anne Flitcraft "Social Knowledge, Social Policy, and the Abuse of Women: The Case against Patriarchical Benevolence," in Richard Gelles, Gerald Hotaling, and Murray A. Straus, eds., *The Dark Side of Families: Current Family Violence Research* (Beverly Hills, Calif.: Sage Publications, 1983). Dobash and Dobash describe two short-lived periods of public concern and social action against wife beating; R. Emerson Dobash and Russell Dobash, *Violence against Wives: A Case against the Patriarchy* (New York: Free Fress, 1979); Mill's (1869) famous essay, "The Subjection of Women," decried the battering of wives and resulted in a report to the British parliament in 1874 (cited in Dobash and Dobash). In the same decade, both British and American legislatures took some limited actions to protect women. The Americans revoked a few laws of chastisement in 1871, while the British offered "meager protection against cruelty and allowed divorce on this ground" (p. 5). During the suffragette movement in the early twentieth century, both British and American women took up the issue until it was obscured by concentration on obtaining the vote.

9. Dobash and Dobash, *Violence against Wives: A Case against the Patriarchy*; Sue Eisenberg and Patrick Micklow, "The Assaultive Wife: 'Catch 22' Revisited," *Women's Rights Law Reporter,* vol. 3 (1977), pp. 138–61; Marjorie D. Fields, "Wife Beating: Government Intervention Policies and Practices," in *Battered Women: Issues of Public Policy* (Washington, D.C.: U.S. Commission on Civil Rights, 1978).

10. Morton Bard, *Training Police as Specialists in Family Crisis Intervention* (Washington, D.C., 1970); Joel Garner and Elizabeth Clemne, "Danger to Police in Domestic Disturbances—A New Look," *National Institute of Justice: Research in Brief* (Washington, D.C.: National Institute of Justice, 1986); Parnas, "The Police Response to the Domestic Disturbance;" James Q. Wilson, "Foreword," in *Domestic Violence and the Police: Studies in Detroit and Kansas City* (Washington, D.C.: Police Foundation, 1977).

11. Donald G. Dutton, "The Criminal Justice Response to Wife Assault," *Law and Human Behavior,* vol. 11, no. 3 (1987), pp. 189–205.

12. Gail A. Goolkasian, "Confronting Domestic Violence: The Role of Criminal Court Judges," *National Institute of Justice: Research in Brief* (Washington, D.C.: National Institute of Justice, 1986); Lisa G. Lerman, "Criminal Prosecution of Wife Beaters, *Response,* vol. 4, no. 3 (January/February 1981).

13. Lawrence W. Sherman and Richard A. Berk, "The Specific Deterrent Effects of Arrest for Domestic Assault," *American Sociological Review,* vol. 49 (1984), pp. 261–72.

14. Jeffrey Fagan and Sandra Wexler, "Crime at Home and Crime in the Streets: The Relationship between Family and Stranger Violence," *Violence and Victims,* vol. 2, no. 1 (1987), pp. 5–24; Merry Morash, "Wife Battering," *Criminal Justice Abstracts,* vol. 18, no. 2 (1986), pp. 252–71.

15. Howard S. Becker, *The Outsiders* (New York: Free Press, 1963); H. Blumer, "Social Problems and Collective Behavior," *Social Problems,* vol. 18 (Winter 1971), pp. 298–306; Social problem theorists focus on the processes by which a social issue is identified, defined, legitimated, and responded to as a public concern. These processes explain how social issues rise to the status of social problem.

16. Jeffrey Fagan et al., *Family Violence and Public Policy: The Final Evaluation Report of the LEAA Family Violence Program* (Washington, D.C.: U.S. Department of Justice, 1984).

17. Herman Schwendinger and Julia Schwendinger, *Rape and Inequality* (Beverly Hills, Calif.: Sage Publications, 1981).

18. Ironically, it was dissatisfaction with the "crisis intervention" and "conflict management" roles adopted by police that led to legislation in Pennsylvania and Massachusetts enabling battered women to obtain protective orders that brought family violence into the criminal jurisdiction. Mandatory arrest statutes and policies followed these developments.

19. Bruno v. McGuire, Consent decree between Carmen Bruno et al. and Robert Maguire et al., 1978, Index 76-21946; Scott v. Hart, U.S. District Court for the Northern District of California, settlement decree between Mary Scott et al. and George Hart et al., 1979, index C76-2395.

20. Fagan et al., *Family Violence and Public Policy: The Final Evaluation Report of the LEAA Family Violence Program.*

21. Goolkasian, "Confronting Domestic Violence: The Role of Criminal Court Judges."

22. Fagan et al., *Family Violence and Public Policy: The Final Evaluation Report of the LEAA Family Violence Program.*

23. Ibid.

24. Donald G. Dutton, *The Domestic Assault of Women* (Boston: Allyn and Bacon, 1988).

25. Later maltreatment of adolescents was also included in the definition of child abuse.

26. Wexler, "Battered Women and Public Policy."

27. Susan Schechter, *Women and Male Violence* (Boston: South End Press, 1982).

28. Richard J. Gelles and Murray A. Straus, "Determinants of Violence in the Family: Toward a Theoretical Integration," in Wesley R. Burr, Ivan Nye, and Ira Reiss, eds., *Contemporary Theories about Family* (New York: Free Press, 1979), vol. 1.

29. Lenore E. Walker, *The Battered Woman Syndrome* (New York: Springer, 1984).

30. Jeffrey Fagan and Sandra Wexler, "Complex Behaviors and Simple Measures: Understanding Violence in Families" (Paper presented at the annual meeting of the American Society of Criminology, San Diego, November 1985).

31. Dobash and Dobash, *Violence against Wives: A Case against the Patriarchy*; Dutton, *The Domestic Assault of Women*; Fagan and Wexler, "Crime at Home and Crime in the Streets: The Relationship between Family and Stranger Violence"; Richard J. Gelles, "Domestic Criminal Violence," in Marvin E. Wolfgang and Neil A. Weiner, eds., *Criminal Violence* (Beverly Hills, Calif.: Sage Publications, 1982).

32. Wexler, "Battered Women and Public Policy," in Ellen Boneparth, ed., *Women, Power, and Policy* (New York: Pergamon Press, 1982).

33. These actions may also be seen as efforts to stake social ownership of the problem, a path followed in similar social problems involving deviant behavior, such as substance use.

34. Law Enforcement Assistance Administration (Department of Justice), Community Services Administration (Department of Housing and Urban Development), Employment and Training Administration (Department of Labor), Social Services Administration, National Institute on Alcohol Abuse and Alcoholism, National Institute of Mental Helath, and the Office of Human Development Services (Department of Health, Education and Welfare).

35. Sandra Wexler, "Battered Women and Public Policy," in Ellen Boneparth, ed., *Women, Power, and Policy* (New York: Pergamon Press, 1982).

36. Other than homicide.

37. In an earlier era, labeling and societal reaction perspectives may have mitigated the concern for sanction, and one can speculate that criminal justice policy may have emphasized diversion, mediation, and treatment intervention in lieu of prosecution. In fact, these approaches characterized the criminal justice response in the era preceding the LEAA program in the mid-1970s.

38. James Q. Wilson *Thinking about Crime* (New York: Basic Books, 1983).

39. Delbert S. Elliott, "Evaluation of Criminal Justice Procedures in Family Violence Crimes," in Lloyd Ohlin and Michael Tonry, eds., *Family Violence*, a special volume of *Crime and Justice: An Annual Review of Research* (Chicago: University of Chicago Press, 1989).

40. Ibid.

41. Dutton, "The Criminal Justice Response to Wife Assault"; Dutton compares this to the finding of Richard Hood and Richard Sparks that police made arrests in 20 percent of the cases where they attended and decided that a crime had been committed (Hood and Sparks, *Key Issues in Criminology*

[New York: McGraw-Hill, 1970]); Dutton, *The Domestic Assault of Women*.

42. Elliott, "Evaluation of Criminal Justice Procedures in Family Violence Crimes."

43. Richard A. Berk and Phyliss Newton, "Does Arrest Really Reduce Wife Abuse?" *American Sociological Review*, vol. 50 (1985), pp. 253–62; Sherman and Berk, "The Specific Deterrent Effects of Arrest for Domestic Assault."

44. Most jurisdictions authorize arrest whenever there is probable cause that a felony assault has occurred. The degree of injury or presence of a weapon generally qualify a felony charge. For misdemeanor cases there are restrictions on arrest in assault cases including corroboration or "in presence" requirements. Lisa G. Lerman, "Prosecution of Wife Beaters: Institutional Obstacles and Innovations," in Mary Lystad, ed., *Violence in the Home: Interdisciplinary Perspectives* (New York: Brunner-Mazel, 1986). Thus victims must initiate a complaint or warrant to efffect an arrest. The intent of mandatory arrest statutes is to eliminate these restrictions on misdemeanor wife assault, the most common charge category for domestic assaults, and to allow officers to make misdemeanor arrests on the basis of either the victim's hearsay or their own probable cause determination. In California these conditions were established by providing concurrent status as both felony and misdemeanor for domestic assault. Other states (such as Washington) have mandated arrest in all domestic assaults based on probable cause or victim complaint.

45. Lee H. Bowker, "Police Services to Battered Women," *Criminal Justice and Behavior*, vol. 9 (1982), pp. 476–94; Peter Jaffe, David A. Wolfe, Anne Telford, and Gary Austin, "The Impact of Police Charges in Incidents of Wife Abuse," *Journal of Family Violence*, vol. 1 (1986), pp. 37–49; Martin, *Battered Wives*; Morash, "Wife Battering"; Sherman and Berk, "The Specific Deterrent Effects of Arrest for Domestic Assault."

46. Sherman and Berk, "The Specific Deterrent Effects of Arrest for Domestic Assault."

47. Richard A. Berk, personal communication with author, 1986.

48. George Tauchen, Helen Tauchen, and Anne D. Witte, "The Dynamics of Domestic Violence: A Reanalysis of the Minneapolis Experiment," University of North Carolina, unpublished.

49. Elliott, "Evaluation of Criminal Justice Procedures in Family Violence Crimes"; Jeffrey Fagan, "Cessation of Family Violence: Deterrence and Dissuasion," in Lloyd Ohlin and Michael Tonry, *Family Violence*, a special volume of *Crime and Justice: An Annual Review of Research* (Chicago: University of Chicago Press, 1989); Lawrence W. Sherman and Richard A. Berk, "The Specific Deterrent Effects of Arrest for Domestic Assault," *American Sociological Review*, vol. 49 (1984), pp. 261–72.

50. Fields, "Wife Beating: Government Intervention Policies and Practices"; Lerman, "Prosecution of Wife Beaters: Institutional Obstacles and Innovations;" Martin, *Battered Wives*.

51. Elliott, "Evaluation of Criminal Justice Procedures in Family Violence Crimes."

52. Fagan et al., *Family Violence and Public Policy: The Final Evaluation Report of the LEAA Family Violence Program*; David A. Ford, "Prosecution as a Victim Power Resource for Managing Conjugal Violence" (Paper presented at the annual meetings of the Society for the Study of Social Problems, San Antonio, August 1984).

53. Elliott, "Evaluation of Criminal Justice Procedures in Family Violence Crimes."

54. Lerman, "Prosecution of Wife Beaters: Institutional Obstacles and Innovations."

55. Fagan et al., *Family Violence and Public Policy: The Final Evaluation Report of the LEAA Family Violence Program*; Lerman, "Prosecution of Wife Beaters: Institutional Obstacles and Innovations."

56. Lerman, "Prosecution of Wife Beaters: Institutional Obstacles and Innovations."

57. Brian E. Forst and Jolene C. Hernon, "The Criminal Justice Response to Victim Harm," *National Institute of Justice: Research in Brief* (Washington, D.C.: National Institute of Justice, 1985).

58. Fagan and Wexler, "Crime at Home and Crime in the Streets: The Relationship between Family and Stranger Violence."

59. Dutton, *The Domestic Assault of Women*.

60. Anne L. Ganley, *Participants Manual: Court Mandated Therapy for Men Who Batter* (Washington, D.C.: Center for Women Policy Studies, 1981).

61. Daniel Saunders and Sandra Azar, "Treatment of Wife Batterers," in Lloyd Ohlin and Michael Tonry, eds., *Family Violence*, a special volume of *Crime and Justice: An Annual Review of Research* (Chicago: University of Chicago Press, 1989); Daniel J. Sonkin, Del Martin, and Lenore E. Walker, *The Male Batterer: A Treatment Approach* (New York: Springer, 1985).

62. Paul Gendreau and Robert R. Ross, "Correctional Potency: Treatment and Deterrence on Trial," in Ronald Roesch and Raymond R. Corrado, eds., *Evaluation and Criminal Justice Policy* (Beverly Hills, Calif.: Sage Publications, 1980).

63. Fagan et al., *Family Violence and Public Policy: The Final Evaluation Report of the LEAA Family Violence Program*.

64. Saunders and Azar, "Treatment of Wife Batterers."

65. EMERGE, *Organizing and Implementing Services for Men Who Batter* (Boston: EMERGE, 1981).

66. Saunders and Azar, "Treatment of Wife Batterers."

67. Dutton, *The Domestic Assault of Women*.

68. Ronald L. Akers et al., "Social Learning and Deviant Behavior: A Specific Test of a General Theory," *American Sociological Review*, vol. 44 (August 1979) pp. 636–55; Albert Bandura, *Aggression: A Social Learning Analysis* (Englewood Cliffs, N.J.: Prentice Hall, 1973); Fagan and Wexler, "Crime at Home and Crime in the Streets: The Relationship between Family and Stranger Violence"; Ganley, *Participants Manual: Court Mandated Therapy for Men Who Batter*.

69. Saunders and Azar, "Treatment of Wife Batterers."

70. Edward Gondolf, "Anger and Oppression in Men Who Batter: Em-

piricist and Feminist Perspectives and Their Implications for Research," *Victimology*, vol. 10, nos. 1–4 (1985), pp. 311–24.

71. Lee H. Bowker, *Beating Wife-Beating* (Lexington, Mass.: D. C. Heath and Company, 1983); Fagan, "Cessation of Family Violence: Deterrence and Dissuasion"; Edward Gondolf, "Fighting for Control: A Clinical Assessment of Men Who Batter," *Social Casework: The Journal of Contemporary Social Work*, vol. 66, no. 1 (1985), pp. 48–54.

72. Angela Browne, *When Battered Women Kill* (New York: Free Press, 1987); Gondolf, "Fighting for Control: A Clinical Assessment of Men Who Batter"; Walker, *The Battered Woman Syndrome*.

73. Browne, *When Battered Women Kill*; Marvin E. Wolfgang, "A Sociological Analysis of Criminal Homicide," in Marvin E. Wolfgang, *Studies in Homicide* (New York: Harper & Row, 1967).

74. Bureau of Justice, "Intimate Victims" (Washington, D.C.: Bureau of Justice Statistics, U.S. Department of Justice, 1980).

75. Browne, *When Battered Women Kill*.

76. See, for example, LaFave and Scott, *Handbook on Criminal Law* (Minneapolis: West Publishing Company, 1972).

77. Browne, *When Battered Women Kill*.

78. Such as threats to children if the woman retaliates or leaves or threats of the assailant's suicide.

79. Browne, *When Battered Women Kill*.

80. Delbert S. Elliott, "The Assumption That Theories Can Be Combined with Increased Explanatory Power: Theoretical Integrations," in Robert F. Meier, ed., *Theoretical Methods in Criminology* (Newbury Park, Calif.: Sage Publications, 1985).

81. Dutton, *The Domestic Assault of Women*; Elliott, "Evaluation of Criminal Justice Procedures in Family Violence Crimes."

82. Dobash and Dobash, *Violence against Wives: A Case against the Patriarchy*; Dutton, *The Domestic Assault of Women*; Fagan and Wexler, "Crime at Home and Crime in the Streets: The Relationship between Family and Stranger Violence."

83. Fagan and Wexler, "Crime at Home and Crime in the Streets: The Relationship between Family and Stranger Violence."

84. Becker, *The Outsiders*; Dobash and Dobash, *Violence against Wives: A Case against the Patriarchy*; Wardell, Gillespie, and Leffler, "Science and Violence against Wives."

85. Paul J. Goldstein, "A Tripartite Typology of Drug-Related Violence," *Journal of Drug Issues* 15 (1985) 493–506; Malcolm W. Klein and Cheryl Maxson, "Street Gang Violence," in Marvin E. Wolfgang and Neil A. Weiner, eds., *Violent Crime* (Newbury Park, Calif.: Sage Publications, 1987); Norman Zinberg, *Drug, Set and Setting* (New Haven, Conn.: Yale University Press, 1984).

86. Murray A. Straus, "Measuring Intrafamily Conflict and Violence: The Conflict Tactics (CT) Scales, *Journal of Marriage and the Family*, vol. 41 (1979), pp. 75–88; Murray A. Straus, "The Conflict Tactics Scales and Its Critics: An Evaluation and New Data on Validity and Reliability," in Murray A. Straus and Richard J. Gelles, eds., *Physical Violence in American Families: Risk Factors*

and Adaptation to Violence in 8,145 Families (New Brunswick, N.J.: Transaction Press, 1987).

87. Criminological research, in contrast, relies on studies of offenders more than on victimization research in developing policy on sanctions.

88. Exceptions, of course, include the nationwide studies: Straus, Gelles, and Steinmetz, *Behind Closed Doors: Violence in the American Family,* and Murray A. Straus and Richard J. Gelles, "Societal Change and Change in Family Violence from 1975 to 1985 as Revealed by Two National Surveys," *Journal of Marriage and the Family,* vol. 48 (1986), pp. 465–79; also studies by Diana H. Russell, *Rape in Marriage* (New York: Macmillan, 1982), that employed representative samples of women in San Francisco.

89. Straus, "Measuring Intrafamily Conflict and Violence: The Conflict Tactics (CT) Scales"; Murray A. Straus, "The Conflict Tactics Scales and Its Critics: An Evaluation and New Data on Validity and Reliability," in Murray A. Straus and Richard J. Gelles, eds., *Physical Violence in American Families: Risk Factors and Adaptation to Violence in 8,145 Families* (New Brunswich, N.J.: Transaction Press, 1987).

90. Elliott, "Evaluation of Criminal Justice Procedures in Family Violence Crimes"; Jeffrey Fagan, Douglas K. Stewart, and Karen V. Hansen, "Violent Men or Violent Husbands? Background Factors and Situational Correlates," in David Finkelhor et al., eds., *The Dark Side of Families: Current Family Violence Research* (Beverly Hills, Calif.: Sage Publications, 1983); Nancy Shields and Christine R. Hannecke, "Patterns of Family and Non-Family Violence: An Approach to the Study of Violent Husbands" (Paper presented at the annual meeting of the American Sociological Association, Toronto, Ontario, 1981).

91. Walker, *The Battered Woman Syndrome.*

92. Franklin E. Zimring, "Jurisprudence of Family Violence," in Lloyd Ohlin and Michael Tonry, eds., *Family Violence,* a special volume of *Crime and Justice: An Annual Review of Research* (Chicago: University of Chicago Press, 1989).

93. James Eisenstein and Herbert Jacob, *Felony Justice: An Organizational Analysis of Criminal Courts* (Boston: Little Brown, 1977); Robert Emerson, "Holistic Effects in Social Control Decision Making," *Law and Society Review,* vol. 17 (1983), pp. 425–55.

94. John Hagan and Karen Bumiller, "Making Sense of Sentencing: A Review and Critique of Sentencing Research," in Alfred Blumstein, et al., eds., *Research on Sentencing: The Search for Reform* (Washington, D.C.: National Academy Press, 1983).

95. Jonathan D. Casper and D. Brereton, "Evaluating Criminal Justice Reforms," *Law and Society Review,* vol. 18 (1984), pp. 122–44.

96. Emerson, "Holistic Effects in Social Control Decision Making."

97. Yeheskel Hasanfeld and P. Cheung, "The Juvenile Court as a People-processing Organization: A Political Economy Perspective," *American Journal of Sociology,* vol. 90 (1985), pp. 801–25; Herbert Jacob, "Courts as Organizations," in Lynn Mather and Kenneth O. Boyum, eds., *Empirical Theories about Courts* (New York: Longman, 1983).

98. Lynn M. Mather, *Plea Bargaining or Trial?* (Lexington, Mass.: D. C. Heath and Company, 1979).

99. Fagan et al., *Family Violence and Public Policy: The Final Evaluation Report of the LEAA Family Violence Program.*

100. Richard J. Gelles and Helen Mederer, "Comparison or Control: Intervention in the Cases of Wife Abuse" (Paper presented at the annual meeting of the National Council on Family Relations, Dallas, November 1985).

101. Browne, *When Battered Women Kill*; Lenore E. Walker, *The Battered Woman* (New York: Harper & Row, 1979); Walker, *The Battered Woman Syndrome.*

102. Fagan et al., *Family Violence and Public Policy: The Final Evaluation Report of the LEAA Family Violence Program.*

103. Dutton, "The Criminal Justice Response to Wife Assault."

104. Alfred Blumstein et al., eds., *Criminal Careers and "Career" Criminals* (Washington, D.C.: National Academy Press, 1986).

105. Alfred Blumstein, David Farrington, and Souymo Moitra, "Delinquency Careers: Innocents, Desisters, and Persisters," in Michael Tonry and Norval Morris, eds., *Crime and Justice: An Annual Review of Research* (Chicago: University of Chicago Press, 1985), pp. 187–220.

106. Fagan, Stewart, and Hansen, "Violent Men or Violent Husbands? Background Factors and Situational Correlates."

107. Ronald V. Clarke and Derek B. Cornish, "Modeling Offenders Decisions: A Framework for Research and Policy," in Michael Tonry and Norval Morris, eds., *Crime and Justice: An Annual Review of Research* (Chicago: University of Chicago Press, 1985); Maurice Cusson and Pierre Pinsonneault, "The Decision to Give Up Crime," in Derek B. Cornish and Ronald V. Clarke, eds., *The Reasoning Criminal* (New York: Springer-Verlag, 1986), pp. 72–82; Shields and Hannecke, "Patterns of Family and Non-Family Violence: An Approach to the Study of Violent Husbands."

108. Ron Stall and Patrick Biernacki, "Spontaneous Remission from the Problematic Use of Substances: An Inductive Model Derived from a Comparative Analysis of the Alcohol, Opiate, Tobacco, and Food/Obesity Literatures," *International Journal of the Addictions*, vol. 2, no. 1 (1986), pp. 1–23.

109. Fagan, "Cessation of Family Violence: Deterrence and Dissuasion."

110. Fagan et al., *Family Violence and Public Policy: The Final Evaluation Report of the LEAA Family Violence Program.*

CHAPTER 6: ALTERNATIVE ANALYTICAL PARADIGMS FOR CONDUCTING POLICY-ORIENTED RESEARCH

1. David G. Gil, *Social Policy: Analysis and Synthesis* (Cambridge, Mass.: Harvard University Press, 1971).

2. Andrea J. Sedlak, *Study of the National Incidence and Prevalence of Child Abuse and Neglect* (Rockville, Md.: Westat, 1988).

3. Donella H. Meadows, "Whole Earth Models and Systems," *CoEvaluation Quarterly* (Summer 1982).

4. Saad Z. Nagi, *Child Maltreatment in the United States* (New York: Columbia University Press, 1977).

5. Albert Gifi, *Non-Linear Multivariate Analysis* (Netherlands: University of Leiden, 1981).

6. J. W. Tukey, "The Future of Data Analysis," *Analysis of Mathematical Statistics* 33 (1962).

7. Norbert Wiener, *Cybernetics* (New York: John Wiley and Sons, 1948).

8. Jay W. Forrester, *Industrial Dynamics,* (Cambridge, Mass.: MIT Press, 1961).

9. Glen H. Elder, Jr., "Approaches to Social Change and the Family," *The American Journal of Sociology Supplement,* vol. 84 (1978).

10. G. P. Richardson and A. L. Pugh III, *Introduction to System Dynamics Modeling with Dynamo* (Cambridge: MIT Press, 1981).

11. Charles P. Gershenson, "An Examination of the 1985 Data for the Duration of Placement for Children in Foster Care," *Child Welfare Research Notes* no. 19, Administration for Children, Youth and Families, Department of Health and Human Services (1988).

12. Roy E. Helfer and C. Henry Kempe, eds., *The Battered Child* (Chicago: University of Chicago Press, 1968); David G. Gil, *Violence against Children* (Cambridge: Harvard University Press, 1970); E. H. Newberger, "The Myth of the Battered Child Syndrome," *Current Medical Dialogue,* vol. 40 (1973), pp. 327–34.

13. David F. Andersen, "An Approach to Analyses of the Military Enlisted Personnel System," Systems Dynamic Group Working Paper D-2369 (Cambridge: A. P. Sloan School of Management, Massachusetts Institute of Technology, 1975), and "How Differences in Analytic Paradigms Can Lead to Differences in Policy Conclusions," in Jorgen Randers, ed., *Elements of the System Dynamics Method,* (Cambridge, Mass.: MIT Press, 1980); J. S. Coleman et al., Equality of Educational Opportunity (Washington, D.C.: Office of Education, U.S. Department of Health, Education and Welfare, 1971).

CHAPTER 7: ASKING THE RIGHT QUESTIONS ABOUT THE FUTURE OF MARITAL VIOLENCE RESEARCH

1. F. Elliot, "The Neurology of Explosive Rage: The Episodic Dyscontrol Syndrome," in M. Roy, ed., *Battered Women: A Psychosociological Study of Domestic Violence* (New York: Van Nostrand Reinhold, 1977); M. Faulk, "Men Who Assault Their Wives," *Medicine, Science and the Law,* vol. 14, 1974, pp. 180–83; M. Symonds, "The Psychodynamics of Violence-Prone Marriages," *American Journal of Psychoanalysis,* vol. 38, 1978, p. 213.

2. Richard Gelles, "Family Violence," *Annual Review of Sociology,* vol. 11, 1985, pp. 347–67; Suzanne Steinmetz, "Family Violence: Past, Present, Future," in M. Sussman and Suzanne Steinmetz, eds., *Handbook of Marriage and the Family* (New York: Plenum Press, 1987).

3. Murray Straus and Richard Gelles, "Societal Change and Change in Family Violence from 1975 to 1985 as Revealed by Two National Surveys," *Journal of Marriage and the Family,* vol. 48, 1986, pp. 465–79.

4. L. A. Davis, "Battered Women: The Transformation of a Social Problem," *Social Work,* July-August, 1987, pp. 306–11; Gelles, "Family Violence"; M. D. Pagelow, *Family Violence* (New York: Praeger, 1984); Steinmetz, "Family Violence: Past, Present, Future."

5. K. E. MacEwen and Julian Barling, "Multiple Stressors, Violence in the Family of Origin, and Marital Aggression: A Longitudinal Investigation," *Journal of Family Violence,* vol. 3, 1988, pp. 73–87; Gayla Margolin et al., "Interaction Patterns Associated with Marital Violence" (Paper presented at the American Enterprise Institute Conference on Research on Family Violence: Identifying and Answering the Public Policy Questions, Washington, D.C., March 1988); Margolin, John, and Gleberman, "Affective Responses to Conflictual Discussions in Violent and Nonviolent Couples," *Journal of Consulting and Clinical Psychology,* vol. 56, 1988, pp. 24–33.

6. Dennis Bagarozzi and Winter Giddings, "Conjugal Violence: A Critical View of Current Research and Clinical Practices," *American Journal of Family Therapy,* vol. 11, 1983, pp. 3–15.

7. Richard Gelles, "Applying Research on Family Violence to Clinical Practice," *Journal of Marriage and the Family,* vol. 44, 1982, pp. 9–20.

8. K. J. Ferraro and J. M. Johnson, "How Women Experience Battering: The Process of Victimization," *Social Problems,* vol. 30, 1983, pp. 325–39; J. S. Pfouts, "Violent Families: Coping Responses of Abused Wives," *Child Welfare,* vol. 57, 1978, pp. 101–11; Douglas Snyder and Lisa Fruchtman, "Differential Patterns of Wife Abuse: A Data-Based Typology," *Journal of Consulting and Clinical Psychology,* vol. 49, 1981, pp. 878–85; Snyder and N. S. Scheer, "Predicting Disposition following Brief Residence at a Shelter for Battered Women," *American Journal of Community Psychology,* vol. 9, 1981, pp. 559–66.

9. Straus and Gelles, "Societal Change and Change in Family Violence from 1975 to 1985."

10. Rebecca Dobash and Russell Dobash, *Violence against Wives* (New York: Free Press, 1979); D. Dutton and S. L. Painter, "Traumatic Bonding: The Development of Emotional Attachments in Battered Women and Other Relationships of Intermittent Abuse," *Victimology,* vol. 6, 1981, pp. 139–55; J. L. Edelson, Z. Eisikovits, and E. Guttmann, "Men Who Batter Women: A Critical Review of the Evidence," *Journal of Family Issues,* vol. 6, 1985, pp. 229–42; Lenore Walker, *The Battered Woman* (New York: Harper & Row, 1979).

11. Straus and Gelles, "Societal Change and Change in Family Violence from 1975 to 1985"; Murray Straus, Richard Gelles, and Suzanne Steinmetz, *Behind Closed Doors* (Garden City, N.Y.: Doubleday, 1980).

12. K. J. Ferraro and J. M. Johnson, "How Women Experience Battering."

13. Straus and Gelles, "Societal Change and Change in Family Violence from 1975 to 1985."

14. Dobash and Dobash, *Violence against Wives.*

15. Straus, Gelles, and Steinmetz, *Behind Closed Doors.*

16. Alan Rosenbaum and K. Daniel O'Leary, "Marital Violence: Characteristics of Abusive Couples," *Journal of Consulting and Clinical Psychology,* vol. 49, 1981, pp. 63–71.

17. K. Daniel O'Leary and A. D. Curley, "Assertion and Family Violence: Correlates of Spouse Abuse," *Journal of Marital and Family Therapy,* vol. 12, 1986, pp. 281–89.

18. Sally Lloyd, "Differentiating Violence from Distress in Marriage" (Paper presented at the International Conference on Personal Relationships, Vancouver, July 1988).

19. Christy Telch and Carol Lindquist, "Violent versus Nonviolent Couples: A Comparison of Patterns," *Psychotherapy,* vol. 21, 1984, pp. 242–48.

20. Karen Coleman, Maxine Weinman, and Bartholomew Hsi, "Factors Affecting Conjugal Violence," *Journal of Psychology,* vol. 105, 1980, pp. 197–202.

21. Julian Barling and Alan Rosenbaum, "Work Stressors and Wife Abuse," *Journal of Applied Psychology,* vol. 71, 1986, pp. 346–48.

22. Randall Morrison, Vincent Van Hasselt, and Alan Bellack, "Assessment of Assertion and Problem-Solving Skills in Wife Abusers and Their Spouses," *Journal of Family Violence,* vol. 3, 1987, pp. 227–38.

23. Gayla Margolin, "Conjoint Marital Therapy to Enhance Anger Management and Reduce Spouse Abuse," *American Journal of Family Therapy,* vol. 7, 1979, pp. 13–23.

24. Gayla Margolin, "The Multiple Forms of Aggressiveness between Marital Partners: How Do We Identify Them?" *Journal of Marital and Family Therapy,* vol. 13, 1987, pp. 77–84.

25. Suzanne Steinmetz, "Wife Beating: A Critique and Reformulation of Existing Theory," *Bulletin of the American Academy of Psychiatry and the Law,* vol. 6, pp. 332–34; Snyder and Fruchtman, "Differential Patterns of Wife Abuse"; M. Penfold, S. Morrow, and C. D. Webster, "Assaultive Behavior Resulting from Marital Conflict," *International Journal of Family Therapy,* vol. 5, 1983, pp. 22–39; Jeanne Deschner, *The Hitting Habit: Anger Control for Battering Couples* (New York: Free Press, 1984).

26. Steinmetz, "Wife Beating," pp. 332–34.

27. Walker, *Battered Woman Syndrome.*

28. Snyder and Fruchtman, "Differential Patterns of Wife Abuse."

29. Penfold, Morrow, and Webster, "Assaultive Behavior Resulting from Marital Conflict."

30. Ibid.

31. Jeanne Deschner, *The Hitting Habit.*

32. N. S. Jacobson and Gayla Margolin, *Marital Therapy* (New York: Brunner/Mazel, 1979); Margolin, "Conjoint Marital Therapy."

33. E. N. Jouriles and K. Daniel O'Leary, "Interspousal Reliability of Reports of Marital Violence," *Journal of Consulting and Clinical Psychology,* vol. 53, 1985, pp. 419–21; M. E. Szinovacz, "Using Couple Data as a Methodological Tool: The Case of Marital Violence," *Journal of Marriage and the Family,* vol. 45, 1983, pp. 633–44.

34. Lloyd, "Differentiating Violence from Distress in Marriage."

35. G. Spanier, "Measuring Dyadic Adjustment: New Scales for Assessing the Quality of Marriage and Similar Dyads," *Journal of Marriage and the Family,*

vol. 38, 1976, pp. 15–30; Murray Straus, "Measuring Intrafamily Conflict and Violence: The Conflict Tactics (CT) Scales," *Journal of Marriage and the Family*, vol. 41, 1979, pp. 75–90.

36. The clustering method used was Ward's method, with Euclidean distance as the distance measure. The decision as to the appropriate number of clusters was based on changes in means for each group; the number of groups presented as the "solution" here represents an attempt to balance uniqueness of group with group size. In this presentation some small groups were included in the table (rather than omitted as outliers) since the emphasis is on an examination of the multiplicity of types of violent relationships. This clustering is meant to be illustrative and would need further replication before its usefulness could be determined. Presumably with a larger sample these "outliers" would be reproduced as groups with larger cell sizes.

37. Differences between levels of husband and wife violence should be interpreted with caution as it is likely that husbands may underreport and wives may overreport their own levels of violence. In addition the CTS does not assess who started the violent episode, whether injuries occurred, or the meaning of the violence to each partner. Clearly a wife's use of violence occurs in a different context and carries different meaning from a husband's use of violence; M. Bogard, "Feminist Perspectives on Wife Abuse: An Introduction," in K. Yllo and M. Bogard, eds., *Feminists' Perspectives on Wife Abuse* (Newbury Park, Calif.: Sage, 1988).

38. C. Kelly, T. L. Huston, and R. M. Cate, "Premarital Relationship Correlates of the Erosion of Satisfaction in Marriage," *Journal of Social and Personal Relationships*, vol. 2, 1985, pp. 167–78.

39. Lloyd, "Differentiating Violence from Distress in Marriage."

40. F. J. Fitch and A. Papantonio, "Men Who Batter: Some Pertinent Characteristics," *Journal of Nervous and Mental Disease*, vol. 171, 1983, pp. 190–92; D. Kalmus, "The Intergenerational Transmission of Marital Aggression," *Journal of Marriage and the Family*, vol. 46, 1984, pp. 11–19; Rosenbaum and O'Leary, "Marital Violence: Characteristics of Abusive Couples"; Straus, Gelles, and Steinmetz, *Behind Closed Doors*; Telch and Lindquist, "Violent versus Nonviolent Couples: A Comparison of Patterns."

41. G. T. Hotaling and D. B. Sugarman, "An Analysis of Risk Markers in Husband to Wife Violence: The Current State of Knowledge," *Violence and Victims*, vol. 1, 1986, pp. 101–24.

42. Pagelow, *Family Violence*; Rosenbaum and O'Leary, "Marital Violence: Characteristics of Abusive Couples."

43. Sally Lloyd, J. E. Koval, and R. M. Cate, "Conflict and Violence in Dating Relationships," in M. Pirog-Good and J. Stets, eds., *Violence in Dating Relationships: Emerging Social Issues* (New York: Praeger, 1988).

44. Margolin, John, Burman, Gleberman, and O'Brien, "Interaction Patterns Associated with Marital Violence."

45. Pagelow, *Family Violence*.

46. R. Cate et al., "Premarital Violence: A Social-psychological Perspective," *Journal of Family Issues*, vol. 3, 1982, pp. 79–90; Sally Lloyd, "Conflict in

Premarital Relationships: Differential Perceptions of Males and Females," *Family Relations*, vol. 36, 1987, pp. 290–94.

47. Gayla Margolin and V. Fernandez, "The 'Spontaneous' Cessation of Marital Violence: Three Case Examples," *Journal of Marital and Family Therapy*, vol. 13, 1987, pp. 241–50.

48. Lloyd, Koval, and Cate, "Conflict and Violence in Dating Relationships."

49. Dobash and Dobash, *Violence against Wives*; Margolin, John, and Gleberman, "Affective Responses to Conflictual Discussions in Violent and Nonviolent Couples"; Margolin, John, Burman, Gleberman, and O'Brien, "Interaction Patterns Associated with Marital Violence."

50. L. A. Coser, *The Functions of Social Conflict* (Glencoe, Ill.: Free Press, 1956); G. Simmel, *Conflict and the Web of Group Affiliations* (New York: Free Press, 1955).

51. Coser, *Functions of Social Conflict*.

52. D. R. Peterson, "Conflict," in H. H. Kelley et al., eds., *Close Relationships* (New York: W. H. Freeman, 1983).

53. Richard Gelles and Murray Straus, "Determinants of Violence in the Family: Toward a Theoretical Integration," in W. R. Burr, et al., eds., *Contemporary Theories about the Family, vol. 1* (New York: Free Press, 1979); W. J. Goode, "Force and Violence in the Family," *Journal of Marriage and the Family*, vol. 33, 1971, pp. 624–36.

54. Jetse Sprey, "Conflict Theory and the Study of Marriage and the Family," in W. R. Burr, R. Hill, F. I. Nye, and I. L. Reiss, eds., *Contemporary Theories about the Family, vol. 1* (New York: Free Press, 1979).

55. Coser, *Functions of Social Conflict*.

56. Jacobson and Margolin, *Marital Therapy*.

57. J. M. Gottman, *Marital Interaction: Experimental Investigations* (New York: Academic Press, 1979).

58. Margolin et al., "Interaction Patterns Associated with Marital Violence"; Margolin, John, and Gleberman, "Affective Responses to Conflictual Discussions in Violent and Nonviolent Couples."

59. Dobash and Dobash, *Violence against Wives*.

60. G. R. Patterson, "A Microsocial Analysis of Anger and Irritable Behavior," in R. Chesney and A. Rosenman, eds., *Anger and Hostility: Behavioral and Cardiovascular Disorders* (Washington, D.C.: Hemisphere Publications, 1985).

61. David Finkelhor, "Common Features of Family Abuse," in David Finkelhor, Richard Gelles, G. Hotaling, and Murray Straus, eds., *The Dark Side of Families* (Beverly Hills, Calif.: Sage, 1983).

62. J. E. Stets and M. Pirog-Good, "Violence in Dating Relationships," *Social Psychology Quarterly*, vol. 49, 1987, pp. 63–71.

63. John Scanzoni, "Social Processes and Power in Families," in W. R. Burr, R. Hill, F. I. Nye, and I. L. Reiss, eds., *Contemporary Theories about the Family, vol. 1* (New York: Free Press, 1979).

64. J. E. Stets, *Domestic Violence and Control* (New York: Springer-Verlag, 1988).

65. Gelles and Straus, "Determinants of Violence in the Family."

66. R. E. Billingham and A. R. Sack, "Courtship Violence and the Interactive Status of the Relationship," *Journal of Adolescent Research*, vol. 20, 1986, pp. 37–44; Straus, Gelles, and Steinmetz, *Behind Closed Doors*.

67. Murray Straus and Suzanne Steinmetz, "Violence Research, Violence Control and the Good Society," in Suzanne Steinmetz and Murray Straus, eds., *Violence in the Family* (New York: Harper & Row, 1974).

68. C. Allen and Murray Straus, "Resources, Power and Husband-wife Violence," in Murray Straus and G. Hotaling, eds., *The Social Causes of Husband-wife Violence* (Minneapolis: University of Minnesota Press, 1980).

69. W. Breines and L. Gordon, "The New Scholarship on Family Violence," *Signs: Journal of Women in Culture and Society*, vol. 8, 1983, pp. 490–531.

70. T. Falbo and L. A. Peplau, "Power Strategies in Intimate Relationships," *Journal of Personality and Social Psychology*, vol. 38, 1980, pp. 618–28.

71. Lloyd, "Conflict in Premarital Relationships."

72. M. D. Schwartz, "Gender and Injury in Spousal Assault," *Sociological Focus*, vol. 20, 1987, pp. 61–75.

73. Karen Coleman, "Conjugal Violence: What Thirty-three Men Report," *Journal of Marital and Family Therapy*, 1980, pp. 207–13.

74. Dobash and Dobash, *Violence against Wives*.

75. Brienes and Gordon, "New Scholarship on Family Violence."

CHAPTER 8: HOW THEORETICAL DEFINITIONS AND PERSPECTIVES AFFECT RESEARCH AND POLICY

1. The latter two factors are discussed as essential to the scientific process by Steven Rose, Leon J. Kamin, and R. C. Lewontin, *Not in Our Genes: Biology, Ideology and Human Nature* (Middlesex, Eng.: Penguin Books, 1984). The impact of ideas is discussed in D. B. P. Kallen et·al., eds., *Social Science Research and Public Policy-making: A Reappraisal* (Windsor, Eng.: NFER-Nelson, 1982).

2. On the three problems of the types of evidence used by biological determinists to generalize from animal to human behavior—inappropriate labeling of behavior, partial observations limited to one or only a few behaviors, and use of data from a few animals or a limited number of species—see Rose, Kamin, and Lewontin, *Not in Our Genes*, pp. 158–60.

3. Ibid., p. 156.

4. Steven Goldberg, *The Inevitability of the Patriarchy* (New York: Marrow, 1974).

5. See Rose, Kamin, and Lewontin, *Not in Our Genes*, pp. 148–49, 151–54, 157.

6. Ibid., p. 149.

7. Ibid., pp. 158–60.

8. Ibid., p. 154.

9. R. Emerson Dobash and Russell Dobash, "If You Prick Me Do I Not Bleed? Reply to 'Wives Who Ask for It,'" *Community Care*, May 1979, pp. 26–28.

10. Ibid., p. 26.

11. Erin Pizzey and Jeff Shapiro, *Prone to Violence* (Middlesex, Eng.: Hamlyn, 1982).

12. R. Emerson Dobash and Russell Dobash, "Explanations of Wife Beating That Blame the Victim," in *Conflict in the Family* (Milton Keynes: Open University, 1980), pp. 29–30.

13. Rose, Kamin, and Lewontin, *Not in Our Genes*, p. 154.

14. Ibid., p. 154.

15. Dobash and Dobash, "If You Prick Me," p. 27.

16. Ibid., p. 27.

17. Ibid., p. 26.

18. Rose, Kamin, and Lewontin, *Not in Our Genes*, p. 23.

19. Ibid., p. 21.

20. L. E. Walker, "Treatment Alternatives for Battered Women," in J. Roberts Chapman and M. Gates, eds., *The Victimization of Women* (Beverly Hills, Calif.: Sage, 1978).

21. E. M. Schneider, "Describing and Changing: Women's Self-Defense Work and the Problem of Expert Testimony on Battering," *Women's Rights Law Reporter*, vol. 9, nos. 3 and 4 (1986), pp. 195–222, p. 207.

22. L. E. Walker, "Victimology and the Psychological Perspective of Battered Women," *Victimology*, vol. 8, nos. 1 and 2 (1983), pp. 82–104, 102.

23. Ibid.; M. Hendricks-Matthews, "The Battered Woman: Is She Ready for Help," *Social Casework*, vol. 63, no. 3 (1982), pp. 131–46.

24. E. M. Schneider, "Describing and Changing."

25. Ibid.

26. E. Pleck, *Domestic Tyranny* (New York: Oxford University Press, 1987); Russell Dobash, R. Emerson Dobash, and S. Gutteridge, *The Imprisonment of Women* (New York: Basil Blackwell, 1986); S. Edwards, *Female Sexuality and the Law* (New York: Basil Blackwell, 1981); A. Sachs and J. H. Wilson, *Sexism and the Law* (New York: Basil Blackwell, 1978).

27. J. M. P. Nielsen et al., "Why Women Stay in Battering Relationships" (Paper presented at the annual meetings of the American Sociological Association, Boston, August 1979); L. E. Walker, *The Battered Woman Syndrome* (New York: Springer, 1984).

28. L. E. Walker, *The Battered Woman Syndrome*, p. 135.

29. R. Emerson Dobash and Russell Dobash, *Violence against Wives* (New York: Free Press, 1979).

30. L. E. Walker, quoted in Schneider, "Describing and Changing," p. 203, n. 49.

31. R. J. Shapiro, "Therapy with Violent Families," in S. Saunders, A. M. Anderson, C. A. Hart, and G. M. Rubenstein, eds., *Violent Individuals and Families* (Springfield, Ill.: Charles C. Thomas, 1984), pp. 112–36.

32. J. Weitzman and K. Dreen, "Wife Beating: A View of the Marital Dyad," *Social Casework*, vol. 63, no. 5 (1982), pp. 259–61.

33. J. Weitzman and K. Dreen, "Wife Beating," pp. 260–61.

34. Shapiro, "Therapy with Violent Families," p. 119.

35. L. Cantoni, "Clinical Issues in Domestic Violence," *Social Casework*, vol. 62 (1981), pp. 3–12.

36. Shapiro, "Therapy with Violent Families," p. 119.

37. Luckenbill, "Criminal Homicide as a Situated Transaction"; Hepburn, "Violent Behavior in Interpersonal Relationships."

38. Luckenbill, "Criminal Homicide as a Situated Transaction."

39. L. Sherman and R. Berk, "The Specific Deterrent Effects of Arrest for Domestic Assault," *American Sociological Review,* vol. 49 (1985), pp. 261–72.

40. Dobash and Dobash, *Violence against Wives.*

41. Ibid.; Pleck, *Domestic Tyranny.*

42. R. Emerson Dobash and Russell Dobash, "The Violent Event," in E. Whitelegg, ed., *The Changing Experience of Women* (New York: Basil Blackwell, 1982); "The Nature and Antecedents of Violent Events," *British Journal of Criminology,* vol. 24, no. 3 (1984), pp. 269–88; "Violence towards Wives," in J. Orford, ed., *Coping With Disorder in the Family* (London: Croom Helm, 1987).

43. Dobash and Dobash, *Violence against Wives;* "Nature and Antecedents of Violent Events"; "Violence toward Wives."

44. Dobash and Dobash, *Violence against Wives.*

45. R. Castel, F. Castel and A. Lovell, *The Psychiatric Society* (New York: Columbia University Press, 1982).

46. D. Adams, "Treatment Models of Men Who Batter: A Profeminist Analysis," in K. Yllo and M. Bograd, eds., *Feminist Perspectives on Wife Abuse* (Beverly Hills, Calif., 1988), pp. 176–99.

CHAPTER 9: JUDGING THE SUCCESS OF INTERVENTIONS WITH MEN WHO BATTER

1. B. A. Bass, "An Unusual Behavioral Technique for Treating Obsessive Ruminations," *Psychotherapy: Theory, Research and Practice,* vol. 10 (1975), pp. 191–92; D. W. Foy, R. M. Eisler, and S. Pinkston, "Modeled Assertion in a Case of Explosive Rages," *Journal of Behaviour Therapy and Experimental Psychiatry,* vol. 6 (1975), pp. 135–37; K. S. Klingbeil, "Interpersonal Violence: A Hospital Based Model from Policy to Program," *Response,* vol. 9, no. 3 (1986), pp. 6–9; M. Pellauer, "Violence against Women: The Theological Dimension," *Christianity and Crisis,* vol. 43 (1983), pp. 206–12; J. Spitzer Ringold, *Spousal Abuse in Rabbinic and Contemporary Judaism* (New York: National Federation of Temple Sisterhoods, 1985).

2. D. R. Cook and A. Frantz-Cook, "A Systemic Treatment Approach to Wife Battering," *Journal of Marital and Family Therapy,* vol. 10 (1984), pp. 83–93; J. A. Geller, "Conjoint Therapy: Staff Training and Treatment of the Abuser and the Abused," in M. Roy, ed., *The Abusive Partner* (New York: Van Nostrand Reinhold, 1982), pp. 198–215; G. Margolin, "Conjoint Marital Therapy to Enhance Anger Management and Reduce Spouse Abuse," *American Journal of Family Therapy,* vol. 7 (1979), pp. 13–24; A. Rosenbaum and K. D. O'Leary, "The Treatment of Marital Violence," in N. S. Jacobson and A. S. Gurman, eds., *Clinical Handbook of Marital Therapy* (New York: Guilford Press, 1986), pp. 385–405; A. Weidman, "Family Therapy with Violent Couples," *Social Casework,* vol. 67 (1986), pp. 211–18; J. Weitzman, and K. Dreen, "Wife Beating: A View of the Marital Dyad," *Social Casework,* vol. 63 (1982), pp. 259–65.

3. C. U. Lindquist, C. F. Telch, and J. Taylor, "Evaluation of a Conjugal Violence Treatment Program: A Pilot Study," *Behavioral Counseling and Community Intervention*, vol. 3 (1985), pp. 76–90.

4. J. Harris, "Counseling Violent Couples Using Walker's Model," *Psychotherapy*, vol. 23 (1986), pp. 613–21.

5. J. W. Taylor, "Structured Conjoint Therapy for Spouse Abuse Cases," *Social Casework*, vol. 65 (1984), pp. 11–18.

6. J. L. Edleson and M. P. Brygger, "Gender Differences in Reporting of Battering Incidences," *Family Relations*, vol. 35 (1986), pp. 377–82; E. N. Jouriles and K. D. O'Leary, "Interspousal Reliability of Reports of Marital Violence," *Journal of Consulting and Clinical Psychology*, vol. 53 (1985), pp. 419–21; M. E. Szinovacz, "Using Couple Data as a Methodological Tool: The Case of Marital Violence," *Journal of Marriage and the Family*, vol. 45 (1983), pp. 633–44.

7. C. Myers, "The Family Violence Project: Some Preliminary Data on a Treatment Program for Spouse Abuse" (Paper presented at the Second National Conference for Family Violence Researchers, University of New Hampshire, Durham, N.H., July 1984).

8. P. H. Neidig, D. H. Friedman, and B. S. Collins, "Domestic Conflict Containment: A Spouse Abuse Treatment Program," *Social Casework*, vol. 66 (1985), pp. 195–204.

9. P. H. Neidig, "The Development and Evaluation of a Spouse Abuse Treatment Program in a Military Setting," *Evaluation and Program Planning*, vol. 9 (1986), p. 278.

10. J. P. Deschner, *The Hitting Habit: Anger Control for Battering Couples* (New York: Free Press, 1984); J. P. Deschner and J. S. McNeil, "Results of Anger Control Training for Battering Couples," *Journal of Family Violence*, vol. 1 (1986), pp. 111–20; J. P. Deschner, J. S. McNeil, and M. G. Moore, "A Treatment Model for Batterers," *Social Casework*, vol. 67 (1986), pp. 55–60.

11. A. Shupe, W. A. Stacey, and L. R. Hazelwood, *Violent Men, Violent Couples* (Lexington, Mass.: Lexington Books, 1987); A. Shupe, W. A. Stacey, and L. R. Hazelwood, "Violent Men and Counseling: Does It Work?" (Paper presented at the Southern Sociological Society, New Orleans, April 1986).

12. Deschner, McNeil, and Moore, "A Treatment Model for Batterers."

13. Deschner and McNeil, "Results of Anger Control Training for Battering Couples."

14. C. S. Feazell, R. S. Mayers and J. Deschner, "Services for Men Who Batter: Implications for Programs and Policies," *Family Relations*, vol. 33 (1984), pp. 217–23.

15. M. Pirog-Good and J. Stets-Kealey, "Male Batterers and Battering Prevention Programs: A National Survey," *Response*, vol. 8 (1985), pp. 8–12.

16. J. L. Edleson et al., "Group Treatment for Men Who Batter," *Social Work Research and Abstracts*, vol. 21 (1985), pp. 18–21.

17. A. Rosenbaum, "Group Treatment for Abusive Men: Process and Outcome," *Psychotherapy*, vol. 23 (1986), pp. 607–12.

18. Ibid., p. 611.

19. Shupe, Stacey, and Hazelwood, *Violent Men, Violent Couples*; Shupe, Stacey, and Hazelwood, "Violent Men and Counseling: Does It Work?"

20. R. M. Tolman, S. Beeman, and C. Mendoza, "The Effectiveness of a Shelter-Sponsored Program for Men Who Batter: Preliminary Results" (Paper presented at the Third Family Violence Conference for Researchers, Durham, N.H., July 1987).

21. Edleson and Brygger, "Gender Differences in Reporting of Battering Incidences."

22. D. G. Dutton, "The Outcome of Court-Mandated Treatment for Wife Assault: A Quasi-Experimental Evaluation," *Violence and Victims*, vol. 1 (1986), pp. 163–75; J. L. Edleson and R. J. Grusznski, "Treating Men Who Batter: Four Years of Outcome Data from the Domestic Abuse Project," *Journal of Social Service Research*, vol. 12, pp. 3–22; Shepard, "Intervention with Men Who Batter: An Evaluation of a Domestic Abuse Program."

23. L. K. Hamberger and J. E. Hastings, "Skills Training for Treatment of Spouse Abusers: An Outcome Study," *Journal of Family Violence*, vol. 3 (1988), pp. 121–30.

24. D. G. Saunders and D. Hanusa, "Cognitive-Behavioral Treatment for Men Who Batter: The Short-Term Effects of Group Therapy," *Journal of Family Violence*, vol. 1 (1986), pp. 357–72.

25. E. W. Gondolf and J. Hanneken, "The Gender Warrior: Reformed Batterers on Abuse, Treatment, and Change," *Journal of Family Violence*, vol. 2 (1987), pp. 177–91.

26. E. W. Gondolf, "Evaluating Programs for Men Who Batter: Problems and Prospects," *Journal of Family Violence*, vol. 2 (1987), pp. 95–108.

27. J. L. Edleson, M. Syers, and M. P. Brygger, "Comparative Effectiveness of Group Treatment for Men Who Batter" (Paper presented at the Third Family Violence Conference for Researchers, Durham, N.H., July 1987).

28. M. Bard, *Training Police as Specialists in Family Crisis Intervention* (Washington, D.C.: U.S. Department of Justice, 1970); R. J. Homant, "The Police and Spouse Abuse: A Review of Recent Findings," *Police Studies*, vol. 8 (1985), pp. 163–72.

29. J. M. Driscoll, R. G. Meyer, and C. F. Schanie, "Training Police in Family Crisis Intervention," *Journal of Applied Behavioral Science*, vol. 9 (1973), pp. 62–82; E. P. Mulvey and N. D. Reppucci, "Police Crisis Intervention Training: An Empirical Investigation.

30. Mulvey and Reppucci, "Police Crisis Intervention Training: An Empirical Investigation."

31. J. B. Pearce and J. R. Snortum, "Police Effectiveness in Handling Disturbance Calls: An Evaluation of Crisis Intervention Training," *Criminal Justice and Behavior*, vol. 10 (1983), pp. 71–92.

32. D. J. Bell, "The Police Response to Domestic Violence: An Exploratory Study," *Police Studies*, vol. 7 (1984), pp. 23–30; D. J. Bell, "The Police Response to Domestic Violence: A Replication Study," *Police Studies*, vol. 7 (1984), pp. 136–44; D. J. Bell, "The Police Response to Domestic Violence: A Multiyear Study," *Police Studies*, vol. 8 (1985), pp. 58–64; L. H. Bowker, "Battered Wives

and the Police: A National Study of Usage and Effectiveness," *Police Studies,* vol. 7 (1984), pp. 84–93.

33. L. W. Sherman and R. A. Berk, "The Specific Deterrent Effects of Arrest for Domestic Assault," *American Sociological Review,* vol. 49 (1984), pp. 261–72.

34. R. A. Berk and P. J. Newton, "Does Arrest Really Deter Wife Battery? An Effort to Replicate the Findings of the Minneapolis Spouse Abuse Experiment," *American Sociological Review,* vol. 50 (1985), pp. 253–62; C. A. Burris and P. Jaffe, "Wife Abuse as a Crime: The Impact of Police Laying Charges," *Canadian Journal of Criminology,* vol. 25 (1983), pp. 309–18; P. Jaffe, D. A. Wolfe, A. Telford, and G. Austin, "The Impact of Police Charges on Incidents of Wife Abuse," *Journal of Family Violence,* vol. 1 (1986), pp. 37–49; A. Jolin, "Domestic Violence Legislation: An Impact Assessment," *Journal of Police Science and Administration,* vol. 11 (1983), pp. 451–56; D. B. Kennedy and R. J. Homant, "Battered Women's Evaluation of the Police Response," *Victimology,* vol. 9 (1984), pp. 174–79.

35. J. Fagan, "Cessation of Family Violence: Deterrence and Dissuasion," in L. Ohlin and M. Tonry, eds., *Family Violence,* Volume II of *Crime and Justice: An Annual Review of Research* (Chicago, Ill.: University of Chicago Press, 1989).

36. L. H. Bowker, "Battered Wives, Lawyers, and District Attorneys: An Examination of Law in Action," *Journal of Criminal Justice,* vol. 11 (1983), pp. 402–12; L. H. Bowker, *Beating Wife Beating* (Lexington, Mass.: Lexington Books, 1983); D. A. Ford, "Wife Battery and Criminal Justice: A Study of Victim Decision-Making," *Family Relations,* vol. 32 (1983), pp. 463–75; D. A. Ford, "Prosecution as a Victim Power Resource for Managing Conjugal Violence" (Paper presented at the annual meeting of the Society for the Study of Social Problems, San Antonio, August 1984); D. A. Ford, "Long-term Impacts of Prosecution Outcomes for Incidents of Conjugal Violence: Evidence from Victim Case Studies" (Paper presented at the annual meeting of the Law and Society Association, San Diego, June 1985); M. McLeod, "Victim Non-cooperation in the Prosecution of Domestic Assault," *Criminology,* vol. 21 (1983), pp. 395–416; D. Rauma, "Going for the Gold: Prosecutorial Decision Making in Cases of Wife Assault," *Social Science Research,* vol. 13 (1984), pp. 321–51.

37. J. Grau, J. Fagan, and S. Wexler, "Restraining Orders for Battered Women: Issues of Access and Efficacy," in C. Schweber and C. Feinman, eds., *Criminal Justice Politics and Women* (New York: Haworth Press, 1985), pp. 13–28.

38. M. Steinman, "Evaluating a System-Wide Response to Domestic Abuse: Some Initial Findings," *Journal of Contemporary Criminal Justice,* vol. 4 (1988), pp. 172–86.

39. M. P. Brygger and J. L. Edleson, "The Domestic Abuse Project: A Multisystems Intervention in Woman Battering," *Journal of Interpersonal Violence,* vol. 2 (1987), pp. 324–36; G. A. Goolkasian, *Confronting Domestic Violence: A Guide for Criminal Justice Agencies* (Washington, D.C.: National Institute of Justice, 1986); E. Pence, "The Duluth Domestic Abuse Intervention Project," *Hamline Law Review,* vol. 6 (1983), pp. 247–75; E. Soler and S.

Martin, *Domestic Violence Is a Crime* (San Francisco: Family Violence Project, 1983).

40. D. J. Gamache, J. L. Edleson, and M. D. Schock, "Coordinated Police, Judicial and Social Service Response to Woman Battering: A Multi-baseline Evaluation across Three Communities," in G. T. Hotaling, D. Finkelhor, J. T. Kirkpatrick, and M. Straus, eds , *Coping with Family Violence* (Newbury Park, Calif.: Sage, 1988); E. Pence, S. Novack, and B. Galaway, "Domestic Abuse Intervention Project: Six Month Research Report" (Duluth, Minn.: Duluth Domestic Abuse Intervention Project, 1982).

41. Dutton, "The Outcome of Court-Mandated Treatment for Wife Assault: A Quasi-Experimental Evaluation."

42. W. W. Hudson and S. R. McIntosh, "The Assessment of Spouse Abuse: Two Quantifiable Dimensions," *Journal of Marriage and the Family*, vol. 43 (1981), pp. 873–85; B. Yegidis Lewis, "The Wife Abuse Inventory: A Screening Device for the Identification of Abused Women," *Social Work*, vol. 30 (1985), pp. 32–35.

43. M. A. Straus, "Measuring Intrafamily Conflict and Violence: The Conflict Tactics (CT) Scales," *Journal of Marriage and the Family*, vol. 41 (1979), pp. 75–86.

44. M. A. Straus, "The Conflict Tactics Scales and Its Critics: An Evaluation and New Data on Validity and Reliability" (Durham: University of New Hampshire Family Research Laboratory, 1987).

45. Deschner, McNeil, and Moore, "A Treatment Model for Batterers," p. 60; M. Shepard, "Intervention with Men Who Batter: An Evaluation of a Domestic Abuse Program" (Paper presented at the Third National Conference for Family Violence Researchers, University of New Hampshire, Durham, N.H., July 1987).

46. Edleson and Grusznski, "Treating Men Who Batter," p. 21.

47. B. Hart, *Safety for Women: Monitoring Batterers Programs* (Harrisburg, Penn.: Pennsylvania Coalition against Domestic Violence, 1988).

48. J. L. Edleson, Z. C. Eisikovits, and E. Guttmann, "Men Who Batter Women: A Critical Review of the Evidence," *Journal of Family Issues*, vol. 6 (1985), pp. 243–44.

49. Edleson and Brygger, "Gender Differences in Reporting of Battering Incidences"; Edleson and Grusznski, "Treating Men Who Batter: Four Years of Outcome Data from the Domestic Abuse Project"; R. M. Tolman, "The Development and Validation of a Scale of Non-Physical Abuse" (Paper presented at the Third Family Violence Conference for Researchers, Durham, N.H., July 1987).

50. Saunders and Hanusa, "Cognitive-Behavioral Treatment for Men Who Batter: The Short-Term Effects of Group Therapy."

51. D. G. Saunders, "Issues in Conducting Treatment Research with Men Who Batter," in G. T. Hotaling, D. Finkelhor, J. T. Kirkpatrick, and M. Straus, eds., *Coping with Family Violence* (Newbury Park, Calif.: Sage, 1988).

52. D. G. Saunders et al., "The Inventory of Beliefs about Wife Beating: The Construction and Initial Validation of a Measure of Beliefs and Attitudes,"

Violence and Victims, vol. 2 (1987), pp. 39–57; Tolman, Beeman, and Mendoza, "The Effectiveness of a Shelter-Sponsored Program for Men Who Batter: Preliminary Results."

53. E. W. Gondolf, "Changing Men Who Batter: A Developmental Model for Integrated Interventions," *Journal of Family Violence,* vol. 2 (1987), pp. 335–49; E. W. Gondolf and D. Russell, "The Case against Anger Control Treatment Programs for Batterers," *Response,* vol. 9, no. 3 (1986), pp. 2–5; Rauma, "Going for the Gold: Prosecutorial Decision Making in Cases of Wife Assault."

54. Hart, *Safety for Women: Monitoring Batterers Programs.*

55. Gondolf, "Changing Men Who Batter: A Developmental Model for Integrated Interventions;" E. W. Gondolf and D. Russell, "The Case against Anger Control Treatment Programs for Batterers," *Response,* vol. 9, no. 3 (1986), pp. 2–5.

56. Ford, "Prosecution as a Victim Power Resource for Managing Conjugal Violence"; R. J. Homant, "The Police and Spouse Abuse: A Review of Recent Findings," *Police Studies,* vol. 8 (1985), pp. 163–72.

57. Bowker, "Battered Wives, Lawyers, and District Attorneys: An Examination of Law in Action"; D. Finkelhor, G. T. Hotaling, and K. Yllo, *Stopping Family Violence: Research Priorities for the Coming Decade* (Newbury Park, Calif.: Sage, 1987).

58. Sherman and Berk, "The Specific Deterrent Effects of Arrest for Domestic Assault."

Chapter 11: Differences among States in Child Abuse Rates and Programs

1. Arnold S. Linsky and Murray A. Straus, *Social Stress in the United States: Links to Regional Patterns in Crime and Illness* (Dover, Mass.: Auburn House Publishing, 1986).

2. Murray A. Straus and Richard J. Gelles, "Societal Change and Change in Family Violence from 1975 to 1985 as Revealed by Two National Surveys," *Journal of Marriage and the Family,* vol. 48 (1986), pp. 465–79.

3. American Association for Protecting Children, *Highlights of Official Child Neglect and Abuse Reporting, 1985* (Denver, Colo.: AAPC, 1987).

4. David Finkelhor, *Sexually Victimized Children* (New York: Free Press, 1979).

5. Murray A. Straus, Richard J. Gelles, and S. K. Steinmetz, *Behind Closed Doors: Violence in the American Family* (New York: Doubleday/Anchor, 1980).

6. Straus and Gelles, "Societal Change and Change in Family Violence from 1975 to 1985 as Revealed by Two National Surveys."

7. Ibid.

8. American Association for Protecting Children, *Highlights of Official Child Neglect and Abuse Reporting* (Denver: AAPC, 1985).

9. Richard J. Gelles and Murray A. Straus, *Intimate Violence* (New York: Simon and Schuster, 1988); Murray A. Straus and Richard J. Gelles, eds., *Physical Violence in American Families: Risk Factors and Adaptations to Violence in 8,145 Families* (New Brunswick, N.J.: Transaction Press, 1988).

10. Murray A. Straus, "Measuring Intrafamily Conflict and Violence: The

Conflict Tactics (CT) Scales," *Journal of Marriage and the Family*, vol. 41 (1979), pp. 75–88; Murray A. Straus, "The Conflict Tactics Scales and Its Critics" (Durham: University of New Hampshire Family Research Laboratory, 1989).

11. Gelles and Straus, *Intimate Violence*; Straus and Gelles, "Societal Change and Change in Family Violence from 1975 to 1985 as Revealed by Two National Surveys"; Straus and Gelles, "How Violent Are American Families?"; Straus, Gelles, and Steinmetz, *Behind Closed Doors*.

12. J. Brutz and B. B. Ingoldsby, "Conflict Resolution in Quaker Families," *Journal of Marriage and the Family*, vol. 46 (1984), pp. 21–26; R. Dembo et al., "Physical Abuse, Sexual Victimization and Illicit Drug Use: A Structural Analysis among High Risk Adolescents," *Journal of Adolescence* (1987); Cristobal Neal Eblen, "The Influence of Stress and Social Support upon Child Abuse" (Ph.D. diss., Arizona State University, 1987); Richard J. Gelles and Ake W. Edfeldt, "Violence towards Children in the United States and Sweden," *Child Abuse and Neglect*, vol. 10 (1986), pp. 501–10; Jean Giles-Sims, "A Longitudinal Study of Battered Children of Battered Wives," *Family Relations*, vol. 34 (1985), pp. 205–10; W. H. Meredith, D. A. Abbott, and S. L. Adams, "Family Violence: Its Relation to Marital and Parental Satisfaction and Family Strengths," *Journal of Family Violence*, vol. 1 (1986), pp. 299–305; David W. Moore and Murray A. Straus, "Violence of Parents toward Their Children: New Hampshire 1987" (Report of a survey submitted to the New Hampshire Task Force on Child Abuse and Neglect, Family Research Laboratory, University of New Hampshire, 1987).

13. Eblen, "The Influence of Stress and Social Support"; Richard J. Gelles, "Violence toward Children in the United States," *American Journal of Orthopsychiatry*, vol. 48, no. 4 (October 1978), pp. 580–92; Richard J. Gelles and Murray A. Straus, "The Cost of Family Violence," *Public Health Reports* (November/December 1957), pp. 638–41; Gerald T. Hotaling, Murray A. Straus, and Alan J. Lincoln, "Violence in the Family and Violence and Other Crime outside the Family," in M. Tonry and L. Ohlin, eds., *Crime and Justice: An Annual Review of Research* (Chicago: University of Chicago Press, 1988); Murray A. Straus, "Family Patterns and Child Abuse in a Nationally Representative American Sample," *Child Abuse and Neglect*, vol. 3 (1979), pp. 213–25; Murray A. Straus, "Ordinary Violence versus Child Abuse and Wife Beating: What Do They Have in Common?" in D. Finkelhor et al., eds., *Issues and Controversies in the Study of Family Violence* (Beverly Hills, Calif.: Sage, 1983); Straus and Gelles, "Societal Change and Change in Family Violence from 1975 to 1985 as Revealed by Two National Surveys"; Straus and Gelles, "How Violent Are American Families?"; Straus, Gelles, and Steinmetz, *Behind Closed Doors*; Murray A. Straus and Glenda Kaufman Kantor, "Stress and Child Abuse," in R. E. Helfer and R. S. Kempe, eds., *The Battered Child*, 4th ed. (Chicago: University of Chicago Press, 1987).

14. Murray A. Straus, "Measuring Physical and Emotional Abuse of Children with the Conflict Tactics Scales," in Murray A. Straus and Richard J. Gelles, eds., *Physical Violence in American Families: Risk Factors and Adaptations to Violence in 8,145 Families* (New Brunswick, N.J.: Transaction Press, 1988).

15. David W. Moore, "Order Effects in Surveys of Illegal Acts: The Case of

Child Abuse" (Durham: University of New Hampshire Family Research Laboratory, 1988); Straus, "Measuring Physical and Emotional Abuse of Children with the Conflict Tactics Scales."

16. Larry Baron and Murray A. Straus, "Cultural and Economic Sources of Homicide in the United States," *Sociological Quarterly* (1988); Larry Baron, Arnold Linsky, and Murray A. Straus, *Four Theories of Rape in the United States* (New Haven, Conn.: Yale University Press, 1989); Arnold Linsky and Murray A. Straus, *Social Stress in the United States: Links to Regional Patterns in Crime and Illness* (Dover, Mass.: Auburn House, 1986); Arnold Linsky, Murray A. Straus, and John P. Colby, Jr., "Stressful Events, Stressful Conditions, and Alcohol Problems in the United States: A Partial Test of Bale's Theory," *Journal of Studies on Alcohol,* vol. 46 (1985), pp. 72–80; Arnold Linsky, John P. Colby, Jr., and Murray A. Straus, "Drinking Norms and Alcohol-related Problems in the United States," *Journal of Studies on Alcohol,* vol. 47 (1986), pp. 86–90; Arnold Linsky, John P. Colby, Jr., and Murray A. Straus, "Social Stress, Normative Constraints, and Alcohol Problems in American States," *Sociology, Science, and Medicine,* vol. 24 (1987), pp. 875–83; John Ost and Murray A. Straus, "Capital Intensive Hospital Technology and Illness: An Analysis of American State Data," *Sociology, Science, and Medicine,* vol. 24 (1987), pp. 875–83; Murray A. Straus, "Primary Group Characteristics and Intra-Family Homicide" (Paper presented at the Third National Family Violence Research Conference, University of New Hampshire, Durham, July 6–9, 1987).

17. Moore and Straus, "Violence of Parents toward Their Children: New Hampshire 1987."

18. Gelles and Straus, "The Cost of Family Violence"; Straus and Gelles, "Societal Change and Change in Family Violence from 1975 to 1985 as Revealed by Two National Surveys."

19. Baron and Straus, "Cultural and Economic Sources of Homicide in the United States."

20. Moore, "Order Effects in Surveys of Illegal Acts: The Case of Child Abuse."

21. Straus, "The Index of Legitimate Violence."

22. Dane Archer and Rosemarie Gartner, *Violence and Crime in Cross-National Perspective* (New Haven, Conn.: Yale University Press, 1984); Larry Baron and Murray A. Straus, "Four Theories of Rape: A Macrosociological Analysis," *Social Problems,* vol. 34 (1987), pp. 468–88; Larry Baron and Murray A. Straus, "Legitimate Violence, Violent Attitudes, and Rape: A Test of the Cultural Spillover Theory," in Robert A. Prentky and Vernon L. Ouinsey, eds., *Human Sexual Aggression: Current Perspectives,* vol. 528 (1988); Nanci M. Burns and Murray A. Straus, "Cross-National Differences in Corporal Punishment, Infant Homicide, and Socioeconomic Factors" (Durham: University of New Hampshire Family Research Laboratory, 1987).

23. Debra S. Kalmuss and Murray A. Straus, "Feminist, Political, and Economic Determinants of Wife Abuse Services in American States," in David Finkelhor et al., eds., *The Dark Side of Families: Current Family Violence Research* (Beverly Hills, Calif.: Sage, 1983).

CHAPTER 12: IS VIOLENCE PREVENTABLE?

1. Federal Bureau of Investigation, *Crime in the United States* (Uniform Crime Reports) (Washington, D.C.: U.S. Department of Justice, 1987), p. 11.

2. Federal Bureau of Investigation, *Crime in the United States* (Uniform Crime Reports) (Washington, D.C.: U.S. Department of Justice, 1964), p. 7.

3. The largest and fastest growing category is unknown relationship. For an effort to attribute these homicides to one or another of the known categories, see K. R. Williams and R. L. Flewelling, "Family, Acquaintance, and Stranger Homicide: Alternative Procedures for Rate Calculation," *Criminology*, vol. 25, no. 3 (1987), pp. 543–60.

4. Marc Reidel, Margaret Zahn, and Lois Mock, *The Nature and Patterns of American Homicide* (Washington, D.C.: U.S. Department of Justice, National Institute of Justice, 1985). All of the descriptive information regarding this study comes from the published report.

5. Police Foundation, *Domestic Violence and the Police: Studies in Detroit and Kansas City* (Washington, D.C.: PF, 1976).

6. Douglas Besharov, "Child Abuse Arrest and Prosecution Decision-Making," *American Criminal Law Review*, vol. 24 (Fall 1986), p. 320.

7. For Boston, see Glen L. Pierce, Susan Spaar, and LeBaron Briggs, *The Character of Police Work: Strategic and Tactical Implications* (Boston: Northeastern University, Center for Applied Social Research, 1988). For Minneapolis, see Lawrence W. Sherman, "Repeat Calls to Police in Minneapolis," *Crime Control Reports Number 4* (Washington D.C.: Crime Control Institute, 1987).

8. Lawrence W. Sherman, Patrick R. Gartin, and Michael E. Buerger, "Hot Spots of Predatory Crime," *Criminology*, vol. 27, no. 1, 1989, pp. 27–56.

9. Attorney General's Task Force on Family Violence, *Final Report* (Washington, D.C.: U.S. Department of Justice, 1984).

10. Alfred Blumstein et al., *Criminal Careers and Career Criminals* (Washington, D.C.: National Academy Press, 1986).

11. See Michael Gottfredson and Travis Hirschi, "Science, Public Policy and the Career Paradigm," *Criminology*, vol. 26, no. 1, 1988, pp. 37–56.

12. Throughout this discussion, we refer to "participation" and "the prevalence rate" interchangeably. Similarly we use the terms "frequency" and "incidence rate" interchangeably.

13. For a review of the current status of the criminal career framework, see Blumstein et al., *Criminal Careers and Career Criminals*, pp. 12–30.

14. Albert S. Reiss, Jr., "Co-offending and Criminal Careers," in *Crime and Justice: A Review of Research*, vol. 10, 1988, pp. 117–70.

15. Marvin E. Wolfgang, Robert N. Figlio, and Thorsten Sellin, *Delinquency in a Birth Cohort* (Chicago: University of Chicago Press, 1972).

16. Blumstein, Cohen, Roth, and Visher, *Criminal Careers and Career Criminals*.

17. Ibid., p. 37. Unless otherwise noted, in this summary of the NAS review of the correlates of participation, we are referring to cumulative participation (D), which is to be distinguished from annual participation rates (d).

Some studies refer to D by age eighteen; others refer to lifetime cumulative participation rates.

18. Patrick Langan and Christopher Innes, *The Risk of Violent Crime*, Bureau of Justice Statistics Special Report (Washington, D.C.: U.S. Department of Justice, 1985); Delbert Elliott, S. Ageton, D. Huizinga, B. Knowles, and R. Canter, *The Prevalence and Incidence of Delinquent Behavior: 1976–1980*, National Youth Survey Report no. 26, 1983.

19. Murray A. Straus, Richard J. Gelles, and Suzanne K. Steinmetz, *Behind Closed Doors: Violence in the American Family* (Garden City, N.Y.: Anchor Press, 1980); Straus and Gelles, "Societal Change and Change in Family Violence from 1975 to 1985 as Revealed by Two National Surveys," *Journal of Marriage and the Family*, vol. 48 (1986), pp. 465–79.

20. M. A. Peterson and H. B. Braiker, *Doing Crime: A Survey of California Prison Inmates*, Report R-2200-DOJ (Santa Monica, Calif.: Rand Corporation, 1980).

21. Reidel, Zahn, and Mock, *Nature and Patterns of American Homicide*.

22. Patrick Langan and Christopher Innes, *Preventing Domestic Violence against Women*, Bureau of Justice Statistics Special Report (Washington, D.C.: U.S. Department of Justice, 1986). This study includes only females.

23. Langan and Innes, *Risk of Violent Crime*.

24. Bureau of Justice Statistics, *Criminal Victimization in the United States*, A National Crime Survey Report (Washington, D.C.: U.S. Department of Justice, 1983). We use the following formula: the victimization rate equals the participation rate times the frequency rate.

25. Langan and Innes, *Risk of Violent Crime*.

26. This is the prevalence rate among all females twelve years of age or older, regardless of whether they have or live with family members. This may not be the most appropriate population base. Additional computations with the National Crime Survey data may be necessary to screen out females who cannot logically be victims of family violence. Note the purposeful household sampling of Gelles and Straus in this regard.

27. What we have labeled "child assault" for the convenience of this table is Gelles and Straus's "very severe" category of violent acts. Apologies to the authors if this leads to misinterpretation of their findings.

28. It would also be interesting to compute the self-report and the victimization rates separately and for males and females.

29. Blumstein et al., *Criminal Careers and Career Criminals*.

30. Ibid., Appendix B, p. 292.

31. The cities were Philadelphia, Newark, Chicago, St. Louis, Memphis, Dallas, Oakland, and "Ashton" (anonymous).

32. The coded data were for the eight cities combined. We did not have the city-by-city data.

33. For children under the age of one year, female offenders killed two girls and five boys. Male offenders killed two boys and six girls.

34. Reidel, Zahn, and Mock, *Nature and Patterns of American Homicide*, p. 34.

CHAPTER 13: HOW RESEARCH MAKES A DIFFERENCE IN POLICY AND PRACTICE

1. M. Bulmer, *The Uses of Social Research* (London: Allen and Unwin, 1982); D. Silverman, *Qualitative Methodology and Sociology* (Aldershot, Eng.: Gower, 1985).

2. Carol Weiss, "The Many Meanings of Research Utilization," *Public Administration Review* (September-October, 1979).

3. D. B. P. Kallen et al., eds., *Social Science Research and Public Policy-Making: A Reappraisal* (Windsor, Eng.: NFER-Nelson, 1982).

4. D. Silverman, *Qualitative Methodology and Sociology* (Aldershot, Eng.: Gower, 1985), pp. 178–96.

5. N. Denzin, *The Research Act in Sociology* (London: Butterworth, 1972), p. 332.

6. C. G. A. Bryant, *Positivism in Social Theory and Research* (London: Macmillan, 1985).

7. Kallen et al., *Social Science Research and Public Policy-Making;* N. Caplan, A. Morrison, and R. Stambaugh, *The Use of Social Science Knowledge in Policy Decisions at the National Level* (Ann Arbor: Institute of Social Research, University of Michigan, 1975), Carol Weiss and M. J. Bucuvalas, *Social Science Research and Decision-making* (New York: Columbia University Press, 1980).

8. Carol Weiss, "Policy Research in the Context of Diffuse Decision-making," in D. B. P. Kallen et al., *Social Science Research and Public Policy-making,* pp. 289–315, 9.

9. Howard S. Becker, "Whose Side Are We On," *Social Problems,* vol. 14 (1967), pp. 239–48.

10. Weiss, "Policy Research in the Context of Diffuse Decision-making," p. 303.

11. Ibid.

12. P. K. Feyerabend, *Against Method: Outline of an Anarchistic Theory of Knowledge* (London: New Left Books, 1975); T. Kuhn, *The Structure of Scientific Revolutions,* 2nd ed. (Chicago: University of Chicago Press, 1970), p. 11; H. L. Dreyfus and P. Rabinow, *Michel Foucault: Beyond Structuralism and Hermeneutics* (Chicago: University of Chicago Press, 1982), pp. 163–65.

13. Silverman, *Qualitative Methodology and Sociology.*

14. R. Bhasker, *The Possibility of Naturalism* (Brighton, Eng.: Harvester, 1979); R. Keat and J. Urry, *Social Theory as Science* (London: Routledge, 1975).

15. J. Stacy and B. Thorn, "The Missing Feminist Revolution in Sociology," *Social Problems,* vol. 32, no. 4 (April 1985), pp. 301–16; K. Yllo, "Political and Methodological Debates in Wife Abuse Research," in K. Yllo and M. Bograd, eds., *Feminist Perspectives on Wife Abuse* (Beverly Hills, Calif.: Sage, 1988), pp. 28–50.

16. Alvin Gouldner, "Anti-Minotaur: The Myth of Value-Free Sociology," *Social Problems,* vol. 9 (1962), pp. 199–213; Becker, "Whose Side Are We On," pp. 239–48.

17. W. Breines and L. Gordon, "The New Scholarship on Family Vio-

lence," *Signs: Journal of Women in Culture and Society,* vol. 8 (1983), pp. 490–531; L. Wardell, D. L. Gillespie, and A. Leffler, "Science and Violence Against Wives," in D. Finkelhor, et al., eds., *The Dark Side of Families* (Beverly Hills, Calif.: Sage, 1983), pp. 69–84.

18. Weiss, "Policy Research in the Context of Diffuse Decision-making," p. 314.

19. Ibid.

20. R. A. Berk and P. J. Newton, "Does Arrest Really Deter Wife Battery? An Effort to Replicate the Findings of the Minneapolis Spouse Abuse Experiment," *American Sociological Review,* vol. 50 (1985), pp. 253–62; S. F. Berk and D. R. Loseke, "Handling Family Violence: The Situational Determinants of Police Arrest in Domestic Disturbances," *Law and Society Review,* vol. 15, no. 2 (1981), pp. 317–46. R. A. Berk et al., "Throwing the Cops Back Out: The Decline of a Local Program to Make the Criminal Justice System More Responsive to Incidents of Domestic Violence," *Social Science Research,* vol. 11 (1982), pp. 245–79.

21. R. Berk, P. J. Newton, and S. F. Berk, "What a Difference a Day Makes: An Empirical Study of the Impact of Shelters for Battered Women," *Journal of Marriage and the Family,* vol. 48 (August 1986), pp. 481–90.

22. Ibid., p. 488.

23. L. Sherman and R. Berk, "The Specific Deterrent Effects of Arrest for Domestic Assault," *American Sociological Review,* vol. 49 (1985), pp. 261–72.

24. Bryant, *Positivism in Social Theory and Research.*

25. D. Willer and J. Willer, *Systematic Empiricism: A Critique of a Pseudo-science* (Englewood Cliffs, N.J.: Prentice Hall, 1973).

26. Murray Straus, Richard Gelles, and Suzanne Steinmetz, *Behind Closed Doors: Violence in the American Family* (New York: Doubleday, 1980), pp. 465–79; Straus and Gelles, "Societal Change and Change in Family Violence from 1975 to 1985 as Revealed by Two National Surveys," *Journal of Marriage and the Family,* vol. 48 (August 1986), pp. 465–79.

27. R. A. Berk et al., "Mutual Combat and Other Family Violence Myths," in D. Finkelhor et al., eds., *The Dark Side of Families* (Beverly Hills, Calif.: Sage, 1983), pp. 197–212; R. Emerson Dobash and Rebecca Dobash, "Research as Social Action: The Struggle for Battered Women," in K. Yllo and M. Bograd, eds., *Feminist Perspectives on Wife Abuse* (Beverly Hills, Calif.: Sage, 1988), p. 4; Dobash and Dobash, "Social Science and Social Action: The Case of Wife Beating," *Journal of Family Issues,* vol. 2, no. 4 (1981), p. 3; M. D. Fields and R. M. Kirchner, "Battered Women Are Still in Need: A Reply to Steinmetz," *Victimology,* vol. 3, nos. 1–2 (1978), pp. 216–22; L. L. Lockhart, "Methodological Issues in Comparative Racial Analysis: The Case of Wife Abuse," *Social Work Research and Abstracts,* vol. 21, no. 2 (1985), pp. 35–41; M. Pagelow, "The Battered Husband Syndrome: Social Problem or Much Ado about Nothing," in N. Johnson, ed., *Marital Violence* (Boston: Routledge, 1985), pp. 172–94; E. Pleck, et al., "The Battered Data Syndrome: A Reply to Steinmetz," *Victimology,* vol. 2 (1977), pp. 680–83; D. G. Saunders, "When Battered Women Use Violence: Husband-Abuse or Self-Defense," *Victims and Violence,* vol. 1 (1986), pp. 47–60; Saunders, "Wife Abuse, Husband Abuse, or Mutual Com-

bat? A Feminist Perspective on the Empirical Findings," in *Feminist Perspectives on Wife Abuse* (Beverly Hills, Calif.: Sage, 1988), pp. 90–113.

28. Murray Straus and Richard Gelles, "Determinants of Violence in the Family: Toward a Theoretical Integration," in W. Burr et al., eds., *Contemporary Theories About the Family*, vol. I (New York: Free Press, 1979), pp. 549–91, 26. See also Straus and Gelles, "Societal Change and Change in Family Violence from 1975 to 1985"; Suzanne Steinmetz, "The Battered Husband Syndrome," *Victimology*, vol. 2 (1977); Straus, "Wife Beating: How Common and Why," *Victimology*, vol. 2 (1977); Straus, "Victims and Aggressors in Marital Violence," *American Behavioral Scientist*, vol. 23 (1980), pp. 681–704.

29. L. H. Bowker, *Beating Wife-Beating* (Lexington, Mass.: D. C. Heath, 1982); D. A. Gaquin, "Spouse Abuse: Data from the National Crime Survey," *Victimology*, vol. 2 (1978), pp. 632–43; M. H. Lystad, "Violence at Home: A Review of the Literature," *American Journal of Orthopsychiatry*, vol. 45, no. 5 (1975), pp. 328–45; D. Martin, *Battered Wives* (San Francisco: Glide, 1976); M. Pagelow, *Woman Battering* (Beverly Hills, Calif.: Sage, 1981); D. Russell, *Rape in Marriage* (New York: Macmillan, 1982); S. Schechter, *Woman and Male Violence: The Visions and Struggles of the Battered Women's Movement* (Boston: South End, 1982); U.S. Commission on Civil Rights, *Battered Women: Issues of Public Policy* (Washington, D.C.: 1978); R. Emerson Dobash and Rebecca Dobash, *Violence against Wives: A Case against the Patriarchy* (New York: Free Press, 1979), p. 3.

30. R. L. McNeely and G. Robinson-Simpson, "The Truth about Domestic Violence: A Falsely Framed Issue," *Social Work* (November–December 1987), pp. 485–90.

31. Murray Straus, "Measuring Intrafamily Conflict and Violence: The Conflict Tactics (CT) Scales," *Journal of Marriage and the Family*, vol. 41 (February 1979), pp. 75–88.

32. Zvi Eisikovits and E. Peled, "Qualitative Research on Spouse Abuse," this volume.

33. Dobash and Dobash, *Violence against Wives*; Dobash and Dobash, "The Nature and Antecedents of Violent Events," *British Journal of Criminology*, vol. 24, no. 3 (1984), pp. 269–88; L. H. Athens, *Violent Criminal Acts and Actors: A Symbolic Interactionist Study* (London: Routledge, 1980); H. Toch, *Violent Men: An Inquiry into the Psychology of Violence* (Chicago: Aldine, 1969); J. R. Hepburn, "Violent Behavior in Interpersonal Relationships," *Sociological Quarterly*, vol. 14 (Summer 1973), pp. 419–29; D. Luckenbill, "Criminal Homicide as a Situated Transaction," *Social Problems*, vol. 24, no. 2 (1977), pp. 176–86.

34. Murray Straus, "The Conflict Tactics Scales and Its Critics: An Evaluation and New Data on Validity and Reliability," in Murray Straus and Richard Gelles, *Physical Violence in American Families: Risk Factors and Adaptations to Violence in Families* (Transaction Press, forthcoming).

35. Dobash and Dobash, *Violence against Wives*; "Nature and Antecedents of Violent Events."

36. Dobash and Dobash, *Violence against Wives*, appendix C; "The Context Specific Approach," in D. Finkelhor et al., *The Dark Side of Families* (Beverly Hills, Calif.: Sage, 1983), pp. 261–76.

37. Dobash and Dobash, "Nature and Antecedents of Violent Events."

38. Hepburn, "Violent Behavior in Interpersonal Relationships"; Luckenbill, "Criminal Homicide as a Situated Transaction."

39. R. Emerson Dobash and Rebecca Dobash, "Community Response to Violence against Wives: Charivari, Abstract Justice and Patriarchy," *Social Problems*, vol. 28, no. 5 (1981), pp. 563–81; "The Contact between Battered Women and the Social and Medical Agencies," in J. Pahl, *Private Violence and Public Policy* (Boston: Routledge, 1985), pp. 142–65.

40. Dobash and Dobash, "Community Response to Violence against Wives"; "Contact between Battered Women and the Social and Medical Agencies."

41. Dreyfus and Rabinow, *Michel Foucault*, pp. 163–65.

42. A Touraine, *The Voice and the Eye* (Cambridge: Cambridge University Press, 1981).

43. Barbara Hart, "Collaboration for change."

Chapter 14: The Effects of Research on Legal Policy in the Minneapolis Domestic Violence Experiment

1. Joan Petersilia, *The Influence of Criminal Justice Research* (Santa Monica, Calif.: Rand Corporation, 1987).

2. Douglas Lipton, Robert Martinson, and Judith Wilks, *The Effectiveness of Correctional Treatment* (New York: Praeger, 1975); Robert Martinson, "What Works?—Questions and Answers about Prison Reform," *Public Interest*, vol. 35 (1974), pp. 22–54; Lee Sechrest, Susan O. White, and Elizabeth Brown, eds., *The Rehabilitation of Criminal Offenders: Problems and Prospects* (Washington, D.C.: National Academy of Sciences, 1979).

3. Alfred Blumstein et al., *Criminal Careers and "Career Criminals"* (Washington, D.C.: National Academy of Sciences, 1986), vol. 1; Peter Greenwood, *Selective Incapacitation* (Santa Monica, Calif.: Rand Corporation, 1982).

4. Stephen E. Feinberg, Kinley Larntz, and Albert J. Reiss, Jr., "Redesigning the Kansas City Preventive Patrol Experiment," *Evaluation*, vol. 3, nos. 1–2 (1976), pp. 124–31; George Kelling et al., *The Kansas City Preventive Patrol Experiment* (Washington, D.C.: Police Foundation, 1974); Richard C. Larson, "What Happened to Patrol Operations in Kansas City?" *Journal of Criminal Justice*, vol. 3 (January 1976).

5. Richard Lempert, "From the Editor," *Law and Society Review*, vol. 18 (1984), pp. 5–10; Lawrence W. Sherman and Richard A. Berk, "The Specific Deterrent Effects of Arrest for Domestic Assault," *American Sociological Review*, vol. 49 (1984), pp. 261–72.

6. Richard Lempert, "Spouse Abuse: Ann Arbor Rushed into Arrest Ordinance without Studying Side Effects," *Ann Arbor News*, June 21, 1987.

7. Lempert, "From the Editor."

8. Ibid.

9. Lempert, "Spouse Abuse: Ann Arbor Rushed into Arrest Ordinance."

10. Lempert, "From the Editor."

11. Bernard Roshco, *Newsmaking* (Chicago: University of Chicago Press, 1975); Leon V. Sigal, *Reporters and Officials: The Organization and Politics of*

Newsmaking (Lexington, Mass.: D. C. Heath, 1973); Herbert J. Gans, *Deciding What's News* (New York: Pantheon, 1979).

12. Sigal, *Reporters and Officials.*

13. "Sociologist-Journalist Sought for Clearinghouse," *Footnotes* (American Sociological Association) (November 1987), p. 2.

14. Gans, *Deciding What's News.*

15. Ibid.

16. Lempert, "From the Editor."

17. Lawrence W. Sherman, Panel presentation on research and the press, American Society of Criminology, Atlanta, November 1986.

18. Gans, *Deciding What's News.*

19. These figures are derived from the Burelle's Clipping Service count for the Police Foundation, which paid Burelle's on a continuing basis to read about 1,000 newspapers nationwide and clip any story mentioning the Police Foundation.

20. Lempert, "From the Editor."

21. Gans, *Deciding What's News.*

22. Kathy Ferraro, Round table presentation, American Sociological Association, Washington, D.C., August 1985.

23. Attorney General's Task Force on Family Violence, *Report* (Washington, D.C.: U.S. Department of Justice, 1984.

24. Lempert, "Spouse Abuse: Ann Arbor Rushed into Arrest Ordinance"; Petersilia, *The Influence of Criminal Justice Research.*

25. Ferraro, Round table presentation; "Dallas Spouse-Abuse Arrests Soar," *Law Enforcement News* (John Jay College), October 27, 1987, p. 3; "Pittsburgh Gets Tough on Domestic Violence," *New York Times,* November 15, 1987, p. 65.

26. Lempert, "From the Editor."

27. Sherman and Berk, "The Specific Deterrent Effects of Arrest for Domestic Assault."

28. Richard A. Berk and Lawrence W. Sherman, "Police Responses to Family Violence Incidents: An Analysis of an Experimental Design with Incomplete Randomization," *Journal of the American Statistical Association* (December 1987).

29. Sherman and Berk, "The Specific Deterrent Effects of Arrest for Domestic Assault."

30. Several continuing replications of the experiment solve this problem by giving most domestic calls to "domestic cars," which can be efficiently observed. One of them has also reduced treatment failures to 3 percent of the first 550 cases (from 18 percent) of the 314 cases in Minneapolis) by screening cases in the field before randomization and then calling the research office, where a sealed envelope containing a prerandomized treatment is opened.

31. Sherman and Berk, "The Specific Deterrent Effects of Arrest for Domestic Assault."

32. Ibid.

33. Alfred Blumstein and Jacqueline S. Cohen, "Estimation of Individual Crime Rates from Arrest Records," *Journal of Criminal Law and Criminology,* vol.

70 (1979), pp. 561–85; Blumstein, et al., *Criminal Careers and "Career Criminals"* (Washington, D.C.: National Academy of Sciences, 1986), vol. 1.

34. Sherman and Berk, "The Specific Deterrent Effects of Arrest for Domestic Assault."

35. Anne Witte, Personal communication.

36. Albert J. Reiss, Jr., "Some Failures in Designing Data Collection That Distort Results," in Leigh Burstein, Howard E. Freeman, and Peter H. Rossi, eds., *Collecting Evaluation Data: Problems and Solutions* (Beverly Hills, Calif.: Sage Publications, 1985), pp. 161–77.

37. Lempert, "From the Editor."

38. Lawrence W. Sherman and Richard A. Berk, *The Minneapolis Domestic Violence Experiment* (Washington, D.C.: Police Foundation, 1984).

39. One of the continuing replications is randomizing the amount of time in jail, to compare the effects of two hours with those of eight hours or more.

40. Albert J. Reiss, Jr., "Consequences of Compliance and Deterrence Models of Law Enforcement for the Exercise of Police Discretion," *Law and Contemporary Problems*, vol. 47, no. 4 (1984), pp. 83–122.

41. Sherman and Berk, "The Specific Deterrent Effects of Arrest for Domestic Assault."

42. Sherman and Berk, *The Minneapolis Domestic Violence Experiment*.

43. Richard A. Berk and Phyllis Newton, "Does Arrest Really Deter Wife Battery? An Effort to Replicate the Findings of the Minneapolis Spouse Abuse Experiment," *American Sociological Review*, vol. 50 (April 1985), pp. 253–62; Lempert, "From the Editor."

44. Thomas D. Cook and Donald T. Campbell, *Quasi-Experimentation: Design and Analysis Issues for Field Settings* (Chicago: Rand-McNally, 1979).

45. Robert Sampson, "Crime in Cities: The Effects of Formal and Informal Social Control," in Albert J. Reiss, Jr., and Michael Tonry, eds., *Communities and Crime: Crime and Justice, A Review of Research* (Chicago: University of Chicago Press, 1986), vol. 8, pp. 271–311.

46. Stuart J. Pocock, Michael D. Hughes, and Robert J. Lee, "Statistical Problems in the Reporting of Clinical Trials: A Survey of Three Medical Journals," *New England Journal of Medicine*, vol. 317, no. 7 (1987), pp. 426–32.

47. Charles Lindblom and David Cohen, *Usable Knowledge: Social Science and Social Problem-Solving* (New Haven, Conn.: Yale University Press, 1979).

48. Sarah Fenstermaker Berk and Donileen R. Loseke, "Handling Family Violence: Situational Determinants of Police Arrest in Domestic Disturbances," *Law and Society Review*, vol. 15 (1980), pp. 315–46; Black, *The Manners and Customs of the Police* (New York: Academic Press, 1980); Charles D. Emerson, "Family Violence: A Study by the Los Angeles County Sheriff's Department," *Police Chief*, vol. 46 (1979), pp. 48–50; James A. Fagin, "The Effects of Police Interpersonal Communications Skills on Conflict Resolution" (Ph.D. diss., Southern Illinois University, 1978); Thomas Ketterman and Marjorie Kravitz, *Police Crisis Intervention: A Selected Bibliography* (Washington, D.C.: National Criminal Justice Reference Service, 1978); Richard Langley and Roger C. Levy, *Wife Beating: The Silent Crisis* (New York: E. P. Dutton, 1977); Nancy Loving, *Responding to Spouse Abuse and Wife Beating* (Washington, D.C.:

Police Executive Research Forum, 1980); Jeanie K. Meyer and Theodore Lorimer, "Police Intervention Data and Domestic Violence: Exploratory Development and Validation of Prediction Models" (Report submitted to National Institute of Mental Health under Grant Number R01MH27918, 1977); Raymond I. Parnas, "The Police Response to the Domestic Disturbance," in Leon Radzinowicz and Marvin E. Wolfgang, eds., *The Criminal in the Arms of the Law* (New York: Basic Books, 1972), pp. 206–36; Jane Potter, "The Police and the Battered Wife: The Search for Understanding," *Police Magazine*, vol. 1 (1979), pp. 40–50; Maria Roy, ed., *Battered Women* (New York: Van Nostrand Reinhold, 1977); P. B. Wylie et al., "Approach to Evaluating a Police Program of Family Crisis Intervention in Six Demonstration Cities: Final Report" (Washington, D.C.: National Criminal Justice Reference Service, 1976).

49. Morton Bard, *Training Police as Specialists in Family Crisis Intervention* (Washington, D.C.: U.S. Department of Justice, 1970).

50. Ibid.

51. Donald A. Liebman and Jeffrey Schwartz, "Police Programs in Domestic Crisis Intervention: A Review," in J. R. Snibbe and H. M. Snibbe, eds., *The Urban Policeman in Transition* (Springfield, Ill.: Charles C. Thomas, 1973), pp. 421–72.

52. Cook and Campbell, *Quasi-Experimentation: Design and Analysis Issues for Field Settings.*

53. Meyer and Lorimer, "Police Intervention Data and Domestic Violence."

54. Lempert, "From the Editor."

55. Ibid.; Lempert, "Spouse Abuse: Ann Arbor Rushed into Arrest Ordinance."

56. Stuart J. Pocock, *Clinical Trials: A Practical Approach* (London: John Wiley, 1983).

57. Ibid.

58. Food and Drug Administration, *Bureau of Drugs Clinical Guidelines* (Washington, D.C., 1977); Pocock, *Clinical Trials.*

59. Allen S. Keller, "Treatment by Chance: Some Doctors Raise Ethical Questions about Randomized Studies," *Washington Post*, June 26, 1985.

60. June Goodfield, "Vaccine on Trial," *Science 84*, March 1984, pp. 78–84.

61. "AZT's Early Test Results Prompt Release of Drug," *Washington Post*, September 20, 1986, p. A1; Margaret A. Fischl et al., "The Efficacy of Azidothymidine (AZT) in the Treatment of Patients with AIDS and AIDS-related Complex," *New England Journal of Medicine*, vol. 317 (1987), pp. 185–91.

62. Philip M. Boffey, "U.S. to Back Gene-engineered Drug for Clotting," *New York Times*, November 13, 1987, p. A1.

63. Lempert, "From the Editor."

64. Keller, "Treatment by Chance."

65. Howard Hiatt, "Will Your Next Hospital Stay Be Necessary?" *Wall Street Journal*, November 18, 1986, p. 32.

66. Thor Hanson, "Put Treatments to a Double-blind Test," *Wall Street Journal*, July 5, 1985.

67. B. Fisher et al., "Five Year Results of a Randomized Trial Comparing

Total Mastectomy and Segmental Mastectomy with or without Radiation in the Treatment of Breast Cancer," *New England Journal of Medicine,* vol. 312 (1985), pp. 665–73.

68. Michael Specter, "FDA to Approve New Drug for Heart Attacks: Experts Say Anticlotting Medication May Save Thousands of Lives," *Washington Post,* November 13, 1987, p. A1.

69. Seymour Perry, "The NIH Consensus Development Program: A Decade Later," *New England Journal of Medicine,* vol. 317, no. 8 (1987), pp. 485–88.

70. Joel Garner, Personal communication.

71. Black, "The Boundaries of Legal Sociology," *Yale Law Journal,* vol. 81 (May 1972), pp. 1086–100.

A NOTE ON THE BOOK

This book was edited by the publications staff
of the American Enterprise Institute.
The figures were drawn by Hördur Karlsson.
The text was set in Palatino, a typeface designed by Hermann Zapf.
Coghill Book Typesetting Company, of Richmond, Virginia,
set the type, and Edwards Brothers Incorporated,
of Ann Arbor, Michigan, printed and bound the book,
using permanent, acid-free paper.

The AEI PRESS is the publisher for the American Enterprise Institute for Public Policy Research, 1150 Seventeenth Street, N.W., Washington, D.C. 20036: *Christopher C. DeMuth,* publisher; *Edward Styles,* director; *Dana Lane,* editor; *Ann Petty,* editor; *Andrea Posner,* editor; *Teresa Fung,* editorial assistant (rights and permissions). Books published by the AEI PRESS are distributed by arrangement with the University Press of America, 4720 Boston Way, Lanham, Md. 20706.